Learning FrontPage 2000

Learning FrontPage 2000

DDC Publishing, Inc.
275 Madison Ave.
New York, NY 10016-1161
techsupp@ddcpub.com
www.ddcpub.com

Author	Quessing Courseware
Managing Editor	Susan Alcorn
Content Editors	Curt Robbins
	Amy Towery
Technical Editor	Erich Rainville
Proofreader	Eileen Levandoski

Legal Notice

Table of Contents

DDC Publishing • www.ddcpub.com

Course Conventions

General Conventions

File and directory names	All caps, Courier font: The files will be copied to the directory `C:/QUESSING/FRONTPAGE-1`.
Text to be typed by student	Bold Courier font: **This is my first frames-enabled page.**
Web page hyperlinks	Bold and underlined: Click **here** to view a different Web page.
New terms, text to be emphasized, Web page titles	Italic: Lengthy data in frames is viewed by *scrolling*.
Keyboard functions	All caps, enclosed in wickets: Press <TAB> to advance to the next field.
Icons, buttons, text fields, keyboard functions, dialog boxes, pulldown menus & menu items	Bold: On the toolbar, click the **Back** button.

Internet Addresses

Uniform Resource Locator	Bold Courier font: **www.ddcpub.com**
E-mail address	Bold Courier font: **webmaster@ddcpub.com**

Keyboard Shortcuts

Advance to next e-mail header field	<TAB>
Advance to next Web page form field	<TAB>
Find (in page or document using Web browser)	<CTRL + F> (Netscape Navigator and MS Internet Explorer)
Return to previous e-mail header field	<SHIFT + TAB>
Return to previous Web form field	<SHIFT + TAB>
Toggle active desktop software application	<ALT + TAB>

Icon Legend

 Definition — A definition or clarification of a new term.

 Example — An illustration of the subject matter being reviewed.

 Java Note — Java-specific information or tips driven by the core learning objectives of the course.

 NetQuote — Quote by a famous or significant individual regarding the history or any other characteristic of the Internet. NetQuotes are sometimes enlightening or entertaining, but always provide perspective to the subject matter being reviewed.

 NetResult — In exercises, the result of specific actions taken. Most exercises have multiple NetResults.

 Note — Supplemental, but important, information regarding the subject matter being reviewed.

 Scenario — Typically preceding an exercise, Scenarios are examples that "set the stage" or provide a real-world context in which to analyze the subject matter being reviewed.

 TechTip — Technical supplement to the core course. TechTips are intended to expand your knowledge beyond the primary goals of this course.

 TriviaTip — Trivial information regarding the Internet. Similar to NetQuotes, TriviaTips lend substance, perspective, and background.

 Warning — Important—sometimes critical—information; unlike TriviaTips or NetQuotes, Warnings are *not* supplemental, but pertain directly to the subject matter being reviewed.

DDC Publishing • www.ddcpub.com

"It's one of his favorite sites."

Mastering FrontPage 2000: Part 1

Creating & Managing Web Sites without Programming

*"In times of change, learners shall inherit the earth, while the learned
are beautifully equipped for a world that no longer exists."*

— Eric Hoffer

Part 1 Description

Mastering FrontPage 2000: Part 1 is an introduction to both FrontPage 2000 and to the fundamentals of building a basic Web site. This section will walk you through the installation of FrontPage 2000, provide you with an overview of HTML and Web page imaging, and help you establish and configure your first FrontPage web. No HTML experience is required for this course.

Please Note: Microsoft FrontPage 2000 can be used to develop and administer Web sites that are published to Windows, Macintosh, and UNIX Web servers. However, the full range of FrontPage 2000 features are best supported within the Microsoft development environment.

This course has been optimized for use in creating Web sites that will run on Web servers that support the FrontPage 2000 Server Extensions (such as Microsoft's Internet Information Server or Personal Web Server). Also, some of the FrontPage components may be viewed only in Microsoft's Internet Explorer. Such requirements are noted as they arise throughout this course.

The solutions files provided include folders which FrontPage does not display in its Folders view. If you wish, you can use Windows Explorer to confirm the presence of these folders on computers used by students to complete the course exercises. Please note that solutions files may not be identical to student files because the student is asked to modify page and web elements to personalize the web they have created during the course.

Course Objectives

By completion of this course, you will have learned how to:

- Install and configure FrontPage 2000
- Recognize and use simple HTML tags
- Create a FrontPage web from "scratch"
- Incorporate and manipulate graphics in your FrontPage webs
- Use FrontPage 2000 themes
- Import an existing FrontPage web
- Publish a FrontPage web

Required Software

- Microsoft FrontPage 2000
- A Web browser (Microsoft Internet Explorer recommended)

Part 1 Setup

Installing the Student Files

The student files necessary for *Mastering FrontPage 2000: Part 1* are archived on the Student Files CD-ROM. Follow these steps to install the student files:

1. Insert the Student Files CD-ROM into the appropriate drive on your computer.

2. Using Windows Explorer (file manager) or another file management utility, locate the file named FP-1.EXE and copy it to your Windows Desktop.

   - On the CD-ROM, single-click FP-1.EXE and right-click.

   - On the shortcut menu that appears, select **Copy**.

   - On your Desktop, be sure your mouse pointer is not on an icon or application and right-click.

   - Select **Paste**. This will copy the FP-1.EXE file from the Student Files CD-ROM to your Windows Desktop.

3. On your Desktop, double-click FP-1.EXE.

4. The **WinZip Self-Extractor** dialog box will appear. Click the **Unzip** button.

5. The files will be decompressed and stored in a folder called FP-1 on your Desktop. If the files were decompressed and installed correctly, an alert box will appear that indicates this.

Lesson 1
FrontPage 2000—
Overview &
Installation

Lesson Topics

► FrontPage 2000 Overview

► FrontPage 2000 Installation

► FrontPage 2000 Views

► FrontPage 2000 Toolbars

► Lesson Summary

FrontPage 2000 Overview

FrontPage 2000, developed and marketed by Microsoft Corporation, is currently the most popular Web page/Web site creation and management tool on the market. The latest version of Microsoft's highly successful FrontPage series allows both novices and experts to create, edit, design, manage, and maintain Web sites and related Web-based multimedia content.

Why Use FrontPage?

Before the advent of FrontPage and other HTML editors—such as HoTMetaL PRO, Net Objects Fusion, and HotDog Pro—Web page designers were required to learn the HyperText Markup Language (HTML), the scripting language in which all Web pages are written. While HTML is a relatively simple scripting language (other scripting languages, such as JavaScript, SGML, and VBScript are significantly more complex), it can take several months or even years to master.

Goodbye to HTML Learning Curve

FrontPage 2000 makes a solid knowledge of HTML unnecessary. It decreases the learning curve of users because it closely resembles other Microsoft Office applications (Word, Excel, PowerPoint, Access, and Outlook). This makes it considerably easier for any user familiar with, for example, creating documents in Microsoft Word to create Web pages with FrontPage.

FrontPage is more than simply an HTML editor. It also facilitates the creation of dynamic Web pages and Web-based applications and the management of an entire Web site.

Goodbye to Cumbersome Scripting

Before FrontPage, a Webmaster needed to become familiar not only with HTML, but also with the scripting languages used to create dynamic, interactive effects, including:

- Java

- JavaScript & VBScript

- Perl

More than Just HTML Automation

FrontPage is also a fully automated Web content management system. You can create and edit Web pages and manage your entire Web site. You can implement security restrictions on portions of your site, assign the maintenance of different parts of the Web site to a particular individual or group, or apply a theme that gives the entire site a consistent look and feel.

What's New in FrontPage 2000?

FrontPage 2000 is the fourth version of FrontPage. While this new version builds on the strengths of FrontPage 97 and FrontPage 98, it also includes many new features. Some of the most frustrating limitations, design flaws, and "features" of previous FrontPage versions—such as the tendency to make unexpected and often unwanted alterations to HTML coding—have been corrected in FrontPage 2000.

Explorer + Editor Combo

The biggest difference that users familiar with FrontPage 98 will notice is the marriage of the FrontPage Explorer and the FrontPage Editor. Separate applications in FrontPage 98, the Explorer and Editor are now combined as a single application in FrontPage 2000.

Major New Features

Listed below are a few of the major new features of FrontPage 2000:

- Source code preservation: earlier versions of FrontPage frequently made unwanted changes to HTML coding. FrontPage 2000, however, will not make any changes without your consent.

- Animation effects: FrontPage 2000 has integrated many features from other MS Office 2000 applications, including many dynamic HTML animation and page transition effects.

- Cascading Style Sheets (CSS) support: the CSS standard was introduced by the World Wide Web Consortium (W3C)[1] to give Webmasters the ability to control the format and style of pages throughout an entire Web site, creating more uniformity and consistency. Previous versions of FrontPage already supported a proprietary version of CSS, in the form of FrontPage themes. However, FrontPage 2000 CSS support for the CSS 2.0 standard is fully realized.

- Microsoft Script Editor: developed by Microsoft as a stand-alone application for developing scripts, the MSE now comes bundled with FrontPage to aid in coding scripts for use in your FrontPage webs.

- MS Access database connectivity: FrontPage 2000 is fully integrated with other Office 2000 applications, including Access 2000. This integration makes it easy to use Access as a "back-end" database solution for developing your Web site.

These and many of the dozens of new features and improvements in FrontPage 2000 will be discussed throughout this course.

---

[1] The World Wide Web Consortium (W3C) maintains and publishes the official HTML 4.0 Specification. The W3C Web site, at www.w3c.org, is a valuable resource for any Webmaster or Web programmer.

FrontPage 2000 Installation

This section details the process of installing FrontPage 2000 on your computer. If you have already installed FrontPage, a cursory look at this lesson is all you need. You should note that the FrontPage 2000 installation process, unlike that of many other software applications, allows a newer version of FrontPage to be installed without affecting earlier installations. For example, if you have FrontPage 98 on your computer, you can install FrontPage 2000 and keep the installation of FrontPage 98 intact.

The exercises in this section assume you are installing FrontPage 2000 from the Office 2000 Premium CD-ROM. The install process is very similar if you are using the standalone FrontPage 2000 CD.

Standard Installation

Standard installation of FrontPage 2000 copies the parts of FrontPage most frequently used to create and manage Web sites to your hard drive. If you have a previous installation of FrontPage, the Standard Installation will upgrade the existing version (such as FrontPage 97 or 98) to FrontPage 2000.

- If you want to retain a previous version of FrontPage on your computer, follow the Standard Installation instructions provided in Exercise 1-1.

- If you plan to use the more advanced features of FrontPage 2000, follow the Custom Installation instructions provided in Exercise 1-2.

Be sure to close all other applications before beginning the FrontPage 2000 installation. It is especially important to ensure that you are not running any Microsoft Office applications during the FrontPage 2000 installation.

Exercise 1-1: Standard Installation of FrontPage 2000

In this exercise, you will go through the steps involved in the standard installation of FrontPage 2000. If you already have FrontPage 2000 installed, you can skip over this exercise. (You should refer back to this exercise if you need to reinstall at a future time).

1. Place your Office 2000 Premium CD-ROM in your computer's CD-ROM drive. An alert box will appear, informing you that the install software is preparing to install Office 2000.

2. After the alert box completes its task, a window will appear, as shown in Figure 1-1.

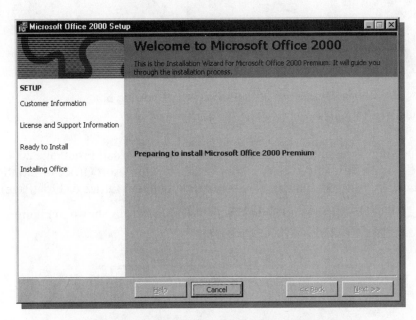

Figure 1-1: Welcome to Microsoft Office 2000 window

3. After the **Welcome to Microsoft Office 2000** window appears, you will see the **Customer Information** dialog box. Type your name, initials, company name, and CD-Key (located on the back of your Office 2000 jewel case).

4. Click **Next**.

5. The Microsoft Office 2000 End-User License Agreement window appears. Peruse the agreement and select "I accept the terms in the License Agreement."

6. Click **Next**.

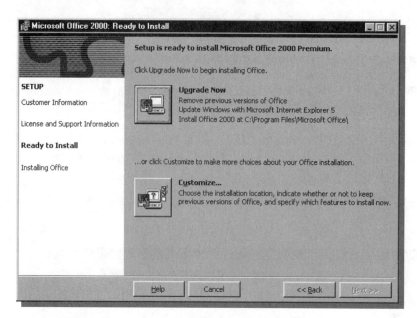

Figure 1-2: Office 2000 Ready to Install dialog box

7. The following screen informs you that you are ready to install FrontPage 2000. Click either **Upgrade Now** (if you have a prior version of Microsoft Office or FrontPage) or **Install** (if you do not have an existing version of either Office or FrontPage).

8. Office 2000 will begin an automated installation process, as shown in Figure 1-3.

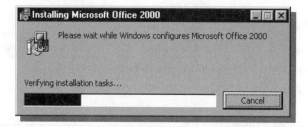

Figure 1-3: Installing Microsoft Office 2000

Custom Installation

The standard installation of FrontPage 2000 includes only its basic features. If you want or need to install features that are outside of these basic parameters, FrontPage 2000 allows you to perform a *custom installation*. You would also use the custom installation option if you have a previous installation of FrontPage that you do not want to upgrade (thus maintaining two separate versions of FrontPage on your computer).

Exercise 1-2: Custom Installation of FrontPage 2000

In this exercise, you will go through the steps involved in the custom installation of FrontPage 2000. Custom installation allows you to choose exactly which FrontPage components you desire to install.

1. Complete Steps 1 through 6 of Exercise 1-1.

2. When the **Ready to Install** screen appears, as shown in Figure 1-4, select **Customize**.

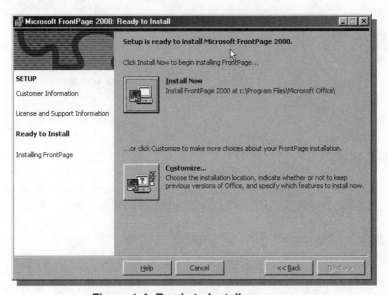

Figure 1-4: Ready to Install screen

3. On the next screen, select your own installation location or leave the default installation directory. Click **Next**.

4. On the **Remove Previous Versions** screen, if you do not want the programs listed to be removed, select the **Keep these programs** checkbox and click **Next**.

5. If you have a version of Internet Explorer previous to 5.0, the next screen will prompt you to upgrade. Make your selection and click **Next**.

6. Select the components you wish to install by using the pull-down menus to the left of the component names as shown in Figure 1-5, and click **Install Now**.

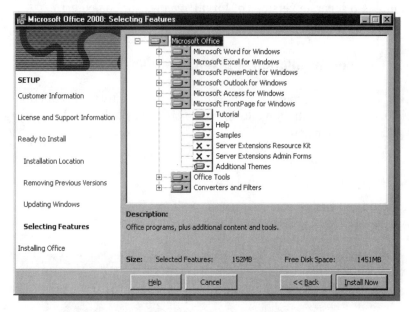

Figure 1-5: Microsoft 2000: Selecting Features screen

Running FrontPage 2000

Once your installation is complete, you will be prompted to restart your computer. After your computer reboots, you can launch FrontPage 2000 by selecting:

Start ▶ Programs ▶ Microsoft FrontPage. (You can also create a Windows shortcut to FrontPage and place it on your desktop.

The first time you run FrontPage 2000, it will ask if you want it to be your default HTML editor. For the purposes of this course, choose **Yes**.

Throughout this course, you will note that both the terms *HTML document* and *web* are used to describe HTML pages. An HTML document is a *single* Web page. A "web" (lower case "w") is a group of related HTML documents when viewed or worked with while *in FrontPage*. A collection of Web (upper case "W") pages regarding a particular company, organization, or topic is universally referred to as a *Web site*.

FrontPage 2000 Views

Now that FrontPage 2000 is installed and running on your computer, you should take a few minutes to explore the screen elements that comprise the user interface to begin to understand and gain a comfort level for FrontPage 2000. One of the most important elements of the FrontPage 2000 user interface is a collection of six *views*.

 If you wish to become productive and efficient using FrontPage, you must become very familiar with all six views.

As indicated earlier, FrontPage 2000 has combined into a single application the features of the FrontPage Editor and FrontPage Explorer from FrontPage 98. New to version 2000, FrontPage now includes six views. Each view provides a different perspective of your FrontPage web or a page within the web and special tools for managing Web pages or the entire Web site.

Table 1-1 outlines the various views and their uses.

View	Description
Page	Basic text and layout editor used for editing Web page content. Most of the exercises in this course will be carried out in the Page View. Page View also includes several "tabs" for viewing a document in a variety of contexts, including "Normal," "HTML," and "Preview."
Folder	Overview of the directory and file structure of a FrontPage web.
Reports	Used for managing site files and links.
Navigation	Graphical tool for building Web site structure (layout) and hierarchy.
Hyperlinks	Graphical representation of hyperlinks between each page of a web.
Tasks	Site management tool for multiple authors and/or site maintenance.

Table 1-1: FrontPage 2000 views

You select an individual view using the View Panel. The View Panel, by default, is located to the left of the FrontPage window. In this course, you will explore the Page View, Folders View, and Hyperlinks View in depth. The other FrontPage views are discussed in greater detail in *Parts 2* and *3*.

Page View

Page View, which displays the current Web page, is unique because it displays three different but similar views. The three Page views are accessed via:

- tabs in the Page View dialog box

- tabs in the bottom left corner of the editor screen

Table 1-2 lists the Page View tabs and their respective functions.

Page View Tab	Description
Normal	The view you will most often use. This is the view in which you develop your pages.
HTML	The view in which you can see and edit the HTML code of your document. If you are familiar with HTML, there may be some tasks that you are more comfortable performing in the HTML tab.
Preview	Displays a close approximation of what visitors to your site will see through their Web browser. NOTE: the preview tab is an approximation and cannot mimic with 100% accuracy what visitors to your site will see.

Table 1-2: Page View tabs

 FrontPage is a WYSIWYG (what-you-see-is-what-you-get) HTML editor. This results in the contents of the Normal tab and the Preview tab being virtually indistinguishable. To avoid confusion, remember the differences between these tabs.

Figure 1-6 shows the same Web page displayed in the three different tab views of Page View (Normal, HTML, and Preview).

Figure 1-6: Page View tabs: Normal, HTML, and Preview (left to right)

Folders View

Folders View displays your web from a directory perspective, much like Windows Explorer displays the files on your hard drive. Most of your images, for example, will be stored in the IMAGES folder. Folders View helps you organize the files composing your Web site. Figure 1-7 shows an example of the Folders View.

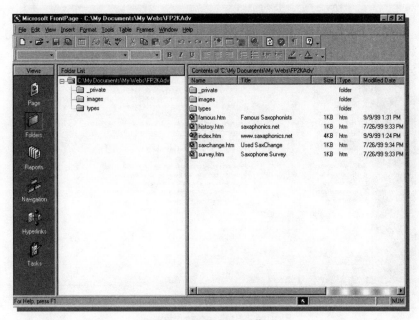

Figure 1-7: Folders View

In the Folders View, you can examine:

- file names

- document titles

- document size (in kilobytes)

- document type (HTML document, image file, Active Server Page, etc.)

- date and time last modified

- who last modified the document

- comments (if available)

Reports View

Reports View provides useful information and statistics regarding your FrontPage webs. A detailed discussion of the Reports View and its uses is provided in *Part 3*. The Reports View is shown in Figure 1-8.

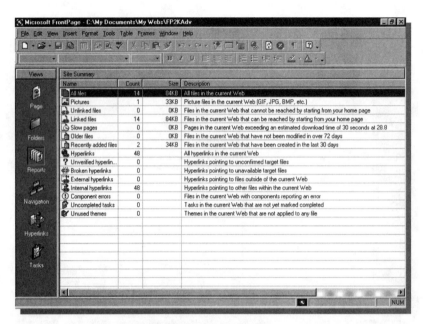

Figure 1-8: Reports View

Some of the more useful reports are described in Table 1-3.

Report	Description
All Files	List of all documents in the current FrontPage web
Pictures	List of all picture files in the current FrontPage web
Linked files	List of all documents to which there are links from other documents in the current FrontPage web
Unlinked files	List of all documents to which no other documents in the current FrontPage web have links
Broken Hyperlinks	List of all hyperlinks pointing to unavailable target files or outside URLs
Uncompleted Tasks	List of tasks that are not marked complete
Unverified Hyperlinks	List of all hyperlinks pointing to unconfirmed target files

Table 1-3: Reports View described

Navigation View

Navigation View is used to build a hierarchical map of your FrontPage web. This provides you with a valuable overview of the hierarchy of your site.

Graphical Display of Hyperlinks

Navigation View also allows you to see which pages and files are linked to each other (or links outside of your web) and which pages stand alone with no interconnections.

Drag & Drop to Rearrange

By clicking and dragging, you can rearrange the map and linking scheme of your site. Navigation View also allows you to:

- add new pages or files

- delete pages or files

- change the site hierarchy

The uses of Navigation View will be fully explored in *Part 2*. Figure 1-9 shows a FrontPage web displayed in Navigation View.

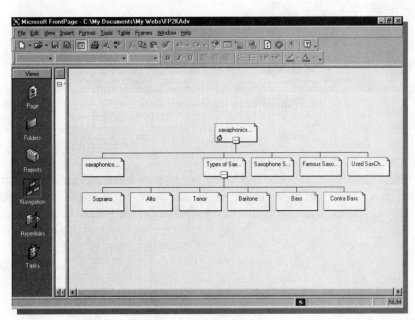

Figure 1-9: Navigation View

Hyperlinks View

Using Hyperlinks View, you can determine the links *to* and *from* any Web page and how many other documents within the same web are interlinked. Hyperlinks View is actually two separate displays configured in a two-paned window, as shown in Figure 1-10:

- each of your web directories and pages is listed in the left pane (Folder List)

- a hierarchical map of all of the hyperlinks in your web is displayed in the right pane (Hyperlinks View)

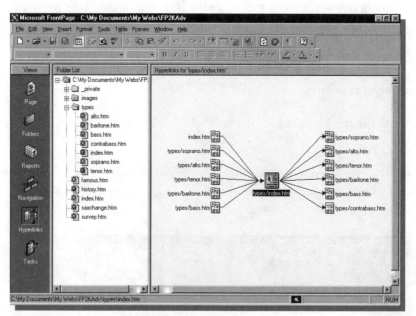

Figure 1-10: Hyperlinks View

When you select an individual document in the left pane, a hierarchical link map for that document appears in the right pane. Thus, the "center" of the right pane is determined by the active web document, which you choose by clicking in the Folder List (left pane).

Tasks View

Tasks View allows you to assign particular Web site project tasks to yourself or others. This view is particularly useful when managing a large, complex Web site with multiple authors and editors.

Task management is covered in greater detail in *Part 3*. Figure 1-11 displays the Tasks View window.

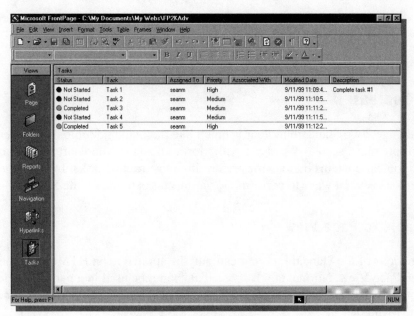

Figure 1-11: Tasks View

FrontPage 2000 Toolbars

Efficient navigation of the FrontPage interface and utilization of FrontPage's tools requires a solid familiarity with FrontPage's various toolbars. This section introduces you to the most commonly used toolbars and their major functions.

 Like all Microsoft toolbars, the FrontPage 2000 toolbars are movable. If you prefer to move any FrontPage toolbar, simply drag it to any location on the FrontPage 2000 window.

The toolbars can be "docked" at the top, bottom, left, or right of your screen, or can be "free-floating" anywhere on your desktop.

Standard Toolbar

The FrontPage 2000 Standard toolbar is much like the Standard toolbars in other Microsoft products, such as Word. As with most toolbars in Microsoft applications, the Standard toolbar contains buttons for performing most routine tasks. In virtually every case, there are several ways to perform the various tasks found on the Standard toolbar.

Applicable to Page View

Most functions of the Standard toolbar can only be applied to an HTML document viewed in Page View, Normal tab. Buttons that cannot be used in a particular view are grayed out. By default, the Standard toolbar appears at the top of the screen, directly below the Menu bar.

Typically the most frequently used toolbar in FrontPage 2000, the Standard toolbar helps you perform most routine tasks, such as:

- opening pages

- saving and printing pages

- publishing pages and files to your Web server

- obtaining help

The twenty-two buttons of the Standard toolbar are displayed in Figure 1-12 and listed in order from left to right in Table 1-4 on the following page.

Figure 1-12: Standard toolbar

Icon	Function
New Page	Opens a new, blank page for editing.
Open	Opens an existing page for editing.
Save	Saves the current page to your local machine or network.
Publish Web	Saves and uploads the current page to your Web server.
Folder List	Displays a list of your folders.
Print	Prints the current page.
Preview in Browser	Displays the current document in your default Web browser.
Spelling	Checks spelling for the current document.
Cut	Removes information from the current document and stores it in the clipboard.
Copy	Copies information from the current document and stores it in clipboard.
Paste	Pastes information stored in clipboard to current document at location of cursor.
Format Painter	Copies HTML format to text within the current page.
Undo	Undoes last command within the current page.
Redo	Redoes last undo within the current page.
Insert Component	Inserts FrontPage 2000 specific components into the current page (requires FrontPage Extensions on the Web server).
Insert Table	Inserts a table into the current page.
Insert Picture From File	Inserts pictures or graphics from your local computer into the current page.
Hyperlink	Inserts a hyperlink into the current page.
Refresh	Refreshes the screen in the current page.
Stop	Stops loading page in preview window.
Show All	Displays all hidden formats in the current page.
Microsoft FrontPage Help	Displays the FrontPage Help menu.

Table 1-4: Standard toolbar functions

Formatting Toolbar

The Formatting toolbar in FrontPage 2000, located by default below the Standard toolbar, is used to control the look of the text in your FrontPage documents. The Formatting toolbar will only work in Page View, Normal tab. Like the Standard toolbar, the Formatting toolbar's functions are grayed out in other Views.

The Formatting toolbar allows you to change many characteristics of Web page text, including:

- font size, type, color, and styles (**bold**, *italic*, <u>underline</u>)

- text alignment and spacing

- bullet lists and numbered lists

 FrontPage 2000 supports a wide range of font styles, but it is important to remember that not all visitors to your site will have support for those same fonts. It is recommended you use standard fonts in your Web pages.

The Formatting toolbar is displayed in Figure 1-13 and its functions listed in order from left to right in Table 1-5 on the following page.

Figure 1-13: Formatting toolbar

Icon	Function
Style	A drop-down menu that allows you to change the text style in the current Web page.
Font	A drop-down menu that allows you to change the font in the current Web page.
Font Size	A drop-down menu that allows you to change the size of the font in the current Web page.
Bold	Bold faces fonts in the current page.
Italic	Italicizes fonts in the current page.
Underline	Underlines fonts in the current page.
Align Left	Aligns text with the left margin in the current page.
Center	Centers text in the current page.
Align Right	Aligns text with the right margin in the current page.
Numbering	Creates an ordered list (i.e., 1., 2., 3., 4., etc.) in the current page.
Bullets	Creates an unordered list (i.e., a bulleted list) in the current page.
Decrease Indent	Sets the current margin of the page further to the left.
Increase Indent	Sets the current margin of the page further to the right.
Highlight Color	Changes the background color of the selected object or text in the current page.
Font Color	Changes the font color in the current page.

Table 1-5: Formatting toolbar functions

Tables Toolbar

The Tables toolbar in FrontPage 2000 is used to create and edit tables in your Web pages. Tables are the easiest way to manipulate the layout of your Web pages. Tables are discussed in greater detail in Lesson 5. Hidden by default, the Tables toolbar appears when you are creating or editing a table. You can use the Tables toolbar to modify the alignment, layout, or background of a table.

The Tables toolbar is displayed in Figure 1-14 and its functions listed in order from left to right in Table 1-6.

Figure 1-14: Tables toolbar

Icon	Function
Draw Table	Draws a new table or edits the layout of an existing table in the current page.
Eraser	Erases table features such as rows and columns in the current page.
Insert Rows	Inserts rows into the selected table.
Insert Columns	Inserts columns into the selected table.
Delete Cells	Deletes cells in the selected table.
Merge Cells	Merges multiple cells into a single cell.
Split Cells	Splits a single cell into multiple cells.
Align Top	Aligns the text in the selected cell to the top.
Center Vertically	Aligns the text in the selected cell to the center.
Align Bottom	Aligns text in the selected cell to the bottom.
Distribute Rows Evenly	Makes the height and width of selected rows equal.
Distribute Columns Evenly	Makes the height and width of selected columns equal.
Fill Color	Allows you to select the background color of rows, columns, cells or the entire table.
Autofit	Allows cells or text to automatically fit within the selected container.

Table 1-6: Tables toolbar icons

Pictures Toolbar

The FrontPage 2000 Pictures toolbar is used to insert, edit, and arrange pictures and images in your Web pages. You will work with images more extensively in Lesson 4.

The Pictures toolbar allows you to:

- add text or a border to an image

- resize or rotate an image

- adjust the brightness or contrast of an image

- alter the coloration of an image

- define *hotspot* regions for the creation of image maps

The Pictures toolbar is displayed in Figure 1-15 and its functions are listed in order from left to right in Table 1-7 on the following page.

Figure 1-15: Pictures toolbar

 Hotspot regions contain hyperlinks that allow users to click a specific area of an image and send that request to a Web server to download another Web page, or begin the download of a file, for example.

Icon	Function
Insert Picture from File	Inserts a picture from your local machine or network into the current HTML document.
Text	Adds text to the selected picture.
Auto Thumbnail	Replaces a picture or image with a smaller version and creates a hyperlink to the larger version.
Position Absolutely	Forces the content of the HTML document to wrap around the picture.
Bring Forward	Brings overlapping picture to the front.
Send Backward	Sends overlapping picture to the back.
Rotate Left	Rotates selected picture 90 degrees to the left.
Rotate Right	Rotates selected picture 90 degrees to the right.
Flip Horizontal	Reverses the selected picture from left to right.
Flip Vertical	Reverses the selected picture from top to bottom.
More Contrast	Increases the contrast of selected picture.
Less Contrast	Decreases the contrast of selected picture.
More Brightness	Increases the brightness of selected picture.
Less Brightness	Decreases the brightness of selected picture
Crop	Allows you to cut out parts of the selected picture.
Set Transparent Color	Converts any color in a picture to transparency.
Black and White	Converts selected picture to monochrome.
Wash Out	Adds whiteness to each of the colors in selected picture.
Bevel	Adds a three-dimensional border around selected picture.
Resample	Converts a picture to actual desired size.
Select	Selects a picture by clicking it.
Rectangular Hotspot	Marks a rectangular area within a picture as a hotspot.
Circular Hotspot	Marks a circular area within a picture as a hotspot.
Polygonal Hotspot	Marks an irregular shaped area within a picture as a hotspot.
Highlight Hotspots	Displays all current hotspots within an image.
Restore	Returns an image to its original appearance.

Table 1-7: Pictures toolbar buttons

Other FrontPage 2000 Toolbars

In addition to the toolbars listed in the previous sections—which are the most commonly used—there are several other toolbars that can be used to assist with some of the more advanced FrontPage 2000 features. These toolbars are discussed in greater detail in *Parts 2* and *3*.

The other toolbars and their functions are listed in Table 1-8.

Toolbar	Function
DHTML Effects	Allows you to add and manipulate DHTML (Dynamic HTML) effects.
Navigation	Used in Navigation View, allows you to add or remove pages from the navigation scheme, or change the alignment of the schematic.
Positioning	Allows you to control the position of images and text.
Reporting	Used in Reports View, allows you to define and manipulate report settings.
Style	Allows you to define styles for use with Cascading Style Sheets (CSS).

Table 1-8: Additional FrontPage 2000 toolbars

You can use the **Customize** window to design custom toolbars for FrontPage 2000. To do so, click the **New** button and type the name of your custom toolbar. Next, choose the **Commands** tab and drag the icons you desire to your new toolbar. It's that simple!

"I've gone from sheer hatred of Microsoft FrontPage 98 to a raving fan of FrontPage 2000."

– Bill Machrone, columnist, PC Week Magazine, 1999

Lesson Summary

▶ FrontPage 2000 is an HTML editor and is a GUI-based application that simplifies the creation of dynamic Web sites which otherwise would require extensive knowledge of HTML and scripting languages and much greater time and effort.

▶ FrontPage is also a tool for the management of a complex Web site, granting site administrators vast control over site content management.

▶ FrontPage 2000 can be installed side-by-side with earlier versions of FrontPage. FrontPage 2000 combines the FrontPage Explorer and FrontPage Editors of earlier FrontPage versions into a single, powerful application. Unlike earlier versions of FrontPage, FrontPage 2000 does not make arbitrary alterations to HTML source code. There are several other new features in FrontPage 2000.

▶ Two important navigation methods offered by the FrontPage 2000 user interface are toolbars and views.

▶ There are six FrontPage views: Page, Folders, Reports, Navigation, Hyperlinks and Tasks. Each view serves a unique function in the development and administration of a FrontPage web.

▶ Most of the development of a FrontPage web is done in Page View. Within Page View, there are several tabs that allow you to view your FrontPage documents in a number of contexts.

▶ FrontPage 2000 has more than a half dozen different toolbars to assist you in developing your web. Of these, the Standard, Formatting, Tables, and Picture toolbars are the most frequently used.

▶ FrontPage 2000 allows you to easily create your own custom toolbars. To create a custom toolbar, click the **New** button and type the name of your custom toolbar. Next, choose the **Commands** tab and drag the icons you desire to your new toolbar.

DDC Publishing • www.ddcpub.com

Lesson Review

Matching

___ 1. Use this to check the files that are linked to a given document.

a. Page View

___ 2. Most FrontPage development is done with this.

b. Formatting toolbar

___ 3. Use this to adjust font or alignment settings.

c. Tasks View

___ 4. FrontPage components and Form elements are added from here.

d. Hyperlinks View

___ 5. This allows you to keep track of what needs to be done for your web.

e. Insert menu

Fill in the Blank

6. _____ and _____ are two elements of FrontPage 98 that are combined in FrontPage 2000.

7. _____ in Office 2000 applications can be repositioned.

8. You would find spell check in the _____ menu.

9. Images can be manipulated with the _____ toolbar.

True or False?

T / F   10. Multiple versions of FrontPage can be installed on the same computer.

T / F   11. Dynamic HTML effects can be added to a Web page using the Edit menu.

T / F   12. You can create customized toolbars in FrontPage.

T / F   13. Only with a graphics application can you use FrontPage 2000 to hack into the White House Web site and give the president a mustache and rabbit ears to the First Lady.

T / F   14. FrontPage's five views are critical to helping you manage your Web site.

DDC Publishing • www.ddcpub.com

Lesson 2
Getting Started
With FrontPage
2000

Lesson Topics

► HTML Primer

► HTML Tags

► HTML Document Components

► Creating a New FrontPage Web

► Lesson Summary

HTML Primer

If you are planning to use FrontPage 2000 to develop your Web site, there is a good chance that one of your principal reasons for doing so is that you are not familiar with HTML, or HyperText Markup Language. This section provides an HTML primer to give you a basic knowledge that is important, even when using a highly automated HTML editor such as FrontPage.

Universal Markup Language

HTML is the *markup language* upon which the World Wide Web is based. All Web pages on the Web (all 900 million of them!) are written in HTML, and possibly enhanced with JavaScript, Java, RealAudio, RealVideo, and Shock animation. But HTML is the foundation on which all Web pages and Web sites are created, regardless of the "icing on the cake" that may have been applied in addition to HTML.

HTML is a non-proprietary, standard, World Wide Web publishing document format that can be generated or applied to existing text-based (ASCII) and word processor formats (MS Word, Corel WordPerfect) by a wide range of tools, including a plain text editor (such as Wordpad or Notepad) or dedicated HTML editor, such as FrontPage 2000.

HTML Knowledge Less Important

Automation tools such as FrontPage 2000 prevent you from having to be an HTML expert. You can now create powerful, attractive, and appealing Web pages without understanding the details of HTML. However, you should realize that FrontPage does not change the fact that Web pages are written in HTML.

HTML Tags

Tags are an integral part of HTML. This lesson is not intended to serve as a comprehensive overview of HTML or its tags (collectively known as the *HTML tag set*). Rather, this lesson is meant to supplement your use of FrontPage 2000. For an extensive overview of HTML, refer to DDC's HTML course series[2].

 HTML formatting commands are enclosed in <angle brackets> called *wickets*, while regular (non-code) text is not.

Tag Components

HTML tags have several basic components with which you should be familiar. The most important are outlined below and shown in Figure 2-1, including:

- opening and closing tags

- standalone tags

- tag elements

- attributes and attribute values

- closing tag switches

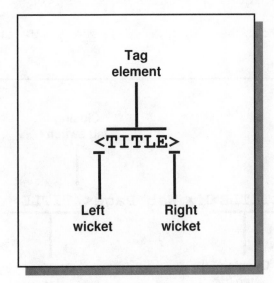

Figure 2-1: Basic anatomy of an HTML tag

---

[2] DDC's HTML series includes *HTML 4.0 Fundamentals*, *HTML 4.0 Intermediate*, and *HTML 4.0 Advanced*.

Tag Elements

The first word within the tag determines the identity of the tag and is called the *tag element*. The element differentiates one tag from other tags. The tag element is typically an abbreviated or acronym-like form of the tag name.

For example:

- <HR> = Horizontal rule tag element

-
 = Break tag element

- <A> = Anchor tag element

Opening & Closing Tags

Most HTML tags appear in the form of a *tag set*, as shown in Figure 2-2. A tag set begins with an opening tag *<tag element>* and ends with a closing tag *</tag element>*. Everything between the opening and closing tags is affected by the tags. Thus, everything between the opening and closing bold tags will appear in bold.

Common examples of opening and closing tag sets are bold and italic text formatting and the Anchor tag (used to create hyperlinks to other Web documents). For example:

- `Erich's Porsche was the <B>`**`fastest`**`</B> in town.`

- `Erich's Porsche was the <I>`*`fastest`*`</I> in town.`

- `Erich's Porsche was the <U>`<u>`fastest`</u>`</U> in town.`

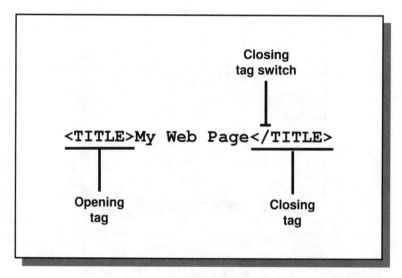

Figure 2-2: Example of a tag set

Standalone Tags

It is only the minority of tags in HTML that are standalone, but it is important to note the difference between tag sets and standalone tags. Common examples of standalone tags are the Break tag, <BR>, which inserts a line break (sometimes called a *soft return*) into a Web page, the Paragraph tag, <P>, which inserts a paragraph break (sometimes called a *hard return*), and the Horizontal Rule tag. <HR>, (shown in Figure 2-3).

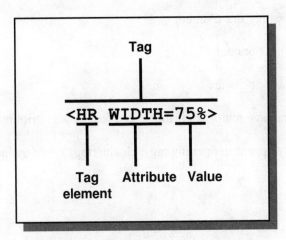

Figure 2-3: Example of a standalone tag

Standalone tags do not require a corresponding closing tag. For example,

```
Erich's Porsche is the coolest and fastest car in town.<BR>
Erich likes me but is in jail.<P>

Janet's Toyota is the slowest and ugliest car in town.<BR>
Janet is mad at me but is not in jail.<P>
```

Attributes

Terms within a tag (i.e., within the wickets) specify characteristics of the element the tag defines. Thus, `<HR WIDTH="60%">` instructs a user's browser to display the horizontal rule as 60% of the width of the browser window. This second part of the tag is called an *attribute*.

Note the following characteristics of HTML tag attributes:

- a tag can have only one element

- all attributes are optional

- not all tags have attributes

- those tags that have multiple attributes can feature all attributes simultaneously

- attributes only appear in opening tags; closing tags never include attributes

For example:

```
<HR WIDTH=50% ALIGN=left SIZE=8>
```

The defaults of a horizontal rule are: width = 100%, alignment = center, size = 2 points. If no attributes are specified, these defaults will be invoked by a user's Web browser.

HTML tags are *not* case sensitive. <TABLE>, <table>, and <TaBLe> are identical in function and browser interpretation.

HTML Document Components

An HTML document will normally have two sections, the HEAD and the BODY. The beginning and end of an HTML document are marked with the <HTML>...</HTML> tags.

HEAD Section

In the <HEAD> section, you will find the document title as well as information about the document itself, such as the author, date created, method of creation, and keywords.

Metadata

This information about the document is called *metadata*. Metadata is used by search engines to index a Web page in a database. Metadata is not required, but is helpful if you want users to be able to locate your Web site using a search engine[3].

Some scripts, such as Java applets, are also defined within the HEAD section. Aside from the title of the document, which will be displayed in the uppermost status bar when the page is viewed in a browser, the rest of the information in the HEAD section is invisible to a visitor to your site unless they view the HTML source code. The HEAD section is enclosed by the <HEAD>...</HEAD> tags.

BODY Section

The <BODY> section of an HTML document contains the actual content of the document. Everything you want visitors to your site to see in their browser window when they access the page must be included in the BODY section. The BODY section is enclosed by the <BODY>...</BODY> tags.

---

[3] See DDC's *Promoting Your Web Site* for detailed information regarding metadata and how to include <META> tags in your HTML documents in order to promote your site in search engine databases.

Common HTML Tags

Table 2-1 includes some of the most commonly used HTML tags. A complete list of HTML 4.0 elements and attributes can be found in Appendix A.

Tag	Description
<HTML>...</HTML>	Marks the beginning and end of an HTML document
<HEAD>...</HEAD>	Marks the beginning and end of the HEAD section of an HTML document
<BODY>...</BODY>	Marks the beginning and end of the BODY section of an HTML document
<TITLE>...</TITLE>	Defines the title of the document
<H1>...</H1> <H2>...</H2> <H3>...</H3> <H4>...</H4> <H5>...</H5> <H6>...</H6>	Headings, sizes 1-6 (H1 being the largest, H6 the smallest)
<P>...</P>	Marks the beginning and end of a paragraph
<FONT>...</FONT>	Defines the font for the enclosed text (attributes required)
<B>...</B>	Displays enclosed text as **bold**
<I>...</I>	Displays enclosed text in *italics*
<U>...</U>	Displays enclosed text as <u>underlined</u>
<UL>...</UL>	Creates an unordered (bullet) list
<OL>...</OL>	Creates an ordered (numbered) list
<LI>...</LI>	List item within a bullet list
<HR>	Draws a horizontal rule across the page

	Inserts a line break
<TABLE>...</TABLE>	Marks the beginning and end of a table
<TR>...</TR>	Marks the beginning and end of a table row
<TD>...</TD>	Marks the beginning and end of a table cell
<A>...</A>	Defines a hyperlink (has a required attribute HREF=)
<IMG>	Defines an inline image (has a required attribute SRC=)

Table 2-1: Essential HTML tags

Exercise 2-1: Creating an HTML Document Using a Text Editor

Before you create your first FrontPage web, it is useful to understand how an HTML document is created in a text editor. In this exercise, you will create an HTML document using a plain text (ASCII) editor and add HTML tags to that document.

1. Launch Notepad (or another text editor). Do not use Microsoft Word or WordPerfect.

2. Type the following text:

   We, the people of the United States, in order to form a more perfect Union, establish Justice, ensure Domestic Tranquility, provide for the Common Defense, promote the General Welfare, and secure the Blessings of Liberty for ourselves and our posterity do ordain and establish this Constitution for the United States of America.

3. Save this document twice in Notepad, once as PREAMBLE_NP.HTML, and once as PREAMBLE_FP.HTML.

4. Open PREAMBLE_NP.HTML in your Web browser. It should resemble Figure 2-4.

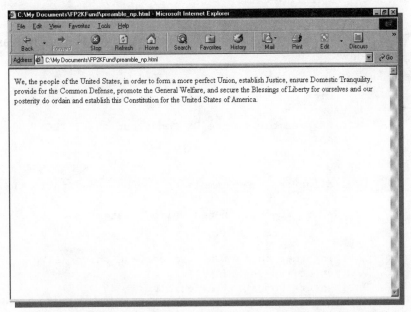

Figure 2-4: Document (without HTML tags) as viewed in a browser

5. Toggle over to PREAMBLE_NP.HTML in Notepad (<ALT> + <TAB>) and add opening and closing HTML tags (<HTML>...</HTML>) to the beginning and end of the document.

6. Under the opening <HTML> tag, add a head (<HEAD>...</HEAD>) section to the document and insert the following tags and text:

   `<TITLE>Preamble to the US Constitution</TITLE>`

7. Add opening and closing body tags (<BODY>...</BODY>) around the body of the document.

8. Enclose the text of the preamble within paragraph tags (<P>...</P>).

9. Make bold "We the people of the United States" by enclosing it within Bold tags (<B>...</B>).

10. Italicize the term "Constitution" by enclosing it within Italic tags (<I>...</I>).

11. Create an unordered (bullet) list by enclosing the text "in order to form a more perfect Union, establish Justice, ensure Domestic Tranquility, provide for the Common Defense, promote the General Welfare, and secure the Blessings of Liberty for ourselves and our posterity" within unordered list tags (<UL>...</UL>) and replacing the commas with list item tags (<LI>).

12. Create an H1 formatted heading (<H1>...</H1>) at the top of the page that reads **`Preamble to the US Constitution`**. Use ALIGN=center as the header tag's attribute (<H1 ALIGN=CENTER>...</H1>).

Your finished HTML document in Notepad should now appear as below:

```
<HTML>

<HEAD>
<TITLE>Preamble to the US Constitution</TITLE>
</HEAD>

<BODY>
<H1 align=center>Preamble to the US Constitution</H1>
<P>
<B>We, the people of the United States</B>,

<UL>
<LI>in order to form a more perfect Union</LI>
<LI>establish Justice</LI>
<LI>ensure Domestic Tranquility</LI>
<LI>provide for the Common Defense</LI>
<LI>promote the General Welfare</LI>
<LI>and secure the Blessings of Liberty for ourselves and
our posterity</LI>
</UL>

do ordain and establish this <I>Constitution</I> for the
United States of America.</P>
</P>

</BODY>
</HTML>
```

13. Save PREAMBLE_NP.HTML and refresh (reload) your browser. Figure 2-5 displays the newly formatted document.

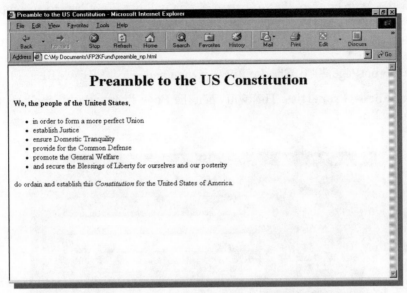

Figure 2-5: ASCII text document featuring HTML formatting

Using FrontPage to Edit HTML Documents

From the previous exercise, you can see that HTML is a relatively simple scripting language. However, when working with larger documents in a complex Web site, HTML coding can become time-consuming, tedious, and very cumbersome. You must always remember to close the tags that you open, and it can be very difficult to visualize the appearance of your Web pages when interpreted by a user's browser. Using a WYSIWYG editor such as FrontPage can make managing large, complex Web pages (and entire Web sites) easier.

Exercise 2-2: Creating an HTML Document with FrontPage 2000

In the previous exercise, you added HTML tags to the document in order to format it for viewing with a Web browser. In this exercise, you will use FrontPage to accomplish the same ends.

1. Launch FrontPage 2000. Choose **File ▶ Open** and select PREAMBLE_FP.HTML.

2. Choose **File ▶ Properties**. This will open the **Page Properties** dialog box, as shown in Figure 2-6.

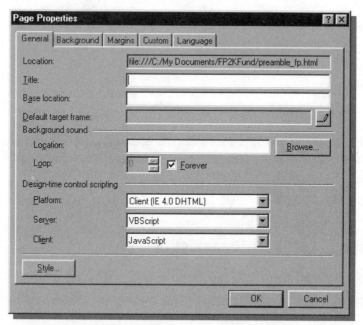

Figure 2-6: General tab in the Page Properties dialog box

3. Type **Preamble to the US Constitution** in the **Title** field.

4. Click **OK** to close the **Page Properties** dialog box.

5. Type **Preamble to the US Constitution** at the top of the document.

6. Highlight this text and select **Heading 1** from the Formatting toolbar. Center the text using the Formatting toolbar.

7. Highlight the text "We, the people of the United States" and apply bold formatting using the Formatting toolbar.

8. Insert a line break before the phrase "in order to form a more perfect Union" by placing your cursor in front of the phrase and pressing <ENTER>.

9. Insert another line break after the word "posterity."

10. Highlight the section that begins "in order to form a more perfect Union, establish Justice…", and ends "secure the Blessings of Liberty for ourselves and our posterity".

11. Create a bulleted list by pressing the bullet button on the Formatting toolbar. This will create one bullet at the beginning of the highlighted section. Insert line breaks at the location of each comma (removing the commas) to create the subsequent bullet points.

12. Highlight the term "Constitution" and italicize it using the Formatting toolbar.

13. Before saving your changes, open PREAMBLE_FP.HTML in your browser.

14. Save your changes to PREAMBLE_FP.HTML in FrontPage. Choose **File ▶ Save**.

15. In your browser, reload PREAMBLE_FP.HTML. Compare the view in the browser with that in FrontPage. View the document in the HTML and Preview tabs (bottom).

Your finished HTML document in FrontPage should now appear as in Figure 2-7 (in Normal tab) and as it should appear in your browser in Figure 2-8 on the following page.

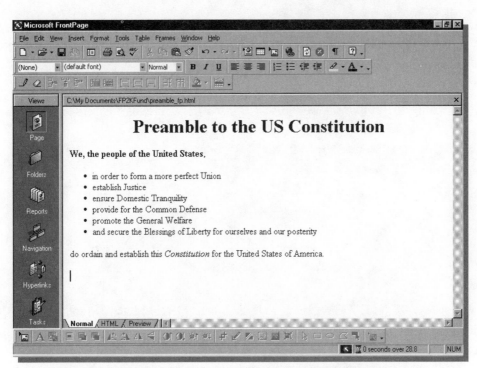

Figure 2-7: Completed HTML document in FrontPage (Normal tab)

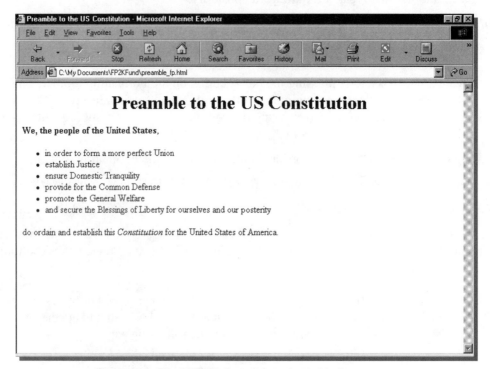

Figure 2-8: Final HTML document viewed in browser

16. Close both FrontPage and your browser when you are finished with this exercise.

Creating a New FrontPage Web

As mentioned earlier, a group of Web pages created, viewed, or edited using FrontPage is called a FrontPage web.

FrontPage offers several methods of creating new webs.

- import an existing Web site

- create a web using a Wizard

- create a web using one of several templates

- create a new web from scratch

To create a new web, open FrontPage and select **File ▶ New ▶ Web**. This opens the **New Web Sites** dialog box, as shown in Figure 2-9.

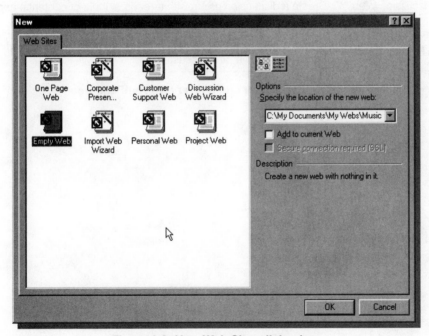

Figure 2-9: New Web Sites dialog box

Your options for creating a new FrontPage web are listed in Table 2-2.

Web type	Description
One Page Web	Create a new web with a single blank page
Empty Web	Create a new multi-page web with nothing in it
Corporate Presence Wizard	Create a professional Internet presence for your organization
Import Web Wizard	Create a web filled with documents from a directory on your computer or a remote file system
Customer Support Web	Create a web to improve your customer support services, particularly for software companies
Personal Web	Create a personal web with pages on your interests, photos, and favorite web sites
Discussion Web Wizard	Create a discussion group with threads, a table of contents, and full text searching
Project Web	Create a web for a project containing a list of members, schedule, status, an archive, and discussions

Table 2-2: Options for creating a new FrontPage web

Working with Wizards & Templates

The other Web Creation Wizards and the pre-formatted templates provided with FrontPage simplify the creation of some common types of Web sites. If you do not have much time to spend on developing your site, these templates and wizards can be very helpful. The Wizards walk you through a step-by-step process for creating a Web site, and do much of the work for you in the background. All of them are fairly self-explanatory; thus, this course will not cover them in detail. You can also create your own custom templates for oft-repeated Web site hierarchies.

Creating Your First FrontPage 2000 Web

The real power of FrontPage is in using it as a tool to develop a new Web site from start to finish. When FrontPage creates a new web, it copies several hidden files to a directory you have created for your Web document. This directory is called the *Root Web*.

The Root Web

The Root Web can reside on:

- your local PC
- a remote file system
- a remote Web server

If you are creating a new FrontPage web on a remote Web server, you must ensure that *FrontPage Server Extensions* have been installed. Check with the server administrator if you are unsure of the status of FrontPage Server Extensions on the remote Web server.

Whenever you create a new FrontPage web, FrontPage will automatically create several hidden files and directories, and two visible directories under the Root Web:

- _PRIVATE
- IMAGES

FrontPage Server Extensions are installed on a server to allow Web sites residing on the server to take advantage of many of the features of FrontPage. It is possible to publish a FrontPage web on a server without Server Extensions, but many FrontPage features will not function. A complete list of components requiring extensions is provided in Appendix B.

Exercise 2-3: Creating Your First FrontPage 2000 Web

In this exercise, you will create an empty FrontPage web. This web will be a site for a used musical instruments store called *Music 4 a Song.* During the balance of this course, you will develop different types of Web pages for the store's new site one the Internet.

1. Ensure that there are no other webs open in FrontPage.

2. Select **File ▶ New ▶ Web**.

3. Specify the location of the new web as C:\MY DOCUMENTS\MY WEBS\MUSIC4ASONG.

4. Choose **Empty Web** and click **OK**.

5. FrontPage will now create the new web, as shown in Figure 2-10.

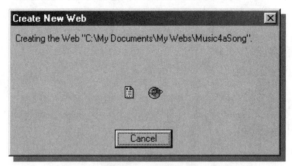

Figure 2-10: Creating a new FrontPage web

6. Once the web is created, switch to FrontPage's Folders View.

 Note that the web folder and two subdirectories called _PRIVATE and IMAGES have been created.

Lesson Summary

▶ HyperText Markup Language (HTML) is the basis of the World Wide Web. HTML is a meta-language, which is to say that it is a language that describes how a document is to be interpreted. A browser interprets HTML much in the same way that a reader interprets punctuation.

▶ HTML is made up of tags. All tags are enclosed within angle brackets (<...>), sometimes known as wickets. Most tags have corresponding open and closing tags, though some standalone.

▶ All HTML tags must include only one element. Some tags may also include one or more attributes, which supplement the appropriate element.

▶ Most HTML documents consist of two sections, the HEAD and the BODY. The HEAD of a document may contain information about the document, known as metadata, and may also include the title of the document and some scripts or applets. The BODY of a document includes the content visible to the average Web site visitor.

▶ Any text editor, such as Notepad, can be used to create HTML documents. Viewing an HTML document in a simple text editor may or may not give you a good sense of how a browser will render the page.

▶ Editing an HTML document in FrontPage or another WYSIWYG editor enables you to get a better sense of how that document will appear in a browser.

▶ You can create new FrontPage webs in several ways. You can import an existing Web site, use a Web Creation Wizard or template, or create your own web from scratch. You can also create new templates for oft-repeated webs.

▶ A new FrontPage web can be created in a directory on your local machine or on a remote Web server. If created on a remote Web server, that server must have FrontPage Server Extensions installed. When FrontPage creates a new FrontPage web, it automatically creates several hidden directories and files, and two visible directories, _PRIVATE and IMAGES, under the Root Web.

Lesson Review

Matching

____ 1. All HTML tags are enclosed in these

a. metadata

____ 2. Information about a document

b. Import Web Wizard

____ 3. Used to create a new FrontPage web from an already existing Web site

c. Discussion Web Wizard

____ 4. Section of an HTML document that contains the document's content

d. wickets

____ 5. Used to create a new FrontPage web for threaded discussion

e. body

Fill in the Blank

6. _____ and _____ are two directories automatically created by FrontPage when a new web is created.

7. All HTML tags must contain at least one and only one _____ and may or may not contain one or more _____.

8. To create a new FrontPage web from scratch, choose **File ▶ New ▶ Web ▶** and select _____.

9. HTML stands for _____.

True or False?

T / F   10. <hr> is an example of a stand-alone tag.

T / F   11. In <p align="center">, the p is the attribute and align="center" is the element.

T / F   12. You can create custom FrontPage web templates.

T / F   13. FrontPage cannot be used to develop sites on servers without FrontPage Server Extensions installed.

Lesson 3
Elements of Web Page Creation

Lesson Topics

► Creating a New Page

► Text Characteristics of Web Pages

► Hyperlinks

► Horizontal Lines & Symbols

► Page Banners

► Lesson Summary

Creating a New Page

Now that you have created a web, it is time to start working with page content. Before you can do that, you need to create a new page. Creating a new page in FrontPage is very similar to creating a new web. In Page View, choose **File ▶ New ▶ Page**, which will bring up the **New Page** dialog box, shown in Figure 3-1.

 You can also create a new page in Folders View, Navigation View, or Hyperlinks View. Only if you create the new page in Page View, however, will you be able to use the **New Page** dialog box.

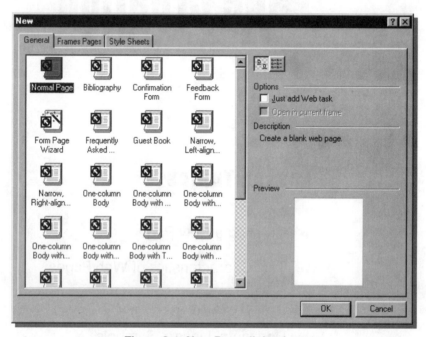

Figure 3-1: New Page dialog box

New Page Layouts

There are three tabs in the **New Page** dialog box:

- General

- Frames Pages

- Style Sheets

Frames Pages and Style Sheets are covered in depth in *Part 2* of this course. Table 3-1 lists the options available on the General tab.

Page Type	Description
Normal Page	Creates a blank web page
Bibliography	Creates a bibliography page that makes reference to printed or electronic works
**Confirmation Form	Creates a page to acknowledge receipt of user input from Discussion, Form Result, or Registration
*Feedback Form	Creates a page where users can submit comments about your web site, products, or organization
*Form Page Wizard	Creates a form page by selecting the types of information you need to collect
Frequently Asked Questions	Creates an FAQ page that answers common questions about a given topic
*Guest Book	Creates a page where visitors to your web can leave their comments in a public guest log
Narrow, Left-aligned body	Creates a page with a narrow, left-aligned body
Narrow, Right-aligned body	Creates a page with a narrow, right-aligned body
One-column body	Creates a page with a centered body
One-column body with contents and sidebar	Creates a page with a one-column body with contents listed on the left and a sidebar on the right
One-column body with contents on left	Creates a page with a one-column body with contents listed on the left
One-column body with contents on right	Creates a page with a one-column body with contents listed on the right
One-column body with staggered sidebar	Creates a page with a one-column body and a two-column, staggered sidebar on the left
One-column body with two sidebars	Creates a page with a staggered sidebar on the left and a sidebar on the right
One-column body with two-column sidebar	Creates a page with a one-column body and a two-column sidebar on the right
*Search Page	Creates a page where users can search for keywords across all the documents in a web
*Table of Contents	Creates a page with links to every document in your web, displayed in outline format
Three-column body	Creates a page with a three-column body
Two-column body	Creates a page with a two-column body

Page Type	Description
Two-column body with contents and sidebar	Creates a page with a two-column body with contents listed on the left and a sidebar on the right
Two-column body with contents on left	Creates a page with a two-column body with contents listed on the left
Two-column staggered body	Creates a page with a body containing two staggered columns
Two-column staggered body with contents and sidebar	Creates a page with a two-column, staggered body with contents listed on the left and a sidebar on the right
**User Registration	Creates a page where users can self-register for a protected web. Only useful in a root web.
Wide body with headings	Create a page with a wide body and subheadings

Table 3-1: New Page general layouts

For many of the layouts in the above table, you will need to experiment in order to determine whether a particular layout works for the page you are creating.

Page Properties

Once you have selected a layout, your next consideration is the page itself. The **Page Properties** dialog box (select **File ▶ Properties**), shown in Figure 3-2 on the following page, allows you to configure:

- document title

- background color or images

- text color

- margins

- background sound effects*

- metadata (custom)**

- language**

- workgroup**

---

* covered in greater depth in *Part 2*.
** covered in greater depth in *Part 3*.

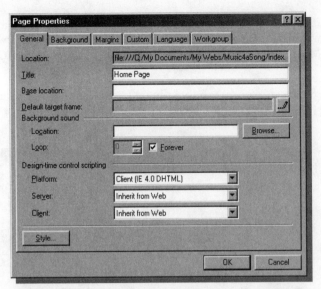

Figure 3-2: Page Properties dialog box, General tab

Document Title

As you will recall from Lesson 2, the title of a document, as defined in the **Title** field of the **General** tab of the **Page Properties** dialog box, is displayed in the uppermost status bar of a browser window when a page is viewed.

Note that when a new page is created in FrontPage, the default naming convention for the file is NEW_PAGE_X.HTM where x is a number signifying this particular page's order of creation.

After you define a page title, the file name will change to reflect that title. If you do not wish to use the page title as the file name, you should rename the file by saving it under a different name.

Background Colors & Images

The **Background** tab of the **Page Properties** dialog box, shown in Figure 3-3 on the following page, allows you to select a color for the background of your document.

If you do not define a background color for your Web page, a user's browser will display a default background color. The default color is white in Microsoft Internet Explorer and gray in Netscape Navigator/Communicator.

You can also use the **Background** tab to define a background image. Background images will be discussed in greater detail in Lesson 4.

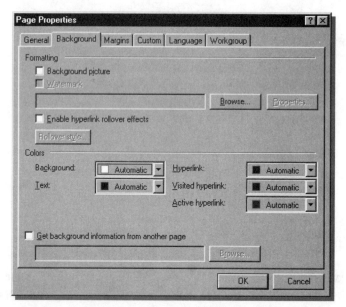

Figure 3-3: Page Properties dialog box, Background tab

Text Color

You can define the text color as well, using the **Background** tab. There are four different text types for which you can define a color:

- Text: all non-hyperlinked text

- Hyperlink: links that have not been followed

- Visited hyperlink: links that have been followed recently

- Active hyperlink: links that are currently being followed

A hyperlink will become "active" when it is clicked. If the linked page loads quickly, this link will only appear "active" for an instant. Many Web designers will set the color of an active hyperlink identical to the background color of the page, creating the effect that the link seems to disappear when clicked. Visited hyperlinks remain for a set period, defined by a user within the browser. Usually this is for just a few days.

If you do not define colors, the default colors will be used. These defaults are:

- <u>Text</u>: black

- <u>Hyperlink</u>: blue

- <u>Visited hyperlink</u>: purple

- <u>Active hyperlink</u>: red

 Use care when selecting colors for text. Be sure to take into consideration the background color and how a given text color will appear against that background. If you have a dark background, it is best to use a bright or complementary color in your text.

Margins

The **Margins** tab of the **Page Properties** dialog box, shown in Figure 3-4, allows you to set the top and left margins of your page in pixels. The bottom and right margins cannot be set, as they are dependent on the size of the user's browser window (highly variable) and the amount and size of content on a given page.

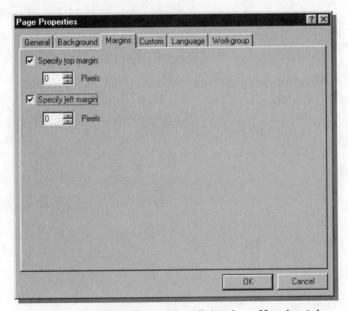

Figure 3-4: Page Properties dialog box, Margins tab

Exercise 3-1: Creating a New Page and Setting Page Properties

In this exercise, you will create a new page and set its properties using the **Page Properties** dialog box.

1. If it is not already, open the *Music 4 a Song* web you created in Exercise 2-3.
2. In **Page View**, create a new page by selecting **File ▶ New ▶ Page**.
3. Select **Normal Page** from the **General** tab of the **New** dialog box and click **OK**.
4. Select **File ▶ Properties** to open the **Page Properties** dialog box.
5. On the **General** tab, define the **Title** of the page as `Welcome to the Music 4 a Song Used Instrument Shop`.
6. On the **Background** tab under Colors, define the background color as **olive**.
7. Define the following colors for your text:
   - Text: white
   - Hyperlink: yellow
   - Visited hyperlink: purple
   - Active hyperlink: green
8. On the **Margins** tab, specify only the top margin as **12** pixels.
9. Click **OK** to apply these changes and exit the **Page Properties** dialog box.
10. Choose **File ▶ Save As...** and save this file as INDEX.HTM in the MUSIC4ASONG folder.

Text Characteristics of Web Pages

One of the most important aspects of any Web site is the content of its text. No matter how impressive the colors and images, if a visitor cannot locate or understand the information he or she requires, your site will not be useful. While this course cannot make you an excellent writer, understanding the various ways you can work with text in a document will make your site more user-friendly.

There are three elements that define text in a Web page:

- format
- font
- alignment

Text Formats

All text in a Web document falls into one of the following formats, defined by the far-left drop-down menu in the formatting toolbar:

- standard body text
- addresses
- headings
- formatted text
- lists

Standard Body Text

Unless otherwise specified, all text in a Web document is considered Normal text. By default, FrontPage uses 12-point Times New Roman font, though this can be modified based on user preferences and customization. This is also the default font used by most Web browsers, though again, it is subject to user preference.

When typing prose paragraphs in FrontPage:

- <ENTER> to begin a new paragraph
- <SHIFT>+<ENTER> to force a line break (sometimes called a *soft return*); this does not begin a new paragraph

Addresses

This format is a hold-over from the early days of HTML (circa 1994), when it was used to format the e-mail address of the Webmaster. It is almost never used in "modern" Web documents.

Headings

Headings are used for page or paragraph titles, and in other cases where text needs to be larger or smaller. There are six Heading sizes (Heading Levels 1 through 6), where Heading 1 is the largest and Heading 6 is the smallest. As with all text in Web documents, Headings are subject to user preference and are relative in size. See Figure 3-5 to get a sense of the relative sizes of the various Headings. Since the advent of the use of various fonts in Web pages, the use of Headings—particularly the smaller ones—has diminished.

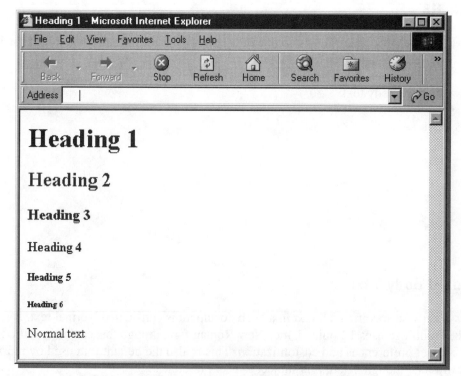

Figure 3-5: Relative size of headings and normal text

 Heading formats and styles can be defined in greater detail with Cascading Style Sheets (CSS). CSS are explored in depth in *Part 2*.

Formatted Text

Formatted text is rendered in a fixed width font, typically Courier or Courier New. Formatted text is useful for maintaining spacing or for making a document previously written for another format available on the Web. The utility of formatted text has been effectively diminished by the advent of tables (for spacing) and the **Save as HTML** feature now available in Microsoft Word, Corel WordPerfect, and other popular word processing applications.

Lists

Lists are very useful in organizing information on a Web page. There are several types of lists, including:

- unordered (bullet) lists
- ordered (numbered) lists
- definition lists
- directory lists
- menu lists

Creating a List

To create any type of list, select it from the drop-down menu on the left side of the Formatting toolbar.

Nesting Lists

Lists can also be nested inside one another, using the increase and decrease indent buttons on the formatting toolbar:

To begin a nested list, press <ENTER> as you would to add another list item, then press the increase indent button twice. To end the nested list, press <ENTER> as you would to add another list item, then press the decrease indent button twice. Lists can be nested within both bulleted and numbered lists.

Bullet & Number Lists

For the bullet and number lists, you can also use their specific buttons on the Formatting toolbar:

To add items to a bulleted or numbered list, press <ENTER> after each list item. Pressing <ENTER> twice ends a bullet list. To end a numbered list, press the down cursor button after the last list item.

Definition Lists

Definition lists are used to create a list of definitions, where the definition is on an indented line beneath the term. To create a definition list, select it from the drop-down Formatting toolbar for Style.

Menu lists and Directory lists work in much the same way as bulleted lists.

List Properties

List Properties can be changed using the **List Properties** dialog box, which can be accessed by selecting **Format ▶ Bullets and Numbering**.

Like headings, lists can also be used in conjunction with Cascading Style Sheets (CSS) to define specific styles for list text. CSS are explored in depth in *Part 2*.

DDC Publishing • www.ddcpub.com

The **List Properties** dialog box features four tabs, as shown in Figure 3-6.

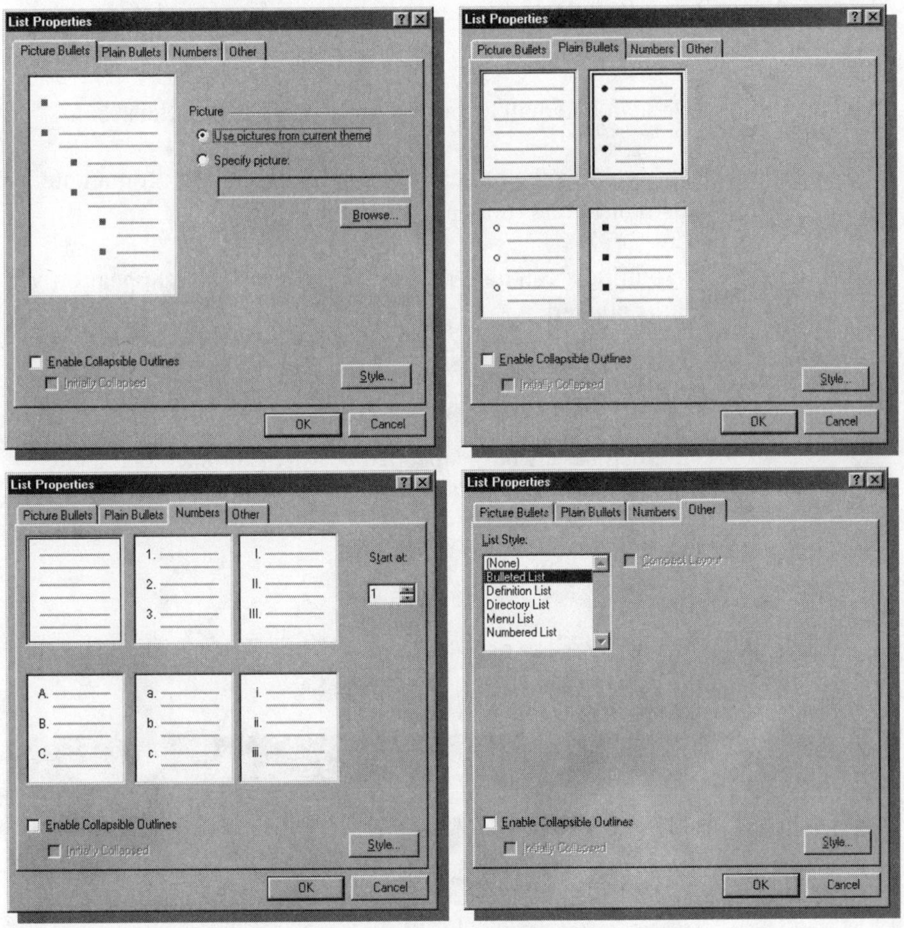

Figure 3-6: List Properties dialog box tabs

The List Properties dialog box can be used to:

- <u>substitute image for standard bullets</u>: can be a specified image or an image included as part of a FrontPage theme (see Lesson 6 for more information regarding FrontPage *themes*)

- <u>change bullet style</u>: can be small or large, round or square bullets

- <u>change numbering style or scheme</u>: can use Arabic numerals, Roman numerals (upper or lowercase) or letters (upper or lowercase)

- <u>enable collapsible outlines</u>: can hide nested lists, having them appear only when the parent list item is clicked

Collapsible outlines are only supported by Microsoft Internet Explorer version 4.0 or later, and are not currently supported in *any* version of Netscape Navigator/Communicator.

Figure 3-7 shows examples of a variety of lists.

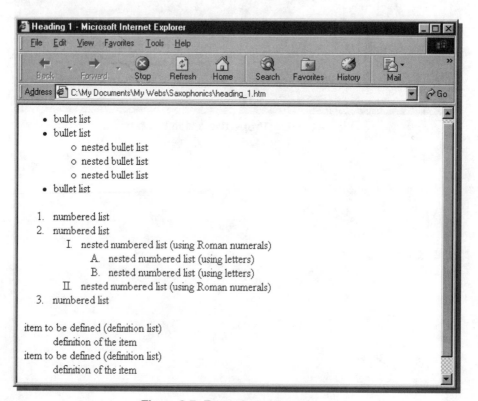

Figure 3-7: Examples of list types

Working with Fonts

The first Web pages were written in straight text, and HTML developers had only the formatting options discussed in the previous chapter to control the appearance of their text, in addition to the bold, italic, and underline effects.

As the Web has evolved, the options for Web developers with respect to the appearance of text have evolved as well. Developers can now define the fonts for use in particular areas of a Web site.

When changing any font in a FrontPage web document, the following font properties can be changed:

- type

- style and effects

- size

- color

 Like headings and lists, fonts can also be used in conjunction with Cascading Style Sheets (CSS) to define specific styles for fonts. CSS are explored in depth in *Part 2*.

Font Type

Font type is changed using the **Font** menu on the Formatting toolbar or through the **Font** dialog box, accessed by selecting **Format ▶ Font**.

Some common fonts and their characteristics are detailed in Table 3-2.

Font	Style	Comment
Times New Roman	Serif	▪ Also called Times Roman ▪ Industry standard serif font
Arial	Sans serif	▪ Industry standard sans serif font ▪ Helvetica is an appropriate industry-standard sans serif substitute
Verdana	Sans serif	▪ Similar to Arial but with wider characters
Courier	Serif	Industry standard monospaced font

Table 3-2: Common fonts and their characteristics

Not all fonts are available to all users or all browsers. If you use fonts other than those listed above, not all users will be able to see them. If a font is called for that is not installed on a given user's machine, the default font will be used instead. There are fonts designed specifically for use with web browsers, such as Verdana and Trebuchet MS.

Font Style & Effects

HTML supports only three font styles (**bold**, *italic*, and <u>underline</u>) and one text effect, blinking. To make text bold, italic, or underline, use the buttons pictured below from the Formatting toolbar:

Font Effects

FrontPage makes a variety of other styles and effects available. Some of the more common font effects include those listed in Table 3-3.

Text Effect	Example	Common Uses
Strikethrough	Regular ~~Strikethrough~~ regular	To show editing of documents
All Caps	regular ALL CAPS regular	To add emphasis to words
Small Caps	regular SMALL CAPS regular	▪ Titles ▪ Headers
Superscript	regular ^{Superscript} regular	▪ Footnote references ▪ Copyright/trademark notations ▪ Mathematical equations
Subscript	regular _{Subscript} regular	▪ Copyright/trademark notations ▪ Fractions ▪ International symbols

Table 3-3: Common font effects

Font Dialog Box

Additional font effects are available in the Font dialog box, as shown in Figure 3-8.

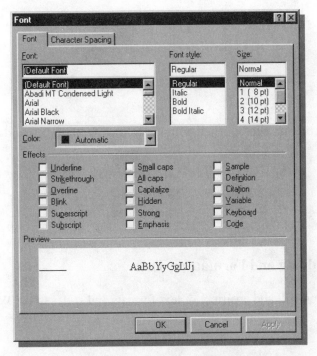

Figure 3-8: Font dialog box

 The blink effect can be annoying; its use is not recommended by many Web page design experts. Think very carefully before using the blink effect (trust us on this one).

Font Size

The size of a given font in a Web document can only be increased or decreased relative to other text. To change the font size, you can either use the pull down menu in the Formatting toolbar or the **Font** dialog box.

Since Web users can custom configure their browsers' default fonts, there is the possibility that the viewer will not see the page exactly as you have specified.

Font Color

Already mentioned with regard to Page Properties, you can also modify the font color for a given word or phrase using the **Font Color** button on the Formatting toolbar or through the **Font** dialog box.

Text Alignment

All text in a FrontPage document (with the exception of lists) can be aligned in one of the following ways:

- left

- right

- center

Alignment formatting is accomplished with the following buttons found on the Formatting toolbar:

Exercise 3-2: Adding and Formatting Text

In this exercise, you will add a variety of text formats and styles to the Web page you created in Exercise 3-1.

1. If it is not already, open INDEX.HTM in **Page View**, **Normal** tab.

2. Insert and center the text **Music 4 a Song** in Heading 1 format at the top of the page.

3. On the next line below, insert the text **Used Musical Instruments You Can Afford** in an 10 point Verdana font. Center the text.

4. On the next line, insert the text **1234 Bargain Hunter Plaza, Nashville, TN 23456** flush right on the page in Heading 4 format. (Be sure to reset your font type to default and size to normal). Insert a line break between the words "Way" and "Arlington."

5. Return to flush left on the following line and create a definition list. In the Style box, click Defined Term and insert the term **Music**. Press ENTER and the next line is automatically formatted with the Definition styles.

6. Insert the definition **any sweet, pleasing or harmonious sound** and press <ENTER> twice.

7. Create an unordered list (bullet list) containing the following:

- **About Our Shop**

- **Instruments We Sell**

- **Most Musical Sites on the Web**

8. Create a nested ordered (number) list under "Instruments We Sell" containing the following:

   `Accordions`

   `Banjos`

   `Cellos`

   `Flutes`

   `Guitars`

   `Keyboards`

   `Violins`

9. Below the above lists, insert the title **About Our Shop** in Heading 2 format. Enter the following text in the Normal format under this title:

   `On one cold winter evening back in 1992, two gentlemen by the names of Johnny "Broken Horn" Murry and Brian "I've got the blues so bad because I lost my guitar again" Jones, were in a desperate situation. They had a gig to play in just a few hours and needed a horn and guitar fast, and cheap too. If they blew this gig they'd have to find another line of work.`

   `As they sat in a corner of a quiet coffee shop, tired cold and down on their luck since they couldn't find a place to sell them a new horn and a guitar, the idea hit them. They would open a shop the sold used musical instruments that hip cats like them could afford.`

   `This was the start of Music 4 a Song.`

10. In the above paragraphs, make bold the two names and italicize the word name of the shop in the last paragraph.

11. Save your work.

12. Preview in your browser (**File ▶ Preview in Browser**).

Remember to use the Formatting toolbar to apply underline, bold, and italic formatting to text.

Your finished page should appear similar to Figure 3-9 and when previewed in a browser.

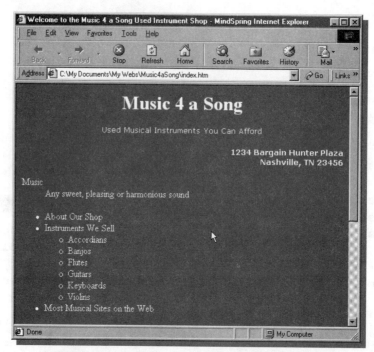

Figure 3-9: Completed page previewed in a browser

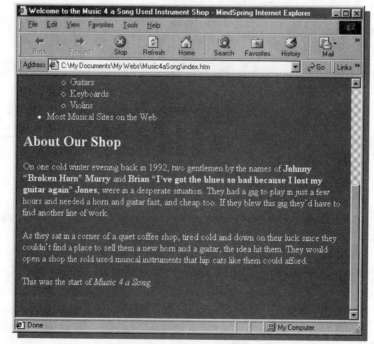

Figure 3-10: Bottom of the completed page previewed in a browser

Hyperlinks

Hyperlinks are hotspots that allow users to click a word or block of text and send a request to a Web server. Hyperlinks allow users to navigate your Web site, progressing from one page to another in whatever path the user chooses. In this respect, hyperlinks are the glue that holds together the Internet.

A hyperlink, or simply *link*, is a selectable connection from one word, picture, or information object to another. In a multimedia environment such as the World Wide Web, hyperlinks can download audio, video, and new emerging types of multimedia data.

The most common form of a link is a word, icon, or photo that is somehow identified or highlighted (such as with underlining or simply in context), can be selected by a user (by clicking a mouse or other pointing device), and results in an immediate request for additional data (although the actual receipt of this data may be delayed or even prevented by various technical problems or nuances of the Internet).

Technically, a link is called an *anchor*. The combination of the anchor and the anchor reference (data object) constitute a hyperlink.

Creating Hyperlinks

With FrontPage, you can easily create hyperlinks to other pages, both within and outside of your own web. Hyperlinks can be created that link to:

- another document within the same web

- a specific point within the current document

- a specific point within another document

- a remote file or Web site

- a file that can be downloaded

- an e-mail address for providing feedback

You can create hyperlinks within your page by highlighting the text to be "anchored" and selecting **Insert ▶ Hyperlink,** or by pressing the **Hyperlink** button on the Standard toolbar:

Create Hyperlink Dialog Box

The **Create Hyperlink** dialog box, shown in Figure 3-11, appears whenever you create a new hyperlink or edit an existing hyperlink.

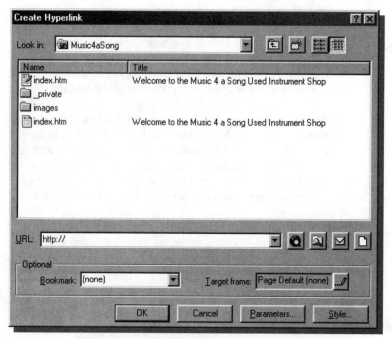

Figure 3-11: Create Hyperlink dialog box

Within the URL field of the **Create Hyperlink** dialog box, you can manually enter the URL or file name to which you want to create a link. You can also use one of the four buttons to the right of that field to create a link to:

- an external Web site or remote file system

- a file within your local file system

- an e-mail address

- an empty file within your web (that will be created once linked)

Exercise 3-3: Creating Hyperlinks

In this exercise, you will use FrontPage 2000 to create hyperlinks to other files in your web, to external Web sites, and to an e-mail address.

1. If it is not already, open INDEX.HTM in **Page View**, **Normal** tab.

2. Highlight the text "Instruments We Sell" and create a hyperlink to the file INSTRUMENTS.HTM. You will have to manually enter this in the URL field because this file does not yet exist and be sure to remove the " http:// " from the text field.

3. Insert a single line break below the mailing address and add the text **Contact Us** Create a hyperlink to your e-mail address **youname@yourdomain.com** by selecting **Insert ▶ Hyperlink** and the envelope icon to the right of the URL line.

4. Highlight the text "Most Musical Sites on the Web" and create a hyperlink. Choose the button to the far right of the URL line to create a new page and link to that page. The **New** Page dialog box will appear. Choose **Normal Page**.

5. Set the title of the new page to "Musical Links" using the **Page Properties** dialog box (**File ▶ Properties ▶ Page Properties**).

6. Place the title **Most Musical Sites on the Web** at the top of the page in Heading 2 and center the text.

7. Create a bullet list with links to the following URLs:

   - **House of Blues** linked to **www.hob.com**

   - **Gibson Musical Instruments** linked to **www.gibson.com**

   - **Fender Guitars** linked to **www.fender.com**

   - **Funky Butt Jazz Club** linked to **www.funkybutt.com**

8. Save the newly created file as LINKS.HTM and close the file to return to INDEX.HTM. You will see that the link to the new page has been created for you.

9. Save the changes to INDEX.HTM and preview in your browser. Follow the link to the **Musical Links** page.

Your finished pages should appear similar to Figure 3-12 and Figure 3-13 when previewed in a browser.

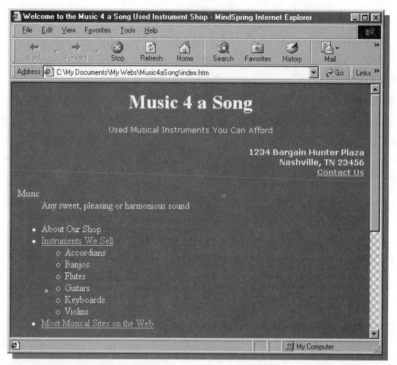

Figure 3-12: Hyperlinks added to INDEX.HTM as previewed in browser

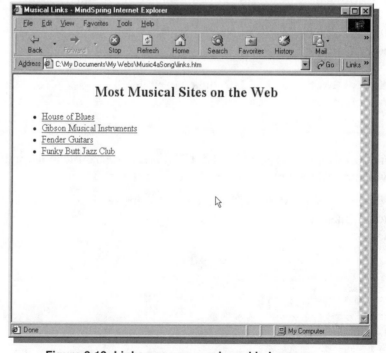

Figure 3-13: Links page as previewed in browser

Bookmarks

Bookmarks, also known as *anchor names* or *internal links*, enable you to create hyperlinks to a specific point within a page. In a particularly long page, for example, you might have a table of contents at the top of the page, and links to the various sections of the page. You can also link from one page to a specific point in another page, provided there is a bookmark defined for that point.

 In most cases, it is better to break a larger page up into smaller pages rather than having a large number of bookmarks.

Creating a Bookmark

Creating a bookmark in FrontPage is simple. Place the cursor at the point you want to insert the bookmark, and choose **Insert ▶ Bookmark** from the menu. You will be prompted to enter a bookmark name. If there are multiple bookmarks on a page, you will see the list of other bookmarks. There cannot be two bookmarks with the same name on the same page.

Linking to Bookmarks

Links to bookmarks are created much in the same way you create other hyperlinks, through the dialog box under **Insert ▶ Hyperlink**. Below the URL field, there is a **Bookmarks** pull-down menu.

- <u>Linking to a bookmark in the current page</u>: the available bookmarks will appear in the **Bookmarks** menu. Simply select the bookmark you desire and click **OK**.

- <u>Linking to a bookmark in another page (within your web)</u>: when the page is selected in the URL field, a list of the available bookmarks will appear in the **Bookmarks** menu. Select the one you desire and click **OK**.

- <u>Manually entering a link to a bookmark</u>: for those located on remote file systems or for bookmarks that have not yet been created. The proper format is 1) the filename, followed by 2) the pound sign (#), followed by 3) the name of the bookmark. No spaces should separate these elements.

 For example, if you had a bookmark called **bookmark** within the file WEBPAGE.HTM, a link to that bookmark should be formatted as: **webpage.htm#bookmark**.

Exercise 3-4: Working with Bookmarks

In this exercise, you will create a link to bookmarks.

1. If it is not already, open INDEX.HTM in **Page View**, **Normal** tab.

2. Highlight the word "About" in the About Our Shop heading. From the **Insert** menu select **Bookmark**. The bookmark name will be automatically set to the highlighted text. Select **OK**. Note that the bookmarked word now has a dashed underline.

3. Create a hyperlink from the text "About Our Shop" in the bulleted list to the newly created bookmark. You should be able to choose the bookmark from the **Bookmarks** menu within the **Create Hyperlink** dialog box.

4. Save your work and preview it in your browser.

Verifying & Recalculating Hyperlinks

An important task for any Web developer is verifying that the links within the Web site and links to outside resources are valid. In a complex site with many links, particularly links to remote file systems, this can be a full time job. Fortunately, FrontPage 2000 makes this task much simpler by providing a number of tools for verifying and repairing hyperlinks.

Hyperlinks View

The FrontPage **Hyperlinks View** displays a schematic of links to and from a given page. Figure 3-14 on the following page shows the **Hyperlinks View** for the current web.

- Valid links: displayed as unbroken lines

- Invalid links: displayed as broken lines (see the link to INSTRUMENTS.HTM for an example)

- Internal links: displayed as black lines

- External links: displayed as a small globe attached to the icon

- Mail links: displayed as envelopes; displayed as broken links

Figure 3-14: Hyperlinks View

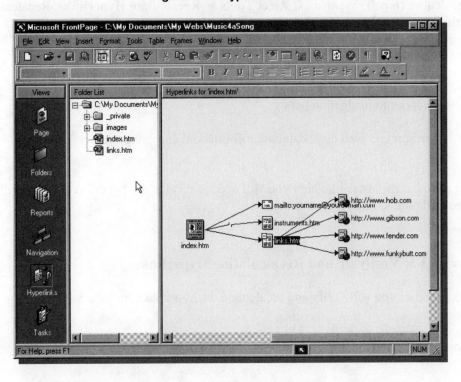

Right-clicking the background brings up a short menu of options:

- <u>Show Page Titles</u>: for internal files, display the title of the page rather than the file name

- <u>Hyperlinks to Pictures</u>: display links to images from a given page

- <u>Repeated Hyperlinks</u>: display multiple instances of the same hyperlink on a single page

- <u>Hyperlinks Inside Page</u>: display hyperlinks to bookmarks within the same page

 To verify external hyperlinks, right-click on the page you wish to verify and select **Verify hyperlink**. If the link is valid the line will remain unbroken. If the line becomes broken, FrontPage could not contact the site. Check to see that you typed the URL correctly and that the site still exists.

Recalculating Hyperlinks

To recalculate (repair) hyperlinks, select **Tools ▶ Recalculate Hyperlinks**. Recalculating hyperlinks accomplishes several goals:

- repairs all hyperlinks in your web

- updates information for all FrontPage-based components, including shared borders and navigation bars

- synchronizes web data, database information, and categories

There are other instances in which you will need to recalculate hyperlinks. These will be discussed throughout the rest of this course.

Exercise 3-5: Verifying and Recalculating Hyperlinks

In this exercise, you will verify and recalculate the hyperlinks for your web.

1. Switch to **Hyperlinks** View and select INDEX.HTM.

 Note that the link to INSTRUMENTS.HTM is broken because that file does not yet exist.

2. Right-click the background and choose **Show Page Titles**.

3. Click the plus (+) sign next to MUSICAL LINKS (LINKS.HTML) to display the six hyperlinks from that file.

4. Right-click each of the external hyperlinks and choose **Verify hyperlink.**

 Note that this will only work if you are currently connected to the Internet. Some hyperlinks may not be valid.

5. Once all of the hyperlinks have been verified, recalculate hyperlinks by selecting **Tools ▶ Recalculate Hyperlinks**.

Horizontal Lines & Symbols

FrontPage 2000 allows you to easily insert horizontal lines and non-keyboard symbols in Web pages.

Horizontal Lines

The horizontal line is one of the earliest and most basic elements of Web design, and has been a mainstay from the earliest versions of HTML. In FrontPage, adding a horizontal line is as simple as choosing **Insert ▶ Horizontal Line**.

If you right-click the line and choose **Horizontal Line Properties**, you can modify several aspects of the line including size, alignment, and color using the **Horizontal Line Properties** dialog box, shown in Figure 3-15.

Figure 3-15: Horizontal Line Properties dialog box

 Some FrontPage themes use an image in place of the standard horizontal line.

Symbols

You will on occasion need to display a character on your Web page that does not appear on the standard keyboard. These include copyright and trademark symbols, fractions and other mathematical symbols, and international characters. To insert one of these non-standard characters, choose **Insert ▶ Symbol**. The full range of available symbols is displayed in Figure 3-16.

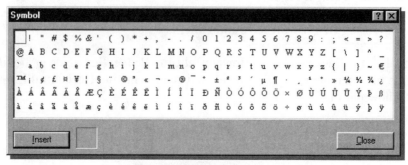

Figure 3-16: Symbols

Exercise 3-6: Inserting Horizontal Lines and Symbols

In this exercise, you will add horizontal lines and symbols to the pages you have already created.

1. If it is not already, open INDEX.HTM in **Page View**, **Normal** tab.

2. Insert a horizontal line beneath the main heading of the page by placing the cursor at the end of the heading and selecting **Horizontal Line** from the **Insert** menu.

3. Right-click the line and modify its properties as follows:

   - Width: 75%

   - Height: 5 pixels

   - Alignment: Center

   - Color: Maroon

4. Insert an identical line beneath the text "Used Musical Instruments You Can Afford" (by default, the second line will retain the properties of the first).

5. Add a horizontal line at the bottom of the page. This line should use the default settings:

   - Width: 100%

   - Height: 2 pixels

   - Alignment: Center

   - Color: Automatic

6. Beneath the line, add and center the text ©2000, `Your Name Here`

7. Save your changes and preview in a browser.

 Your modified page should appear similar to Figure 3-17 when previewed in a browser.

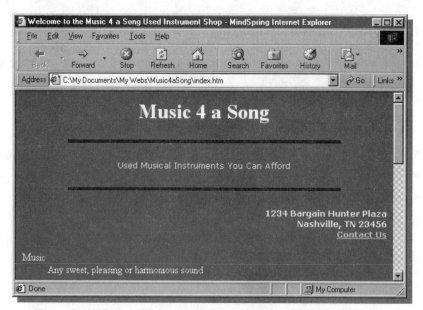

Figure 3-17: Page with horizontal lines as previewed in browser

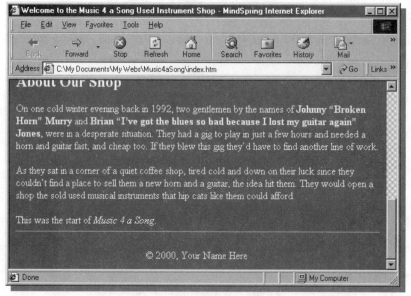

Figure 3-18: Page with symbols as previewed in browser

Page Banners

Page Banners are a FrontPage component similar to Headings. They allow you to display the title of your page prominently. When used in conjunction with a FrontPage theme (see Lesson 6), Page Banners reinforce the theme's look and feel quite prominently.

Adding a Page Banner to your page is very easy. Simply choose **Insert ▶ Page Banner**, and you will be prompted to enter the text of your banner. You will also have the option of displaying the banner as text or as a picture. If you choose text or are not using a FrontPage theme, the banner will display as Heading 1 text.

Exercise 3-7: Adding a Page Banner

In this exercise you will add a Page Banner to INDEX.HTM.

1. If it is not already, open INDEX.HTM in **Page View**, **Normal** tab.

2. Delete the Heading 1 text "Music 4 a Songs" at the top of the page.

3. Select **Insert ▶ Page Banner**.

4. When prompted, choose to display the text **Music 4 a Song** as a picture.

5. Click **OK**.

6. Save the changes to INDEX.HTM and preview in your browser.

 You should not notice any difference in your page now, but when you apply a theme in Lesson 6, the Page Banner will display differently.

Lesson Summary

▶ FrontPage contains a number of templates and wizards to assist in the creation of new Web documents. Web designers can choose from one of FrontPage's templates or can create their own documents from the **Normal Page** template.

▶ Page Properties that can be modified using the **Page Properties** dialog box include document title, background colors or images, text colors, and margins.

▶ The elements of text in a Web document that can be configured using FrontPage are format, font, and alignment.

▶ Most prosaic text within a document is in the format **Normal text**. There are also six levels of headings which are proportional in size. All text in a Web document is relative to the default font set by a user in the browser. Formatted text prints in a fixed-width font.

▶ Lists are very useful for organizing information in a Web document. Types of lists include bulleted lists, numbered lists, and definition lists. Lists can be nested within one another and their properties modified using the **List Properties** dialog box. Among the properties that can be modified are the type of bullet or number and the numbering scheme.

▶ While the font of the earliest Web documents was completely dependent on the user's browser configuration, modern Web designers have a host of fonts at their disposal. In spite of the wide range of fonts supported by FrontPage, not all fonts will be available to all users, though there are some standard fonts that almost all browsers will support.

▶ Using FrontPage, you can modify the font type, style, size, and color. The most common font styles are bold, italic, and underline. Font size is always relative to the user's default font.

▶ Hyperlinks form the basis of the World Wide Web. Hyperlinks are text, images, photos, which, when clicked, open a new document either within the same web or on a remote file system.

▶ Hyperlinks can be made to local files, remote files, e-mail addresses, specific points within the same file, or specific points within a different file. A specific point within a file to which a hyperlink may be directed is called a bookmark.

▶ FrontPage's **Hyperlinks view** allows Webmasters to verify and repair (or recalculate) the links within their sites and to remote file systems.

▶ FrontPage allows you to add horizontal lines and non-keyboard symbols to Web documents with ease. Horizontal lines can be modified with respect to width, height (thickness), color, and alignment.

▶ Page Banners allow you to display your page's title prominently, particularly when used in conjunction with a FrontPage theme.

Lesson Review

Matching

___ 1. Use this to verify hyperlinks

___ 2. Can be nested within one another

___ 3. Specific point within a file to which a hyperlink may be made

___ 4. Utility for repairing hyperlinks

___ 5. Hyperlinks which link to files that do not exist

a. Broken hyperlinks

b. Recalculate hyperlinks

c. Lists

d. Hyperlinks view

e. Bookmark

Fill in the Blank

6. The four types of text that can be configured within the **Page Properties** dialog box are _____, _____, _____, and _____.

7. Three fonts common to almost all web browsers are _____, _____, and _____.

8. Copyright, fractions, and international characters are examples of _____.

9. _____ prints in a fixed width font.

True or False?

T / F   10. The blink effect is an impressive enhancement to any Web page.

T / F   11. The ability to insert horizontal lines in Web documents is a very recent development.

T / F   12. All font sizes within a Web document are defined relative to the user's browser default.

T / F   13. A hyperlink can be made to an e-mail address.

DDC Publishing • www.ddcpub.com

Lesson 4
Web Page Images

Lesson Topics

▶ Images on the Web

▶ Inserting Inline & Background Images

▶ Modifying Image Properties

▶ Thumbnails & Alternative Representations

▶ Lesson Summary

Images on the Web

As the old adage goes, a picture is worth a thousand words. Images have been an integral part of the Web since the NCSA (National Center for Supercomputing Applications) introduced Mosaic, the first graphical Web browser, in 1993.

Uses of Images

Images have many uses in a Web site, both aesthetic and utilitarian. There are essentially two ways to include images on a Web page:

- background images

- inline images

Background images function as their name implies—they provide a backdrop for text and other inline images. Inline images in FrontPage are available in two basic types:

- standard images

- thumbnail images

Standard images may be used as image maps[4], where clicking different areas of an image yields different results.

A thumbnail image is a small version of a picture that a user clicks to view the full-size version.

Common Graphic File Formats

The two most common image file types on the Web are GIF and JPEG. More information regarding these universal Web graphic file formats is provided in Table 4-1.

Graphic File Format	Pronunciation	File Extension
GIF (Graphic Interchange Format)	"jiff"	GIF (e.g., BIGFOOT.GIF)
JPEG (Joint Photographic Experts Group)	"jay-peg"	JPG or JPEG (e.g., BIGFOOT.JPG)

Table 4-1: GIF and JPEG graphics file format characteristics

---

[4] Image maps are discussed in greater detail in *Part 2*.

Newcomer PNG

There is a third image file type called Portable Network Graphics (featuring a PNG file extension and pronounced "ping"). PNG is a relatively new, very functional alternative to GIF and JPEG, but only the latest versions of Microsoft Internet Explorer and Netscape Navigator/Communicator support it. At this time, PNG remains a promising (it has been standardized by the W3C) but unrealized industry standard.

GIF vs. JPEG

Many first-time Web designers are uncertain whether a particular image should be saved in GIF or JPEG format. There really is no single, correct answer; the format you choose will depend on the content and size of the image.

Table 4-2 outlines the main differences between the two formats.

GIF	JPEG
Best for graphics (with large sections of solid colors)	Best for photographs (or any graphic with high levels of color and hue variation)
256 colors per image	16.7 million colors per image
Larger file size	Smaller file size
Retains data if compressed	Becomes blurry or distorted if compressed
One-color transparency	No transparency support
No translucence support	No translucence support
Animation support	No animation support

Table 4-2: GIF and JPEG comparison

Inserting Inline & Background Images

There are several ways to insert images into the pages of your site. You can:

- insert an image from another location on your local file system

- copy images from anywhere on the Internet, including other Web pages

- insert an image from the FrontPage 2000 clip art collection

Use great care and consideration when utilizing images obtained from other Web sites or seemingly "public" sources. Many images available via the Internet or CD-ROM are copyrighted.

It is always courteous to ask permission before using someone else's image in your own site. There are a number of sites on the Web that legally distribute public domain images which can be used free of charge and without asking permission.

Inline Images

Adding inline images to your Web documents is easy with FrontPage. You can insert images by selecting **Insert ▶ Picture**. You can then choose to insert an image from:

- a file (on your local system or on a remote Web site)

- an image from the FrontPage clip art collection

Alternatively, you can add an inline image by selecting the image button from the Standard toolbar:

Choosing to insert an image from a file, through either method, opens the **Picture** dialog box, shown in Figure 4-1.

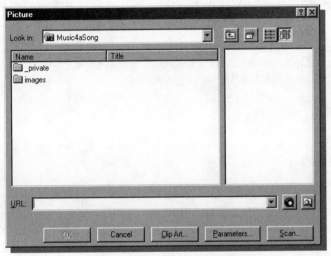

Figure 4-1: Picture dialog box

You can manually enter the image file's location in the URL field, or use the buttons to the right of the field to search for an image on the Web or on your local file system. If you have already added images to this web, you can locate them in the folders window above the URL field.

You also have the option of selecting **Clip Art** from FrontPage's Clip Art Gallery.

Alternate sources of images for use in FrontPage are: 1) using a hardware scanner to scan hardcopy photos or artwork; 2) using a digital camera to capture images in a native digital format for transfer to a PC (most digital cameras, by default, save pictures as JPEG or GIF), or; 3) having standard 35mm film developed and scanned to Kodak Photo CDs, an industry standard digital file format that can easily be converted to JPEG or GIF.

Many Webmasters and FrontPage users get the graphics "bug" after they have begun publishing Web pages. Regardless of your personal desires, it does behoove a Webmaster or any individual or organization that publishes Web pages to know as much as possible regarding Web graphics and to have as many graphics tools as necessary. You should also be aware that graphics add to the overall download size of the page. The more graphics that are added to a page the more time it will require to download and display in the visitor's browser window.

Background Images

Background images are tiled across the screen, with other text and graphics appearing on top of the background image. Background images can be set in the **Background** tab of the **Page Properties** dialog box, discussed in Lesson 3. You can manually enter an image's location or you can choose **Browse** to locate an image on your local file system (or on the Web), as shown in Figure 4-2.

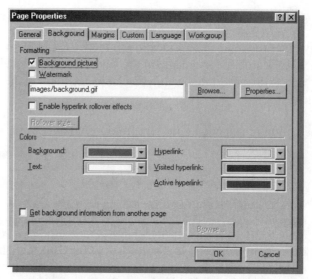

Figure 4-2: Setting a background image

Exercise 4-1: Inserting Inline and Background Images

In this exercise, you will insert inline images from the Clip Art Gallery, from a remote Web site, and from a local file.

1. Open the file INDEX.HTM in **Page View**, **Normal** tab.

2. Insert your cursor after the second horizontal line at the top of the page and press <ENTER>.

3. Choose Insert ▶ Picture ▶ From File.

4. Select the icon to browse files on your computer. Browse to the Student Files folder and select the image BROKENHORN-MURRY.JPG, as shown in Figure 4-3.

Figure 4-3: Image file

5. Insert this image on your page (for now, do not worry about the size of the image).

6. Save the changes to INDEX.HTM. You will be prompted to save the image file along with the page. The name of the file is BROKENHORN-MURRY.JPG. Choose **Rename** and save the file as BROKENHORN.JPG, as shown in Figure 4-4.

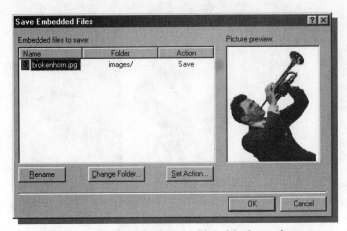

Figure 4-4: Saving the image file with the web page

The other options at this point are:

- <u>Change folder</u>: by default, FrontPage 2000 saves all image files to a root folder. To save the image file in the Images folder, select the file and click Change Folder. In the Change Folder dialog box, click once on the Images folder and select OK.

- <u>Set action</u>: you can choose whether to save image files. In this case, save the file.

7. Create a new page from the **Normal Page** template. Give the page the title `Instruments We Sell` and save this page as `INSTRUMENTS.HTM`.

8. Choose **Insert ▶ Picture ▶ From File**. Find in the student files the image INSTRUMENTS.JPG and click **OK**.

9. Save changes to INSTRUMENTS.HTM. Save the image file into the images folder.

10. Open the file LINKS.HTM in **Page View**, **Normal** tab.

11. Choose **File ▶ Properties** and select the **Background** tab.

12. Select the **Background picture** check box and choose **Browse**. Locate the image `BACKGROUND.GIF` included with the student files for this course and select it. Set the text color to white and the hyperlink color to yellow. Click **OK** to close the **Page Properties** dialog box and apply changes.

13. Save changes to LINKS.HTM. Save the image file. Preview the three modified files.

Figure 4-5, Figure 4-6, and Figure 4-7 show these pages.

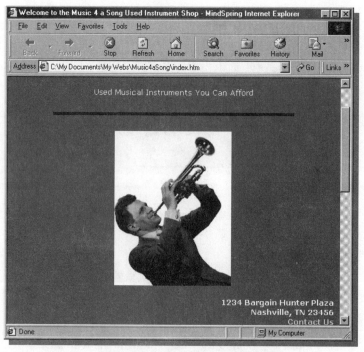

Figure 4-5: Image added to INDEX.HTM

Figure 4-6: Inline image added to INSTRUMENTS.HTM

Figure 4-7: Background image added to LINKS.HTM

Modifying Image Properties

FrontPage allows you to modify several image properties, using the Picture toolbar and the **Picture Properties** dialog box. Among the image properties you can modify are:

- size

- alignment

- appearance

To select an inline image, click anywhere within that image. Selecting an image will cause the Picture toolbar to become active. To bring up the **Picture Properties** dialog box, right-click the image.

Figure 4-8 and Figure 4-9 (on the following page) show the **General** and **Appearance** tabs of the **Picture Properties** dialog box.

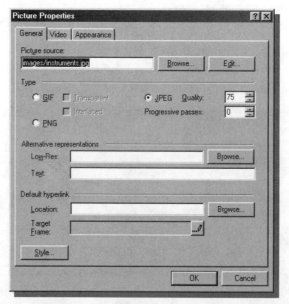

Figure 4-8: Picture Properties dialog box, General tab

Figure 4-9: Picture Properties dialog box, Appearance tab

To modify a background image using the Pictures toolbar, click anywhere on the background. To modify background image properties using the **Picture Properties** dialog box, choose the **Properties** button to the right of the image location in the **Background** tab of the **Page Properties** dialog box.

Modifying Image Size

Images can be resized manually by clicking and dragging the image edge with the mouse, or can be set to specific dimensions using the **Appearance** tab of the **Page Properties** dialog box. When setting an image size to specific dimensions, the dimensions can be set in pixels or as a percentage of the document's height and width. The **Keep aspect ratio** option keeps the width's proportion with respect to the height constant (and vice versa).

Modifying Image Alignment

As with all aspects of web design, it is not only important to have nice images, but to have them placed in an appealing fashion. FrontPage 2000 provides you with a wide range of placement options.

Image Positions in FrontPage

Images can be aligned to the following positions (relative to a page):

Left	Right	Bottom	Baseline	Absbottom
Middle	Center	Absmiddle	Top	Texttop

 Except for Center, these terms refer to alignment of the picture relative to the surrounding text.

- Baseline: refers to the imaginary line on which the text appears.

- Absbottom: refers to the absolute bottom of the text, which is the bottom of the lowest letter.

- Texttop: aligns the image with the top of the tallest character. Generally, this is the same as Top.

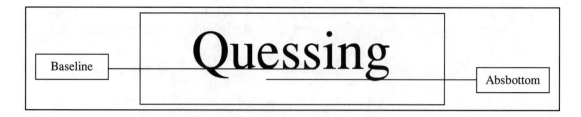

To align an image at the center of a page, you can use the same method as for centering text (the **Center** button on the Formatting toolbar). This can also be set using the **Appearance** tab of the **Picture Properties** dialog box.

To modify alignment of an image relative to surrounding text, you must use the **Appearance** tab of the **Picture Properties** dialog box.

Exercise 4-2: Modifying Image Size and Alignment

In this exercise, you will resize one of the images inserted in Exercise 4-1 and align that image with respect to surrounding text. You will also center an image on a page.

1. If it is not already, open INDEX.HTM in **Page View**, **Normal** tab.

2. Select the image BROKENHORN.GIF and right-click to open the **Picture Properties** dialog box.

3. Choose the **Appearance** tab and select **Specify Size**. Change the value of **Width** to **50** pixels. If you have chosen to **Keep aspect ratio**, the value of **Height** should change accordingly. Click **OK**.

4. In the pave view, select the image and move it to the beginning of the line "Used Musical Instruments …" by cutting and pasting it.

5. Right-click on the image to select the Picture Properties. Change the value of **Alignment** to **Middle**. Click **OK** to apply changes.

You will note that the image is now centered vertically with the words "Used Musical Instruments …"

6. Save the changes to INDEX.HTM.

7. Open INSTRUMENTS.HTM in **Page View**, **Normal** tab.

8. Select the image NSTRUMENTS.JPG, and click the **Center** button on the Formatting toolbar.

9. Save changes to INSTRUMENTS.HTM. Preview both modified files in a browser.

Figure 4-10 and Figure 4-11 (on the following page) show these pages as previewed in a browser.

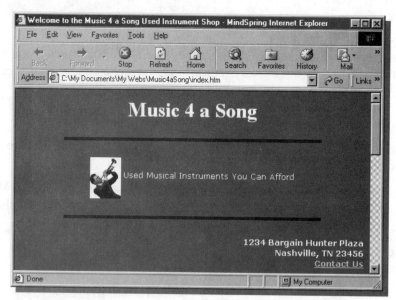

Figure 4-10: Resized and re-aligned image in INDEX.HTM

Figure 4-11: Re-aligned image in INSTRUMENTS.HTM

Modifying Image Appearance

The Pictures toolbar can be used to modify many aspects of an image's appearance. This gives you greater control over the appearance of your images.

The effects you can control using the Pictures toolbar are outlined in Table 4-3.

Buttons	Effect	Description
	Image rotation and flipping	Images can be rotated or flipped around horizontally or vertically
	Contrast and brightness	You can alter the contrast and brightness to create sharper images
	Transparency	Most images are not round, and therefore have a white background when viewed against a non-white page background. Making an image transparent matches the background of the image to the surrounding page
	Wash out	Used primarily for backgrounds, to give an image a faded effect
	Bevel	Creates a raised frame around an image
	Cropping	You can trim a larger image to focus on the picture's subject
	Black and White	Converts a color image to black and white
	Resample	Resampling a picture changes its pixel size to match its current display size

Table 4-3: Modifying image appearance with the Pictures toolbar

Exercise 4-3: Modifying Image Appearance

In this exercise, you will modify the appearance of an image using the Pictures toolbar.

1. Open the Pictures toolbar by selecting **View ▶ Toolbars ▶ Pictures.**

2. Flipping an image:

   - Switch to LINKS.HTM in **Page View**, **Normal** tab.

   - Click anywhere in the background of the page to activate the Pictures toolbar.

   - Click the **Flip Horizontal** button to flip the image so it is facing the opposite direction.

   - Save changes to LINKS.HTM. You will be prompted to overwrite the existing copy of BACKGROUND.GIF. Click **OK**.

3. Setting contrast and brightness:

   - Switch to INSTRUMENTS.HTM in **Page View**, **Normal** tab.

   - Click anywhere within the image to activate the Pictures toolbar.

   - Click the **More Contrast** button three times, and the **More Brightness** button two times. Note the changes in the images appearance.

   - Save changes to INSTRUMENTS.HTM. You will be prompted to overwrite the existing copy of INSTRUMENTS.JPG. Click **OK**.

4. Setting transparency:

   - Switch to INDEX.HTM in **Page View**, **Normal** tab.

   - Click the image to activate the Pictures toolbar.

   - Click the **Set Transparent Color** button.

   - Your mouse pointer will change into a pencil. Click within the white background of the image with the pencil. The background will now match the background of the rest of the page. Note that since transparency can only be achieved with gif files, FrontPage will warn you that it will need to convert the JPG image to a gif. Select **OK**.

   - Save changes to INDEX.HTM. You will be prompted to save the image with a gif extension, as BROKENHORN.GIF. Click **OK**.

5. Cropping an image:

- Open INSTRUMENTS.HTM in **Page View**, **Normal** tab.

- Click anywhere in the image to activate the Pictures toolbar.

- Click the **Crop Picture** button from the Pictures toolbar.

- A dotted line frame will appear within the picture. By clicking and dragging the anchor points on the frame with your mouse, move this frame so that the drum is removed from the image, as shown in Figure 4-12. Click the **Crop Picture** button again.

Figure 4-12: Cropped picture

6. Preview the three modified files in a browser.

 Figure 4-13 and Figure 4-14 on the following page show the changes to LINKS.HTM and INDEX.HTM.

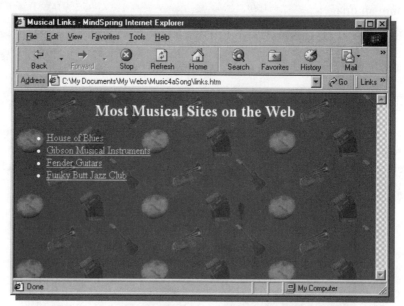

Figure 4-13: Flipped background image on LINKS.HTM

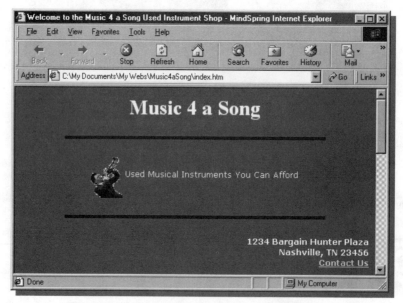

Figure 4-14: Transparent image on INDEX.HTM

Thumbnails & Alternative Representations

Both thumbnails and alternative representations are ways in which you can accommodate users of slow Internet connection. One of the biggest challenges of any Webmaster is catering to the often dramatic differences between users. While one user will have a high-speed Internet connection, a big color monitor, and high-resolution graphics, another may have a very slow connection, have the display of images turned off in his or her browser, or have a small monitor displaying low-resolution graphics.

Thumbnails

If you have a need for very large images within your site, you may want to consider making thumbnail versions of these images available. You can place the smaller, thumbnail version of the image on the page. When clicked, the thumbnail is opened at full size.

Thumbnail is a term used by graphic designers and photographers for a small image representation of a larger image, usually intended to make it easier and faster to look at or manage a group of larger images.

FrontPage makes it easy to create thumbnail versions of your images, using the **Auto-Thumbnail** button on the Picture toolbar:

Alternative Representations

Some users with especially slow Internet connections may choose to turn off the display of images in their browsers to speed page loading. FrontPage allows you to create a text description of an image so that users not displaying images can have a better idea of how a page should appear and understand the overall content of the page.

This is especially important if you are using images to convey information. For example, if you have a graphic that displays your organization's logo, an alternate representation could be your motto or slogan. Thus, if a user cannot see the graphic of your logo, they will still know the name of your organization.

Alternate representations are set in the **General** tab of the **Picture Properties** dialog box.

Exercise 4-4: Setting Alternative Representations

In this exercise, you will set alternate representations of your images.

1. If it is not already, open INDEX.HTM in **Page View**, **Normal** tab.

2. Right-click the image and open the **Picture Properties** dialog box. In the field **Text** under **Alternative representations**, enter `Broken Horn Murry`. Click **OK**.

3. Save changes to INDEX.HTM.

4. Repeat the above for the image in TYPES.HTM. Use the text `Just a few of the instruments we sell` as the alternative representation.

5. Save changes to TYPES.HTM.

Lesson Summary

► Images have been an integral part of the World Wide Web since the first graphical browser was introduced in 1993. Images can be used both for aesthetic value and to convey information.

► The two principal image formats used in Web documents are GIF (Graphic Interchange Format) and JPEG (Joint Photographic Experts Group). Each image format has its pros and cons. GIFs are used primarily for graphics, and JPEGs for photographs.

► Images in a Web document may be background or inline. Background images are tiled across the background of a page, while inline images appear on the page itself.

► FrontPage allows you to insert images from local files, from remote Web sites, and from the FrontPage Clip Art Gallery.

► When saving images with a Web document, FrontPage places all images in the images folder.

► FrontPage allows you to modify the size, alignment, and appearance of an image using the **Page Properties** dialog box and the Pictures toolbar.

► The alignment of an image is set relative to surrounding text, and there is a wide range of options for setting this alignment. Images can also be centered on a page.

► Using the Pictures toolbar, you can modify a number of aspects of an image's appearance. Images can be flipped or rotated. The brightness and contrast of an image can be adjusted. Images can be made to have transparent backgrounds or be faded using the wash out effect. The bevel effect creates a raised frame around the outside of an image. FrontPage also allows you to crop images.

► Thumbnails are smaller versions of larger image files that, when clicked, display the larger image file. Thumbnails are useful when your site includes and depends upon a large amount of images.

► Alternative representations of images should be used to convey the information otherwise depicted by an image for users without access to the images.

Lesson Review

Matching

___ 1. Image format that best retains structure when compressed

a. Bevel

___ 2. Effect that makes an image appear to fade

b. JPEG

___ 3. Smaller version of an image

c. Wash out

___ 4. Image format with wider range of available colors

d. Thumbnail

___ 5. Effect that creates a raised frame around the outside of an image

e. GIF

Fill in the Blank

6. JPEG stands for _____ _____ _____ _____ .

7. GIF stands for _____ _____ _____ .

8. The contrast and brightness of an image can be set using _____ .

9. The term for making the background of an image match that of the page is _____ .

True or False?

T / F   10. The JPEG image format supports animation.

T / F   11. The first graphical Web browser was Lynx, introduced in 1991.

T / F   12. You can use the Pictures toolbar to crop an image.

T / F   13. Images can be aligned only with respect to the surrounding text.

T / F   14. Mosaic was the first Graphical WYSIWYG HTML editor in 1993.

Lesson 5
Creating &
Modifying Tables

Lesson Topics

▶ Designing Basic Tables

▶ Modifying Table Properties

▶ Tables for Complex Page Layouts

▶ Lesson Summary

Designing Basic Tables

Netscape Communications Corporation first introduced tables to the Web with the release of Navigator 2.0 as a way to present data in an orderly fashion. Prior to tables, the only way to order data in an HTML document was to use formatted text. Since their introduction, tables have become much more advanced and more useful in designing complicated Web pages.

Elements of Table Design

At the most basic level, tables consist of three elements:

- rows

- columns

- cells

Every table must have at least one row and one column, and every row and column must have at least one cell.

Supplemental Elements

Other elements that may be included in tables are:

- headers

- captions

Table Properties

When designing tables in FrontPage, it is possible to control a variety of properties, including:

- layout

- borders

- background

Steps to Create a Table in FrontPage

There are several ways to create a table in FrontPage 2000:

- Select **Table ▶ Insert ▶ Table**

- Select the **Insert Table** button on the Standard toolbar:

- Select **Table ▶ Draw Table**

- Convert existing text to a table by selecting **Table ▶ Convert ▶ Text to Table**

How you create your tables is a matter of personal preference. The first two options are by far the most common.

If you choose the first option, select **Table ▶ Insert ▶ Table**, the **Insert Table** dialog box will appear, as shown in Figure 5-1.

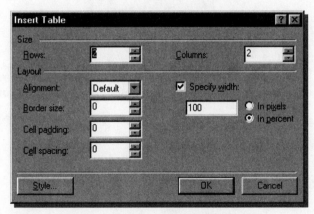

Figure 5-1: Insert Table dialog box

When creating a table in this way, you must specify the table size, in number of columns by number of rows. While it is possible to add rows and columns later, it is best to plan your tables in advance in order to know how many rows and columns you will need.

Other items that can be set when creating a table using this method are:

- Alignment: options are default, right, center, left, and justify; determines a table's placement on a page's horizontal axis

- Border size: thickness, in pixels, of a table's borders

- Cell padding: amount of space between cell content and cell border

- Cell spacing: space, in pixels, between cells

- Specify width: set the width of your tables in pixels or as a percentage of the total page width

If you choose the second method of table creation, after pressing the **Table** button on the Standard toolbar, you will set the number of rows and columns by clicking and dragging your mouse, as shown in Figure 5-2. In this method, the other parameters must be set after the table is created.

Figure 5-2: Creating a table with the Standard toolbar button

Exercise 5-1: Creating a Basic Table

In this exercise, you will create a table to organize information about the various types of saxophones.

1. Open INSTRUMENTS.HTM in **Page View**, **Normal** tab.

2. Beneath the image, insert a table with four columns and six rows. Use whichever method of table creation you desire. Do not worry about spacing or alignment for now.

3. Populate your table with the following data and place the corresponding images in the picture column from the Student Files directory:

Instrument	Brand	Condition	Picture
Six-string electric guitar	Fender	Very good, could use a little tuning	Guitar-electric.jpg
Banjo	Unknown	Good. Needs a new set of strings	Banjo.jpg
Keyboard	Yamaha	Excellent. Previous owner only played it on Sundays	Keyboard.jpg
Classic War Bugle	US Army	Good. Needs a coat of polish. If you're looking for something with a sound that'll wake 'em up, this is it!	War-bugle.jpg
Balo	Hand-made	We're not sure where we picked this one up but it is sure fun to play.	Balo.jpg

4. Save changes to INSTRUMENTS.HTM and preview in a browser.

   Figure 5-3 shows the newly created table as displayed in a browser.

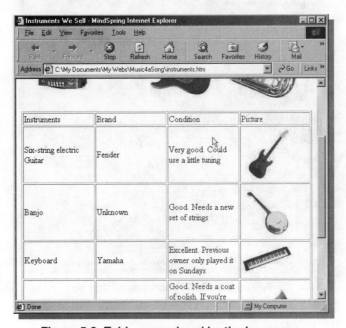

Figure 5-3: Table as rendered by the browser

Modifying Table Properties

Once a table is created, it is easy to modify table properties using the **Table Properties** and **Cell Properties** dialog boxes, shown in Figure 5-4 and Figure 5-5. Either dialog box can be accessed by right-clicking within an existing table. The **Table** menu and Table toolbar can also be used to modify table properties.

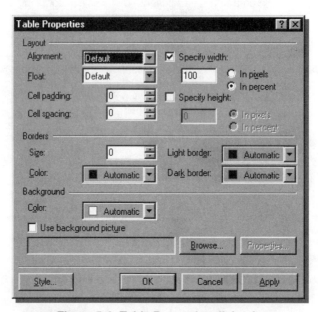

Figure 5-4: Table Properties dialog box

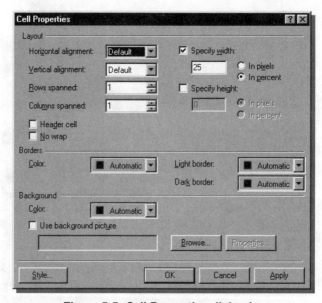

Figure 5-5: Cell Properties dialog box

Table Properties Dialog Box

Using the **Table Properties** dialog box, you can set parameters for the table as a whole. Among the elements you can configure:

- layout

- borders

- background

Modifying Table Layout

The attributes of a table's layout that can be modified are shown in Table 5-1.

Attribute	Description
Alignment	■ Choices are: default, left, right, center, justify ■ Refers to a table's position within a page
Float	■ Choices are: default, left, right ■ If left or right is specified, the table with be flush to the respective margin and text will wrap on the other side. If no float is specified, text will not wrap around a table, but will only be above or below the table
Cell padding	■ Set in pixels ■ Sets spacing between cell content and cell border
Cell spacing	■ Set in pixels ■ Sets spacing between cells
Specify width	■ Can be set in pixels or as a percentage of page width ■ If not set or defined, table will fit itself to its contents
Specify height	■ Refers to the height of table cells ■ Can be set in pixels or as a percentage of table height ■ If not set or defined, cells will fit to contents

Table 5-1: Attributes of table layout

Modifying Table Borders

You can also use the **Table Properties** dialog box to modify a table's borders.

- <u>Size</u>: thickness of outer table border (as measured in pixels)

- <u>Color</u>: color of table borders

- <u>Light and Dark borders</u>: used to create a shadow effect, making a table cell appear to float above the page (a light border appears on the top and left of the cell; a dark border appears on the bottom and right).

Modifying Table Background

Just as you can set a background color or image for an entire page, so too can you set these parameters within a table. If no background color or image is specified, the table will use the same background as the rest of the page.

Cell Properties Dialog Box

Using the **Cell Properties** dialog box, you can set parameters for individual cells. Among the elements you can configure are:

- layout

- borders

- background

Modifying Cell Layout

The attributes of a cell's layout that can be modified are shown in Table 5-2 on the following page.

Attribute	Description
Horizontal alignment	■ Choices are: default, left, right, center, justify ■ Refers to content's horizontal position within a cell
Vertical alignment	■ Choices are: default, top, middle, baseline, bottom ■ Refers to content's vertical position within a cell
Rows spanned	■ Refers to a cell's height with respect to other cells within the same row (used to create cells that span multiple rows)
Columns spanned	■ Refers to a cell's width with respect to other cells within the same column (used to create cells that span multiple columns)
Specify width	■ Can be set in pixels or as a percentage of table width ■ By default, cell will be 1/x of the total table width, where x is the number of columns
Specify height	■ Can be set in pixels or as a percentage of table height ■ If not set or defined, cells will fit to contents ■ Can also be set in Table Properties, if there is a conflict, the Cell Properties takes precedence.
Header cell	■ When selected, defines a particular cell as a table header ■ Used with Cascading Style Sheets (CSS)
No wrap	■ When selected, forces all cell content on a single line unless explicitly broken

Table 5-2: Attributes of cell layout

Modifying Cell Borders

You can also use the **Cell Properties** dialog box to modify an individual cell's borders.

■ Color: color of a cell border

■ Light and Dark borders: used to create a shadow effect, making a table cell appear to float above the page (a light border appears on the top and left of the cell; a dark border appears on the bottom and right).

Modifying Table Background

Just as you can set a background color or image for an entire page or table, so too can you set these parameters within a single cell. If no background color or image is specified, the cell will use the same background as the rest of the table.

Several elements can be set in either the **Table Properties** or **Cell Properties** dialog box. In case of conflict, the values set in the **Cell Properties** dialog box will override those set in the **Table Properties** dialog box.

Table Menu & Table Toolbar

You will recall from Lesson 1 that there is both a specific menu and a specific toolbar for use with tables. To review, the **Table** menu is shown in Figure 5-6. The Table toolbar is displayed in Figure 5-7.

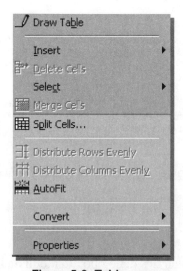

Figure 5-6: Table menu

Figure 5-7: Table toolbar

Many table management tasks can be accomplished using either of these, including:

- adding or deleting rows or columns

- merging or splitting cells

- adding a table caption

- adjusting cell content alignment

Adding a Row to a Table

1. Place your cursor in the row either above or below the location at which you want to insert an additional row.

2. Choose **Table ▶ Insert ▶ Rows or Columns**.

3. A dialog box will appear, asking whether you want to add rows or columns, how many, and whether the row should be added above or below your current location. Make your selections and click **OK**.

- OR -

1. Place your cursor in the row below the location at which you want to insert an additional row.

2. Click the **Insert Row** button on the Tables toolbar:

- OR -

To add an additional row at the bottom of the table, put your cursor in the last cell of the table (bottom right) and press <TAB>.

Adding a Column to a Table

1. Place your cursor in the column either to the left or to the right of the location at which you want to insert an additional column.

2. Choose **Table ▶ Insert ▶ Rows or Columns**.

3. A dialog box will appear, asking whether you want to add rows or columns, how many, and whether the column should be added to the left or right of your current location. Make your selections and click **OK**.

- OR -

1. Place your cursor in the column to the right of the location at which you want to insert an additional column.

2. Choose the **Insert Column** button from the Table toolbar:

Deleting Rows, Columns, or Cells

1. Select the row(s), column(s), or cell(s) you want to remove.

2. Choose **Table ▶ Delete Cells** or click the **Delete Cells** button on the Table toolbar:

Merging Cells

1. Select the cells you want to merge.

2. Choose **Table ▶ Merge Cells** or click the **Merge Cells** button on the Table toolbar:

Splitting Cells

1. Select the cell you want to split.

2. Choose **Table ▶ Split Cells** or click the **Split Cells** button on the Table toolbar:

3. A dialog box will prompt you to indicate whether the cell is to be split into columns or rows, and how many. Make your selections and click **OK**.

Adding a Table Caption

A table caption is simply a label for the table, and appears above the table itself. To add a caption to your table, select **Table ▶ Insert ▶ Caption**.

Adjusting Cell Content Alignment

In addition to the **Cell Properties** dialog box, the alignment of cell content can also be adjusted using these buttons on the Table toolbar:

Exercise 5-2: Modifying Table Properties

In this exercise, you will modify the table you created in Exercise 5-1 using the **Table Properties** and **Cell Properties** dialog boxes, the **Table** menu, and the Table toolbar.

1. If it is not already, open INSTRUMENTS.HTM in **Page View**, **Normal** tab.

2. Right-click within the table and open the **Table Properties** dialog box. Change the following settings:

   - Alignment: center

   - Cell padding: 5

   - Cell spacing: 2

   - Width: 90%

   - Border size: 5

   - Border color: black

3. Click **OK** to apply the changes.

4. Select the top row of the table by placing your cursor on the left cell border of the first cell in the row. When a small black arrow appears, click once to select the entire row. Now you may right-click on any of the highlighted cells, and select the **Cell Properties** dialog box. Change the following settings:

   - Horizontal alignment: center

   - Vertical alignment: middle

   - Header cell: checked

   - Background color: silver

5. Click **OK** to apply the changes.

6. Select the Condition column of the table, right-click, and select the **Cell Properties** dialog box. Change the width to 50%. Click **OK** to apply the changes.

7. Select the first two columns at the left of the table, right-click, and select the **Cell Properties** dialog box. Uncheck the box next to **Specify width**. Click **OK** to apply the changes.

8. Select all of the cells in the table except the top row. Align the text to the top of the cells by selecting **Table ▶ Properties ▶ Cell.** In the **Vertical** alignment properties field, change the selection to **Top**. Click **OK** to apply the changes.

9. Add the caption **Current Instruments For Sale** to the table by selecting **Table** ▶ **Insert** ▶ **Caption**. Use **Heading 3** and the **Small Caps** effect on this text.

10. Save changes to INSTRUMENTS.HTM and preview in a browser.

To add the **Small Caps** effect to text: highlight the text, right click, and select Font. On the Font tab of the dialog box, select the **Small Caps** checkbox.

Figure 5-8 displays the newly modified table in a browser.

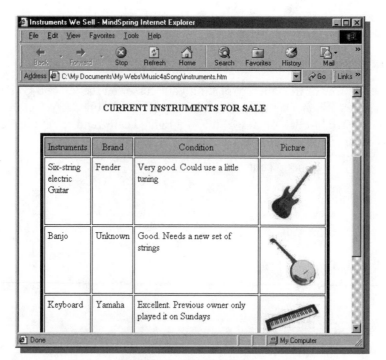

Figure 5-8: Modified table

Tables for Complex Page Layouts

HTML is notoriously limited when it comes to creating complex page layouts. However, through the use of tables, Web developers are free to develop more complex layouts for their sites. Tables can be used as a grid on which the rest of the page is constructed, by merging or splitting cells and adjusting content alignment within the cells of the grid. The more cells your grid has, the more freedom you have to arrange the text within those cells.

Exercise 5-3: Using a Table Grid as a Layout Tool

In this exercise, you will apply a table grid layout to the INDEX.HTM page for greater control over page layout.

1. If it is not already, open INDEX.HTM in **Page View**, **Normal** tab.

2. At the top of the page, create a table six columns across by two rows down.

3. Select the top row of your table and merge all of the cells into a single cell.

4. Highlight the text "Music 4 a Song" and "Used Musical Instruments You Can Afford" and the two horizontal bars, and select **Edit ▶ Cut**. Paste this from the clipboard into the top row of the table.

5. Select the BROKENHORN.GIF image and select **Edit ▶ Cut**. Paste this from the clipboard into the fourth cell from the left in the second row.

6. Merge the two cells to the right of the image into a single cell.

7. Cut and paste the address text into the newly merged cell.

8. Insert a new row at the bottom of the table and merge all of the cells in the row.

9. Cut and paste the definition into the newly merged cell.

10. Modify the table properties so that the table border is 0.

11. Save the changes to INDEX.HTM and preview in a browser.

Figure 5-9 shows the newly modified layout in a browser.

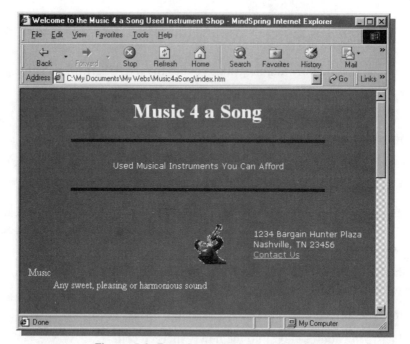

Figure 5-9: Page layout using a table grid

Lesson Summary

▶ Tables were introduced in Netscape 2.0 as a way to present information in an orderly manner. Prior to that, information could only be presented in tables using formatted text.

▶ Tables are made up of rows, columns, and cells, and may include headers or captions. All tables must include at least one row and one column. All rows and columns must contain at least one cell. Table layout, borders, and backgrounds can be modified.

▶ Tables can be modified using the **Table Properties** dialog box, the **Cell Properties** dialog box, the **Table** menu, and the Table toolbar.

▶ The **Table Properties** dialog box controls the alignment of a table on a page, the alignment of cells within the table, the size and color of table borders, and the table background.

▶ The **Cell Properties** dialog box controls the alignment of content within the cell, both horizontally and vertically. The **Cell Properties** dialog box can also be used to set borders and background for a single cell. The **No wrap** option prevents text from spilling onto the next line.

▶ Both the **Table** menu and Table toolbar can be used to add or delete rows, columns, or cells, or to split or merge cells. The Table toolbar can also be used to adjust alignment of content within cells.

▶ A caption is a label that appears above a table, and can be added using the **Table** menu.

▶ Tables can be used to create complex layouts for Web pages that are not otherwise possible with standard HTML. Using a table grid, you can arrange page content with much more freedom. The more cells a table grid has, the more accurate the layout.

Lesson Review

Matching

___ 1. Cell property that prevents text from spilling to the next line

___ 2. Label that appears above a table

___ 3. Space between cells

___ 4. Space between cell content and cell border

___ 5. Used to create a shadow effect

a. cell padding

b. caption

c. light and dark borders

d. cell spacing

e. no wrap

Fill in the Blank

6. All tables must have at least one _____ and _____.

7. All rows and columns must have at least one _____.

8. Captions are added using the _____.

9. Cell padding and cell spacing are set in _____.

True or False?

T / F 10. Tables were introduced in Internet Explorer version 2.1.

T / F 11. When there is a conflict between Cell and Table properties, Cell properties take precedence.

T / F 12. You can adjust the vertical alignment of cell content using the Table menu.

T / F 13. Tables can be used to create complex site layouts.

Lesson 6
FrontPage Themes

Lesson Topics

► FrontPage Web Themes

► Customizing Themes

► Lesson Summary

FrontPage Web Themes

FrontPage 2000 offers a variety of themes that you can apply to your webs. Themes are a way to apply a common format and structure throughout your web. By automatically adding the same images, backgrounds and style to your web, themes can give your web page a uniform look and feel.

Theme Advantages

Creating a themed web allows FrontPage 2000 to make recommendations regarding color and font. In addition, FrontPage 2000 allows you to share your themes with other Office 2000 applications, providing consistency across not only your web, but across all of your organization's documents.

Figure 6-1 shows the **Themes** window. You can access the themes window at any time by right-clicking in your document and selecting **Theme** or by selecting **Format ▶ Theme**.

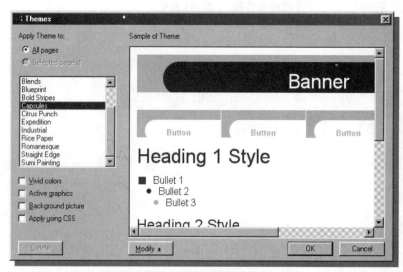

Figure 6-1: Themes window

Theme Elements

Themes apply standard elements to a number of components of your Web site. The main areas that a theme will affect are:

- font: type, size, and color

- background: color and images

- bullets

- horizontal lines

- Page Banners

- buttons

When applying a theme to an already existing FrontPage web, all of these elements will change to reflect the theme.

Applying a Theme to Your Web

 It is important to note that you cannot undo a theme once it has been applied. If you remove a theme from a page, it will revert to its default settings and any style and formatting modifications will be lost. It is always a good idea to make a copy of your web before applying a theme.

Themes can be applied either to an entire web or just to selected pages. This gives you the freedom to create different looks for different parts of your Web site.

Many themes also give you a chance to limit what aspects of the theme are displayed. For example, a theme with many bright colors will allow you to mute the colors, so the page is easier on the eyes of your viewers. Themes that include animated graphics will allow you to choose whether or not to include those animated graphics.

 Before you proceed, take a moment to examine the various FrontPage themes.

Exercise 6-1: Applying a Theme to Your Web

In this exercise, you will apply a theme to your web that will create a standard look across the three pages.

1. Select **Format ▶ Theme** and choose the theme of your choice. (The theme choose in the following screens is Capsules.)

2. Choose the following options:

   ▪ Apply theme to All Pages

   ▪ Enable vivid colors

   ▪ Enable active graphics

   ▪ Enable background image

3. Click **OK** to apply the theme.

4. FrontPage will prompt you with a warning, shown in Figure 6-2, before applying the theme to your web. Click **Yes** in the warning box.

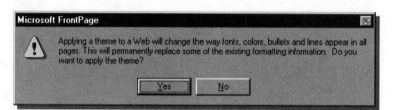

Figure 6-2: Warning box

 It will take a few moments for FrontPage to apply the theme to your web (longer if you have a very large web). Once completed, preview the pages in your browser. Figure 6-3 through Figure 6-10 show the changes to your FrontPage web.

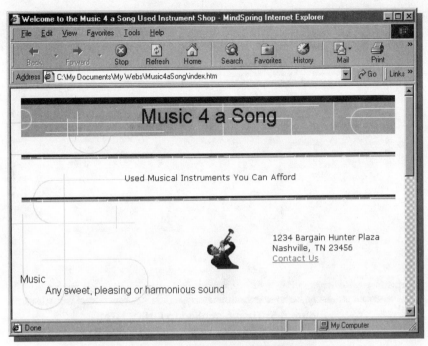

Figure 6-3: Theme applied to INDEX.HTM (1)

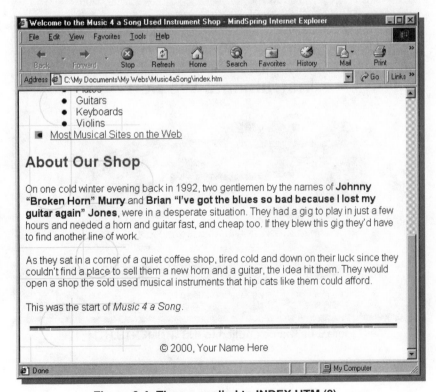

Figure 6-4: Theme applied to INDEX.HTM (2)

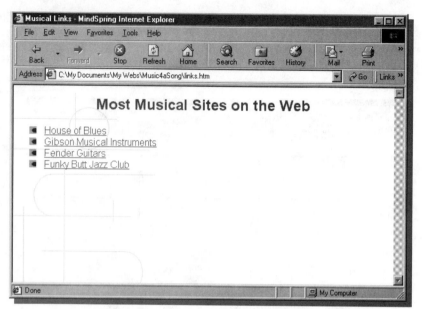

Figure 6-5: Theme applied to LINKS.HTM

Figure 6-6: Theme applied to INSTRUMENTS.HTM (1)

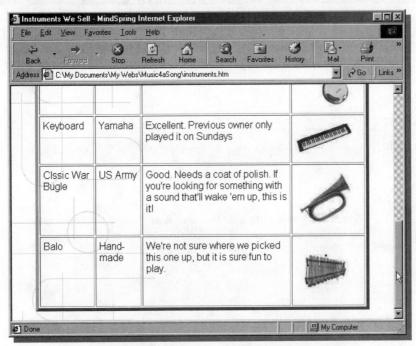

Figure 6-7: Theme applied to INSTRUMENTS.HTM (2)

Customizing Themes

FrontPage is very flexible regarding the use of themes. You can modify the color, text, and images of any theme. In order to modify a theme, choose **Modify** within the **Themes** window. The Themes window allows you to alter the following theme elements:

- text
- colors
- graphics

Whenever you modify a theme, save it as a new file to ensure that the original theme remains unmodified.

Customizing Theme Text

You can customize the font style used by your theme by selecting **Text** from the **Modify Theme** window. This opens a new window, where you can select fonts for use with Normal text and with each of the six Heading levels, as shown in Figure 6-8. The Modify Text window allows you to preview how the various fonts will look with your theme.

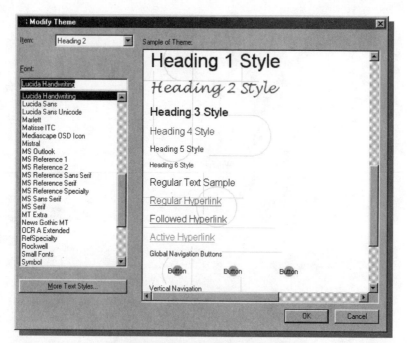

Figure 6-8: Modify Theme dialog box

You can, in fact, select a different font for the body of your document and for each heading level. Keep in mind though that not all users will have access to the same fonts.

Exercise 6-2: Customizing Theme Text

In this exercise, you will set the fonts used by your custom theme.

1. Select **Format ▶ Theme** to open the **Themes** window.

2. Click **Modify** and select **Text**.

3. For the **Item** *Heading 2*, select a new type face of your choise.

4. Click **OK** to apply changes.

5. Click **Save as** and save your new theme as MUSIC 4 A SONG.

6. Click **OK** to apply the new theme to your web.

 Preview your web in a browser. You will see the new text style applied to the text *Musical Links* in LINKS.HTM and *About Our Shop* at the bottom of INDEX.HTM.

Customizing Theme Colors

Customizing theme colors works in much the same way as customizing text. You can customize the colors used by your theme by selecting **Color** from the **Modify Theme** window. This opens a new window, where you can choose from among three options for customizing colors:

- Color Schemes

- Color Wheel

- Custom

Color Schemes

Color schemes are predefined color groupings that can be applied to any theme. Using these color schemes can help you to avoid clashing colors.

Figure 6-9 on the following page displays the **Color Scheme** window. The **Color Scheme** window allows you to preview various colors before applying them to your theme.

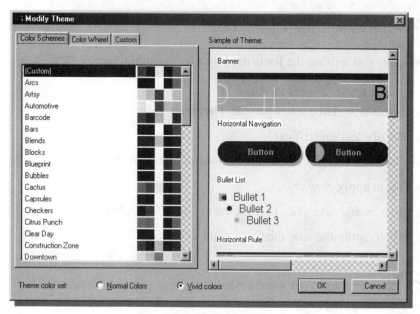

Figure 6-9: Color Schemes

Color Wheel

A second tool for customizing the color of your themes is the Color Wheel. The Color Wheel works with the Color Scheme tool to allow you to adjust the color of the text within the scheme. The advantage of the Color Wheel is that it allows you more freedom to choose colors. Figure 6-10 shows the Color Wheel, which you can also see (in color) by selecting the **Color Wheel** tab from the **Modify Theme Colors** window.

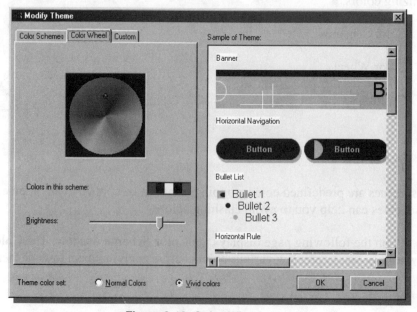

Figure 6-10: Color Wheel

Within the color you should see a little "cursor" between "6 and 7 o'clock" on the Color Wheel. As you move the cursor around the wheel, the color scheme of the text within your chosen scheme changes. This allows you to fine-tune your text colors.

Custom Color

The **Custom** tab allows you to define the color for a variety of elements in your site. Unlike the **Color Scheme** and **Color Wheel** tools, when using the **Custom** tab to set your theme's colors, each element's color is set independently of the colors of other elements.

The Custom tab consists of two pull-down menus:

- the first allows you to choose the page element you want to change

- the second allows you to set the color for that element

Even if you are using a color scheme defined by the **Color Scheme** or **Color Wheel** tools, you can use the **Custom** tab to set the color for individual elements.

As always, use care in your color selection, as not all colors are available to all users.

Exercise 6-3: Customizing Theme Color

In this exercise, you will learn how you can set the colors used by your custom theme.

1. Select **Format** ▶ **Theme**.
2. Click **Modify** and choose **Colors**.
3. Take a look at how each of the different color schemes will affect the theme components by selecting a color theme title. One the right side of the window a preview will display.
4. From the **Custom** tab, select the item **Banner text** and the color **white**.
5. Also select the item **Table border** and the color **red**.
6. If you have found a color theme scheme that you like click **OK** to apply changes and **Save** to save changes to the MUSIC 4 A SONG, otherwise click **Cancel**.
7. Click **OK** to apply the changes to your web.

 Preview the web in a browser. You will see the new color scheme applied, particularly changes to the Page Banner text color in INDEX.HTM and the table border in INSTRUMENTS.HTM.

Customizing Theme Graphics

You can also customize all of the graphics utilized by a theme. The graphics you can modify (as well as any additional customizable attributes) are:

- background picture

- horizontal rule

- bullet list (up to three levels of bullets can be defined for nested lists)

For these items, you can also customize font style, size, and alignment:

- Page Banners

- global navigation buttons

For the items listed below, in addition to customizable fonts, there are also different customizations depending on whether Active or Normal graphics are used. When using Active graphics, three different buttons (normal, selected, and hover) are available. For Normal graphics, normal and selected are available.

- horizontal navigation

- vertical navigation

- quick back button

- quick home button

- quick next button

- quick up button

Exercise 6-4: Customizing Theme Graphics

In this exercise, you will set the graphics used by your custom theme.

1. Select **Format ▶ Theme**.

2. Click **Modify** and choose **Graphics**.

3. For the item **Background Picture**, choose BACKGROUND.GIF.

4. For the item **Banner**, set the font style to **Bold Italic**.

5. Click **OK** to apply changes and **Save** to apply changes to MUSIC 4 A SONG.

6. Click **OK** to apply the changes to your web.

 Preview your web in a browser. You should see the new background image on all pages. You may need to return to the Modify Theme set up to select a new color scheme to match the background or simply remove the background image all together.

Installing Additional Themes

If you would like additional themes, there are many places on the Internet from which you can download them. As with any downloads done from the Internet, it is always important to scan the files for viruses. A downloaded theme is typically a single file with a .MSI extension.

To install a new theme, select **Install Additional Themes** in the **Themes** window.

Below are some Web sites from which you can obtain additional FrontPage themes:

- www.microsoft.com/frontpage

- www.rtbwizards.com/fpthemes

- www.thememart.com

- alysta.com/fpthemes/themes.htm

- www.frontpageusers.com

- www.themepak.com

Lesson Summary

▶ Themes are a means of applying a consistent look across your web. Themes can be shared with other Office applications to create a consistent appearance to all of your documents.

▶ Themes affect background, font style and color, bullets, horizontal lines, Page Banners, and buttons. Once a theme is applied to a web, all previous formatting is lost. Before applying a theme to your web, you should make a backup copy of the web in case you need to revert to a previous version.

▶ FrontPage 2000 comes with close to fifty themes available. These themes can be used as they are, or can be customized. You can also download additional themes from a number of sites on the Web.

▶ While you cannot create a custom theme from scratch, you can alter an existing theme. When doing so, it is best to save the modified theme with a different name. When customizing themes, you can modify font, colors, and graphics.

▶ Fonts can be modified either for all text types in a theme, or for specific text types. The font type, style, size, and color are all configurable. Not all users will have access to the same fonts, so it is best to use standard fonts.

▶ Colors can be modified for text, background, and borders. Three methods are available to set the colors for a theme. You can select a pre-defined Color Scheme, use the Color Wheel to create your own color scheme, or you can create a custom color for a specific element, such as table borders or header text.

▶ A number of related graphics are part of any theme, including background images, horizontal lines, bullet points, and buttons. Any of these individual graphics can be changed when customizing your theme.

Lesson Review

Matching

___ 1. Page element that is not affected by themes

___ 2. Dynamic images that can be enabled or disabled in a theme

___ 3. Tool for creating a custom color scheme

___ 4. Page element that is affected by themes

___ 5. Pre-defined set of colors for use in a theme

a. Color Scheme

b. Color Wheel

c. Active graphics

d. Page Banners

e. table size

Fill in the Blank

6. You can create custom themes by modifying _____, _____, and _____.

7. Themes include _____ different bullet point styles for nesting lists.

True or False?

T / F 8. You cannot alter the size of the font used by Page Banners.

T / F 9. Once a theme is applied to a web, all previous formatting is lost.

T / F 10. You can customize the fonts used in global navigation buttons.

T / F 11. FrontPage themes can be shared with PowerPoint presentations.

T / F 12. You can change the color of a theme's navigation bar using the Color Wheel.

T / F 13. FrontPage will not allow you to choose clashing colors for a theme.

T / F 14. Themes downloaded from the Web have an MST extension and must be accompanied by an FP2 DLL profile file.

Lesson 7
Publishing Your
FrontPage Web

Lesson Topics

► Publishing a FrontPage Web to a Server

► The FrontPage 'Publish' Function

► Lesson Summary

Publishing a FrontPage Web to a Server

Once you have created your FrontPage Web on your local computer, you must upload it to a Web server. You may have access to a Web server physically housed within your organization. Or you might have access to a Web server remotely hosted by an Internet Service Provider (ISP) or Web hosting service. In either case, your FrontPage web is not truly a Web site and available to the world until you upload it to a Web server.

Types of Web Servers

There are a number of different types of Web servers used to host Web sites. Web servers are typically computer platform-specific, meaning they rely upon the operating system of the server computer itself. Some of the most common server configurations include:

- Internet Information Server (Windows NT)

- Netscape Enterprise Server (UNIX/Windows NT)

- Apache (UNIX)

You should know the type of server you will use to host your Web site; it can affect your ability to use FrontPage (as you will learn shortly). If you have not yet selected a hosting provider, you should make your decision based on how well FrontPage works with the type of server supported by the hosting service and how the service supports FrontPage.

FrontPage 2000 Server Extensions

FrontPage 2000 Server Extensions are a group of programs and applications that allow FrontPage to act not only as an HTML editor, but as a scripting and content management tool as well. To get the maximum benefit from FrontPage, a Web site should be hosted on a Web server that supports and has installed the FrontPage Extensions.

Without Extensions

You can design your site in FrontPage without using any features that depend on the FrontPage Extensions. (Many of these features are discussed in *Parts 2* and *3*.) At this level, these might not be as important to you as learning to create a basic site.

However, if your Web server does not have FrontPage Extensions installed, you will not be able to take advantage of one of the unique features of FrontPage: publishing your web via HTTP.

Publishing: HTTP vs. FTP

The basic method of moving files to and from a Web server is FTP (File Transfer Protocol). FTP is an Internet protocol dedicated to moving files between Internet servers and clients or between two servers.

  FTP uses port 23 to connect and transfer documents; HTTP uses port 80.

FrontPage's **Publish** feature uses HTTP to publish, instead of FTP. This type of publishing keeps the FrontPage web intact as a unit, with the relationships between files maintained. With FTP, each file would be uploaded separately, losing those relationships.

HTTP publishing is made possible by the FrontPage Server Extensions. Without them in place, you can upload using FTP, but you will not be able to take full advantage of FrontPage's content management and site administration features.

Web Servers that Support FrontPage Extensions

Microsoft makes many versions of the FrontPage 2000 Extensions. There is a version for almost every type of Web server, even those that do not run on Microsoft operating systems. Theoretically, you should be able to use all the features of FrontPage no matter which platform your site is hosted on.

Server Extensions Run Best on Windows Servers

Server Extensions run best on Windows platforms, however. Administrators of UNIX-based Web servers are sometimes reluctant to install FrontPage Extensions. Most commercial Web hosting providers support the Server Extensions only for their Windows-based servers.

If you do not already have an ISP, FrontPage 2000 provides a list of ISPs that support FrontPage 2000 Extensions. You can sign up with a provider when you publish your web.

  If a Web server is running the FrontPage 98 Server Extensions, you will still be able to publish your FrontPage 2000 web via HTTP, but some of the advanced features will not be supported such as the Database Connection Wizard.

The FrontPage 'Publish' Function

All of the pages you create using FrontPage are never seen by the world if you do not publish your web. This section will show you how to publish your Web and upload pages you have changed to your Web server.

Two Publishing Methods

There are two ways to access the FrontPage **Publish** function: 1) the **Publish Web** icon on the Standard toolbar or 2) **File ▶ Publish Web**.

The first time you publish using the **Publish Web** icon, you are prompted to enter the location of the web to which you are publishing. After this, however, FrontPage assumes you want to publish to the same address and does not prompt you for the location.

The **File ▶ Publish Web** method prompts you to enter the location to which you want to publish. You do this using the **Publish Web** window, as shown in Figure 7-1.

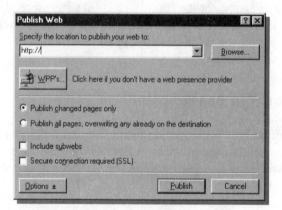

Figure 7-1: Publish Web window

You have several options to customize your publishing:

- **Specify the location to publish your web to**

- **Publish changed pages only** (the safest option)

- **Publish all pages, overwriting any already on the destination** (be careful!)

- **Include subwebs** (subwebs are discussed in *Mastering FrontPage 2000: Part 3*)

- **Secure connection required** for a server that supports Secure Sockets Layer

Exercise 7-1: Publishing Your Web

In this exercise, you will publish the *Music 4 a Song* FrontPage web to a Web server using the FrontPage **Publish** function to publish via HTTP.

To complete this exercise, you must have a Web server to which you can publish your FrontPage web. This Web server must have FrontPage Server Extensions installed.

1. Open the *Music 4 a Song* web.

2. Select **File ▶ Publish Web**.

3. For location, enter the URL of your Web site.

4. Since this will be the first publication of the web site select **Publish all pages**. For future reference when updating the site use the choice **Publish changed pages only**.

5. Click **Publish**.

6. Enter your username and password, if so prompted.

You will see a series of images and text indicating your FrontPage web is being published to your Web server, as shown in Figure 7-2 and Figure 7-3 (on the following page).

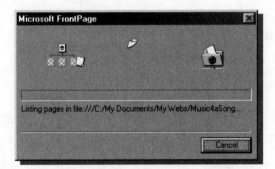

Figure 7-2: Publishing process (1)

Figure 7-3: Publishing process (2)

 When publishing is complete, you will see the message shown in Figure 7-4.

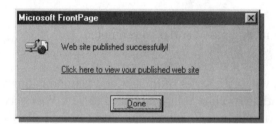

Figure 7-4: Publishing confirmation message

Using the Publish Function to Upload via FTP

If your Web server does not have FrontPage Server Extensions installed, you can still use the FrontPage **Publish** function to publish via FTP.

The only modification you need to make is in entering the location of the Web site to which to publish. Instead of specifying the HTTP transfer protocol:

`http://www.yoursite.com`

you must use the FTP transfer protocol:

`ftp://www.yoursite.com`

Lesson Summary

▶ Once you have created your FrontPage web, you will need to upload it to a Web server so that anyone on the Internet using a Web browser can access it.

▶ There are several types of Web servers running on different operating systems. Not all of them support the FrontPage Server Extensions.

▶ The FrontPage Server Extensions enable you to publish your web via HTTP instead of FTP. This in turn allows FrontPage to create relationships between files in a web, and permits you to use the advanced site management features of FrontPage.

▶ If your Web server does not have the FrontPage Server Extensions installed, you can still upload your files via FTP, but you lose much of FrontPage's unique features.

▶ The FrontPage **Publish** function uses HTTP (or FTP, if you so specify) to simply transfer your FrontPage web to a Web server.

▶ If you do not already have an ISP, and are looking for one to host your Web site, be sure that the ISP you choose supports the FrontPage 2000 Server Extensions.

Lesson Review

Matching

___ 1. File Transfer Protocol   a. Publish function

___ 2. Transfers a FrontPage web to a Web server   b. Port 80

___ 3. Applications that enable publishing via HTTP   c. FTP

___ 4. HTTP port   d. Server Extensions

Fill in the Blank

5. The Publish function uses either _____ or _____ to upload files.

6. _____ must be installed on a Web server to publish via HTTP.

7. Three examples of common Web servers are _____ , _____ , and _____ .

8. FrontPage's Publishing feature uses _____ to publish (instead of _____).

True or False?

T / F   9. The only way to upload a FrontPage web to a Web server is to use FTP.

T / F   10. FrontPage Server Extensions are only available for Microsoft Internet Information Server.

T / F   11. The FrontPage Publish function can be launched from the Menu bar or from the Standard toolbar.

T / F   12. You can publish a FrontPage 2000 web to a server running FrontPage 98 Extensions.

T / F   13. You can publish a FrontPage web to a Web server that does not have FrontPage Server Extensions installed (but you will not enjoy the benefit of FrontPage-specific features in your web).

Lesson 8
Course Review

Applying What You Have Learned

Now that you have the skills necessary to create a Web site using FrontPage 2000, it is time to apply them. Be as creative as you would wish within the parameters of the following exercise. Feel free to add any additional Web page elements or formatting.

Exercise 8-1: Applying Your Knowledge

1. Create a new empty page.

2. Title the new page "Famous Saxophonists" in Heading 1.

3. Create a table on the new page with five rows and three columns.

   - Populate the first two columns of the table as follows:

Saxophonist	Primary Instrument
Kenny G.	Soprano
Dave Koz	Alto
Clarence Clemmons	Tenor
Branford Marsalis	Various

   - Size the table to its contents.

   - Merge the bottom four cells in the right hand (third) column into a single cell.

   - Insert the image MUSIC.GIF in this cell. Adjust the size of the image.

   - Give the entire table a white background.

   - Modify other table and cell properties with regard to borders and alignment according to your preferences.

4. Save the file as FAMOUS.HTM.

5. Add a list item in INDEX.HTM for the Famous Saxophonists page.

6. Create a hyperlink from the list item to the page.

7. In the table in TYPES.HTM, add bookmarks to each of the saxophone types.

8. Verify all of your hyperlinks.

9. Modify the color scheme of your theme as you desire.

10. Publish the modified pages of your web.

"I'm posting my new Web site—'A Vegetarian Thanksgiving.'"

Mastering FrontPage 2000: Part 2

Further Studies with Microsoft's HTML Editor

"FrontPage 2000 improves on FrontPage 98 by eliminating much of the older product's tendency to arbitrarily change HTML tags and offers broader function support. FrontPage 2000 is a Web wizard!"

— Windows Magazine, 1999

Part 2 Description

Welcome to *Mastering FrontPage 2000: Part 2*, the second section in DDC's comprehensive *Mastering FrontPage 2000* series. This intermediate-level course is designed to provide an overview of some of the more sophisticated and powerful features of FrontPage 2000 for Webmasters and users who desire to create Web sites with interactive elements.

In this section, you will learn to use various FrontPage 2000 components and apply them to a static Web site through a series of hands-on exercises.

Course Objectives

- Creating a navigation structure and scheme for your site

- Incorporating shared elements such as borders and frames

- Understanding and using style sheets

- Collecting user feedback through the use of forms

- Indexing your site for searching

- Creating and managing a discussion forum

- Incorporating special effects and multimedia

Part 2 Setup

Mastering FrontPage 2000: Part 2 requires minimal PC configuration and setup. Three primary elements are required for this course:

- Microsoft FrontPage 2000 (either standalone version or bundled with Microsoft Office 2000 Premium)

- A Web browser (Microsoft Internet Explorer 4.*x* or 5.*x* or Netscape Navigator/Communicator recommended)

- Student files accompanying this course

During this entire course, you (or your students) will toggle back and forth between your Web browser and FrontPage as you edit the Web pages you create during the dozens of hands-on exercises integrated into this course.

Installing the Student Files

The student files necessary for *Mastering FrontPage 2000: Part 2* are archived on the Student Files CD-ROM. Follow these steps to install the student files:

1. Insert the Student Files CD-ROM into the appropriate drive on your computer.

2. Using Windows Explorer (file manager) or another file management utility, locate the file named FP-2.EXE and copy it to your Windows Desktop.

   - On the CD-ROM, single-click FP-2.EXE and right-click.

   - On the shortcut menu that appears, select **Copy**.

   - On your Desktop, be sure your mouse pointer is not on an icon or application and right-click.

   - Select **Paste**. This will copy the FP-2.EXE file from the Student Files CD-ROM to your Windows Desktop.

3. On your Desktop, double-click FP-2.EXE.

4. The **WinZip Self-Extractor** dialog box will appear. Click the **Unzip** button.

5. The files will be decompressed and stored in a folder called FP-2 on your Desktop. If the files were decompressed and installed correctly, an alert box will appear that indicates this.

6. Using Windows Explorer, create a new MY WEBS folder inside the C:\MY DOCUMENTS folder. Each web must be in a separate folder. Therefore, if a MY WEBS folder already exists and contains webs, those webs must be deleted or moved before preparing for this course.

7. Open the FP-2 folder from your Desktop. Select and copy all the files and the folder; paste them all in the C:\MY DOCUMENTS\MY WEBS folder.

To further prepare your personal computer for taking this course, complete the following steps to properly configure your installation of FrontPage 2000:

1. Launch FrontPage 2000.

2. Select **File ▶ New ▶ Web**.

3. Single-click **Import Web Wizard**.

4. In the **Options** section, specify the location of the web as C:\MY DOCUMENTS\MY WEBS and click **OK**.

5. A dialog box will appear, asking you whether to convert the folder to a web. Click **Yes**.

6. In the **Import Web Wizard – Choose source** dialog box, choose to import from existing files by selecting the first radio button **From source directory of files on a local computer or network**.

7. In the **Location** field, enter C:\MY DOCUMENTS\MY WEBS.

8. Select the **Include subfolders** checkbox.

9. Click **Next**.

10. The following screen will display a list of the files to be copied.

11. Click **Next**.

12. Click **Finish**.

13. If any alert box appears notifying you that any file already exists, click **Yes to All**.

DDC Publishing • www.ddcpub.com

Lesson 9
Site Structure &
Navigation

Lesson Topics

► Navigating a Web Site

► Creating a Table of Contents

► Navigation Bars

► Image Maps

► Lesson Summary

Navigating a Web Site

As with any project, the first step in building a complex Web site with FrontPage 2000 is to *plan*. Whether you are developing a corporate intranet, a business, academic, or organizational Web presence, or an online store (e-commerce), you should ask yourself the following questions:

- What is the mission or purpose of my site?

- What are the short- and long-term goals of my site?

- Who are the intended audiences?

- Why will people come to my site?

- What monitor size and video resolution am I designing for?

An important factor to remember when developing a Web site using FrontPage 2000 is that many of FrontPage's components are proprietary. Thus, several FrontPage components work only if the Web server on which your site resides has *FrontPage Server Extensions* installed.

Other FrontPage components may only work with Microsoft's Internet Explorer browser (users of Netscape Navigator or Communicator or other browsers may not be able to view content created with these components).

See Appendix A for a list of components that require FrontPage Server Extensions.

Deciding Which Navigation Scheme to Use

There are a number of other things to take into consideration when deciding which of the several navigation schemes to use in your Web site.

- How large will the site be?

- What distinct categories can the information be organized into?

- Do the pages have a logical flow of information?

These factors will help to determine your site's navigation scheme. The versatility of FrontPage 2000 allows you to combine different schemes on the same page or in different places in your site

Linear vs. Hierarchical Structure

There are essentially two types of navigational structure for any Web site (as described in Table 9-1):

- Linear structure: links are provided to the previous and next pages in the series, as well as to return to the home page.

- Hierarchical structure: links provided may be grouped by category or topic.

Navigation Logic Type	Explanation	Example
Linear	<ul><li>Site visitors travel from one page to the next in a set order (determined by you, the Web site author).</li><li>Akin to the linear navigation of a novel or a magazine article.</li><li>Strict navigation structure and logic in order to retain meaning and significance of all site information.</li></ul>	<ul><li>Page 1 to page 2 to page 3 to page 4, etc.</li><li>If a user navigates directly from page 2 to page 4 (passing page 3), the navigation logic is broken and necessary information is left out.</li></ul>
Hierarchical	<ul><li>A site is laid out like a tree or organizational chart, with different levels.</li><li>Allows site visitors to make their own decisions regarding the information they want to see and in what order, without disrupting the intended navigation logic or missing necessary information.</li></ul>	A user may navigate from a main page(s) containing general information about a category to specific items within a category. For example, user may navigate from a page about travel to individual pages about specific travel destinations.

Table 9-1: Characteristics of linear and hierarchical site navigation structures

Within a hierarchical site, there may be areas that are laid out in a linear structure.

Types of Navigation Schemes

Once you have determined the structure of your site, you need to decide how visitors will navigate through the Web site. FrontPage 2000 offers several tools that aid in the creation of a navigation scheme. Certain schemes work better for a site that is hierarchical rather than linear in structure.

FrontPage 2000 components that can be used to create a navigation scheme are:

- tables of contents (TOC)

- site maps

- navigation bars ("nav bars")

- shared borders

You can also use FrontPage 2000 to create a navigation scheme incorporating frames or image maps.

In this lesson, you will learn how to use FrontPage 2000 to incorporate a table of contents, site map, navigation bar, and image map into your site.

 An image map and a navigation bar on your home page could also include links to a table of contents or a site map.

Navigation View

As discussed in *Part 1*, FrontPage 2000 has a variety of different "views" through which you can view the content and structure of your site. These include:

FrontPage View	Function
Page	Displays the content of an individual page for editing
Folders	Displays the directory structure of your site
Reports	Displays a variety of customizable reports on your site
Navigation	Allows you to map out a navigational structure for your site
Hyperlinks	Displays your site as a network of hyperlinked files
Tasks	Allows you to delegate various administrative and editing tasks

Table 9-2: FrontPage 2000 Views

The navigation elements available in FrontPage as shown in Table 9-3 are generated from the structure you create in the program's **Navigation View**. This view shows how pages in your FrontPage Web are related to one another, depending on your site's structure.

The types of pages displayed in FrontPage's **Navigation View** are:

Navigation View Element	Definition
Home page	The first page viewed by a visitor to your site
Top-level page	A page the resides at the same structure level as the sites home page
Parent-level page	A page that is directly below the home page in the sites structure, usually an overview to a particular area of the site
Child-level pages	Pages that support a parent page, usually with more detailed information than the parent page.
Same-level pages	Pages that are on the same level but accessed through a single child page, usually found in a linear navigation structure or slide-show type of presentation

Table 9-3: Navigation View elements

Building a Site's Navigation Structure

You can build out a site's navigation structure by switching to **Navigation View** in the FrontPage Views window. To add a new page to the navigation structure, click the **New Page** button on the toolbar. If you have a page selected, the new page will automatically be added under it. You can also click and drag this page to the desired location in the navigation structure.

Modifying the Navigation Structure

You can modify the navigation structure as you desire:

- To add an existing page to the navigation structure, click the page in the **Folder List** and drag it to the desired location in the navigation structure

- To rename a page, right-click it and select **Rename**

- To remove a page, right-click it and select **Delete**

Figure 9-1 displays a navigational schematic and Folder List in the **Navigation View**.

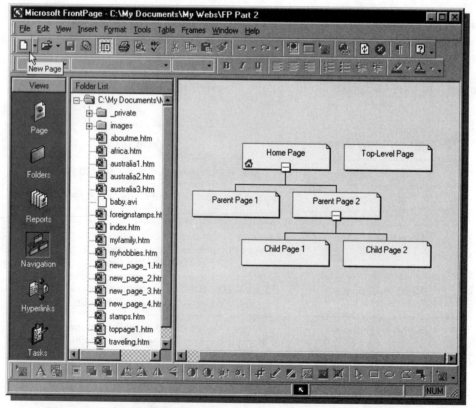

Figure 9-1: Hierarchical navigation structure in the Navigation View

Applying Your Changes

When you are finished making changes to the navigation structure, you must right-click the background and select **Apply Changes**. This will include any new pages added to the structure and apply any name or navigation changes.

Locating a particular file in the navigation structure is difficult in sites with multiple pages. FrontPage 2000 helps you locate a file in the navigational structure.

In **Navigation View**, on the left, right-click the file name in the Folder list and choose **Find in Navigation**. The highlighted page in the navigation structure on the right corresponds to the file that you selected.

Exercise 9-1: Creating a Hierarchical Site Structure with Navigation View

1. Select **Navigation View**.

To move files from the Folder List on the left to the navigation structure schematic on the right, click the file name in the Folder List at the left and, holding down the mouse button, drag the file across to the location you want in the site structure on the right.

2. Drag the files ABOUTME.HTM, MYHOBBIES.HTM, and MYFAMILY.HTM to the navigation side as child pages of the *Home Page* as shown in Figure 9-2.

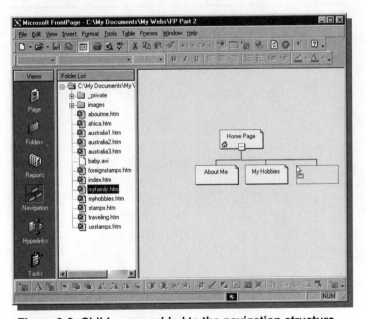

Figure 9-2: Child pages added to the navigation structure

3. Drag the files STAMPS.HTM and TRAVELING.HTM to the structure as child pages of *My Hobbies*.

4. Drag the files FOREIGNSTAMPS.HTM and USSTAMPS.HTM to the structure as child pages of *Stamp Collecting*. Drag the files AFRICA.HTM, AUSTRALIA1.HTM, AUSTRALIA2.HTM, and AUSTRALIA3.HTM to the structure under *Traveling*.

5. Right-click the background and select **Apply Changes**.

 Your final navigation structure should appear similar to Figure 9-3.

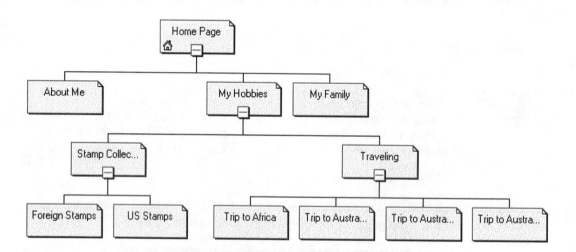

Figure 9-3: Completed navigation structure for the site

Creating a Table of Contents

Now that you have configured the navigation structure of your FrontPage web, you can create a table of contents (TOC) for your site. FrontPage automatically generates a TOC from the navigation structure of your web. You can position the TOC on your home page or on its own page.

 You will probably want to create a separate page for your TOC if you have many pages in your FrontPage web. In such a case, the TOC page would be a second top-level page in your site structure.

TOC Options

When you create the table of contents, you are presented with several options. Figure 9-4 displays the first dialog box of the **Table of Contents Properties**.

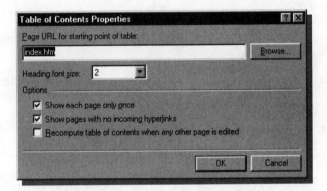

Figure 9-4: Table of Contents Properties dialog box

First, you must choose a page to use as the starting point. The default offered is INDEX.HTM. Then you can select the style for the heading of the table of contents. Here you will choose a font size from **1** to **6**, size **1** being the smallest.

 If you do not want the starting page to be included in the table of contents, you should select **none** for the heading font size.

The **Show each page only once** option prevents a page from appearing more than once in the table of contents if it is the target of multiple links. The **Show pages with no incoming hyperlinks** option allows you to list pages in your web that are not linked to by other pages. **Recompute table of contents when any other page is edited** allows automatic updating of the table of contents. If you do not choose this option, you will have to manually regenerate the table of contents by opening, and then saving, the page containing the table of contents. This will be necessary anytime pages are added, deleted or renamed.

Recompute table of contents when any other page is edited should not be selected if you have a large Web, because it will take longer to save pages when editing.

Exercise 9-2: Creating the Table of Contents

In this exercise, you will create a table of contents for a FrontPage web that provides a user with a convenient "index" of your site that improves navigation and ease of use.

1. Open `INDEX.HTM` in **Page View**, with the **Normal** tab selected (the primary editing area).

2. Insert your cursor wherever you would like to place the table of contents.

3. Select **Insert ▶ Component ▶ Table of Contents**.

4. For **Page URL for starting point of table**, type `index.htm`.

5. Set **Heading font size** to **none**. (This page will not be included in the TOC.)

6. Select all **Options,** except **Recompute table of contents when any other page is edited**. (This is the default.)

7. Click **OK**.

8. Save the file.

Viewing the TOC

In Exercise 9-2, you created a table of contents. However, even after you save the file, you will see a "dummy" table of contents in **Page View**, as shown in Figure 9-5 on the following page. The table of contents is a FrontPage component and, thus, needs to be published in order to be viewed correctly. You can view the TOC if you preview the file in a Web browser.

To do this, select **File ▶ Preview in Browser**. Choose **Internet Explorer** from the menu and click **Preview**. Now the table of contents shows the titles of the pages, as defined in **Navigation View**, and as shown in Figure 9-6 on the following page.

Figure 9-5: Table of contents displayed in Page View

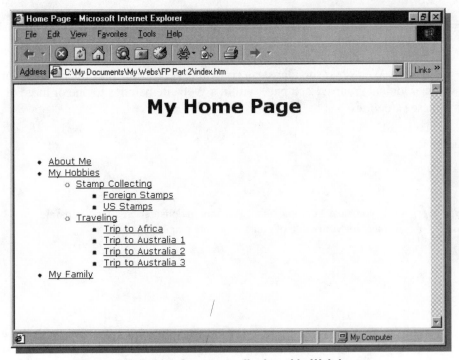

Figure 9-6: Table of contents displayed in Web browser

Modifying the TOC

Any table of contents property can be modified after the TOC has been created.

Exercise 9-3: Modifying the Table of Contents

In this exercise, you will add an option to your table of contents.

1. With INDEX.HTM open in **Page View**, **Normal** tab, right-click the table of contents.
2. Select **Table of Contents Properties**.
3. Select **Recompute table of contents when any other page is edited**.
4. Click **OK**.
5. Save and close the file.

Site Maps

A site map is a navigation scheme that is similar to a table of contents. Site maps are most appropriate for sites with hierarchical structures. A site map lists the pages in your site as determined by the sites navigation structure.

- Simple Web sites: a site map can be as simple as a list of hyperlinks to the various pages in the Web site.

- Complex Web sites: site maps can contain lists of hyperlinks to categories or to other logical groups. Each page within a Web site belongs to one or more of these categories.

 If you have a complex site, you should consider creating a separate page for your table of contents or site map.

Exercise 9-4: Creating a Site Map Page

In this exercise, you will create a Web page containing a site map that aids users in navigating your site.

1. From **Navigation View**, right-click the background of the navigation schematic and select **New Top Page**.

2. Right-click the newly-created page and choose **Rename**. Rename the page *Site Map*.

3. Double-click to edit *Site Map*.

4. Select **Insert ▶ Insert Component ▶ Table of Contents**.

5. For **Heading Font Size**, select **2**. This site map page will be included in the TOC.

6. In the **Options** section, select all except **Recompute table of contents when any other page is edited** (this is the default).

7. Click **OK**.

8. Save the file and preview it in your Web browser.

 The site map appears in your Web browser, similar to Figure 9-7.

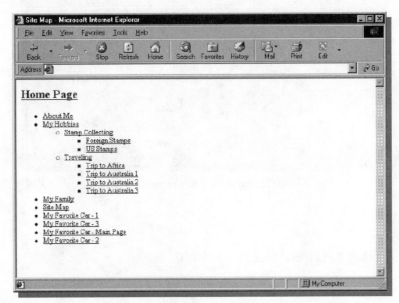

Figure 9-7: Site map page as viewed in a Web browser

Navigation Bars

A navigation bar, or "nav bar," is a group of hyperlinks that provide a user with a means by which to navigate through your Web site. A nav bar is generated based on the navigation structure you create in FrontPage's **Navigation View**.

Navigation Bar Options

The first choice in designing a navigation bar is to decide which hyperlinks will be included. FrontPage cannot make this decision for you, but the interface by which you tell FrontPage which hyperlinks to include in your nav bar is accessed in the **Navigation Bar Properties** dialog box, as shown in Figure 9-8. This dialog box is opened by selecting **Insert ▶ Navigation Bar**.

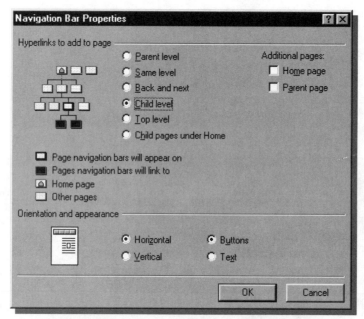

Figure 9-8: Navigation Bar Properties dialog box

Choosing Which Hyperlinks to Include

Choosing which hyperlinks to include in your navigation bar will depend on the structure of your site. If you have a linear structure, you will want to create navigation bars leading to the next and previous pages in the series. You may also want to provide links to a parent page and/or the home page.

Nav Bar Characteristics

Remember the following points when creating nav bars:

- When you select a level of hyperlinks to include, the **Navigation View** chart graphic changes to display the pages that will be affected.

- You can manually add the home page and/or a parent page to the navigation bar by selecting the appropriate boxes.

- You must select the orientation and appearance of your navigation bar

  - a vertical navigation bar is typically used along the side of a page

  - a horizontal navigation bar is more appropriate along the top or bottom of a page.

- A navigation bar can contain text or button hyperlinks.

- When you create a navigation bar, it appears on only one page. To add a navigation bar to multiple pages in your FrontPage web, you should use shared borders[5].

Using a nav bar that is generated by FrontPage is convenient, but it comes at a cost. Because FrontPage applies the same logic to every page in the site structure, navigation bars cannot be customized for individual pages.

---

[5] Shared borders are discussed in detail in Lesson 10.

Exercise 9-5: Creating a Hierarchical Navigation Bar

In this exercise, you will create a hierarchical navigation bar.

1. Open INDEX.HTM.

2. Insert your cursor below the title "My Home Page" and click the icon on the Formatting toolbar to left-justify so that the cursor us about even with the "dummy" TOC line, "Title of a Page."

3. Select **Insert ▶ Navigation Bar**.

4. In the **Hyperlinks to add to page** section, select **Child** level.

5. In the **Orientation and appearance** section, select **Horizontal** and **Text**.

You can only use buttons if you are applying a FrontPage theme to your site. Themes are covered in detail in *Part 1*.

6. Click **OK** and save the file.

7. The results appear in the **Normal** tab, as shown in Figure 9-9.

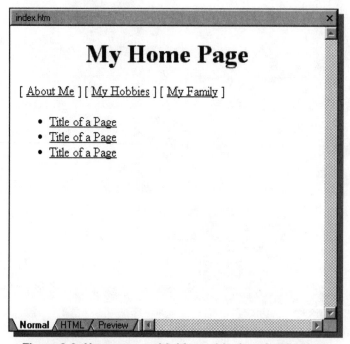

Figure 9-9: Home page with hierarchical navigation bar

Exercise 9-6: Creating a Linear Navigation Bar

In this exercise, you will create a linear navigation bar.

1. Open AUSTRALIA1.HTM.

2. Position your cursor one line under the photo.

3. Select **Insert ▶ Navigation Bar**.

4. In the **Hyperlinks to add to page** section, select **Back** and **Next**.

5. In the **Orientation and appearance** section, select **Horizontal** and **Text**.

6. In the **Additional pages** section, select **Home page** and **Parent page**.

7. Click **OK** and save the file.

8. The results appear on the **Normal** tab, as shown in Figure 9-10.

Figure 9-10: Page with a linear navigation bar

 Navigation bars typically work best for sites with a linear structure. For hierarchical sites, site maps and tables of contents are more appropriate.

Excluding Pages from a Nav Bar

You will note that the navigation bar you have created allows you to move back from *Trip to Australia 1* to *Trip to Africa*. Because this does not follow in the linear progression, you can choose to exclude *Trip to Africa* from the navigation bar.

Exercise 9-7: Excluding a Page from a Navigation Bar

In this exercise, you will exclude a page from the nav bar.

1. From **Navigation View**, right-click *Trip to Africa*.

2. Deselect **Included in Navigation Bars**.

3. Right-click the **Navigation View** background and select **Apply Changes**.

4. Double-click *Trip to Australia 1*.

 Note that **Previous** no longer appears in the navigation bar.

5. Save and close the file.

Modifying Nav Bar Properties

You can format a navigation bar like any other text. You can change the following characteristics of nav bars:

- alignment

- font

- size

- any other text properties

Exercise 9-8: Modifying a Navigation Bar

In this exercise, you will center the navigation bar and change its font.

1. Open `INDEX.HTM`.
2. Right-click the nav bar and select **Paragraph**.
3. Under **Alignment**, select **Center** and click **OK**.
4. Right-click the nav bar again and select **Font**.
5. Under **Font**, select **Arial**.
6. Under **Font style**, select **Bold**.
7. Under **Size**, select **3 (12 pt)**.
8. Click **Apply**.

 You can use the **Preview** tab to see the results.

9. Click **OK**.
10. Save and close file.

 "The automatically-updated navigation bars, one of the best features of FrontPage Webs, have been improved [in FrontPage 2000], giving you a bit more control over what pages will be included..."

— *David Fiedler, WebDeveloper.com, 1999*

Image Maps

Image maps are another tool available to help guide users through your site. They provide a more graphical way for the user to navigate through your site.

 An image map is an image (photo or graphic) in which areas of the image, called *hotspots*, provide hyperlinks to other Web pages.

Image maps can be interpreted on the server (known as *server-side image maps*), or in the browser (known as *client-side image maps*). FrontPage 2000 enables you to easily create client-side image maps by helping you to quickly define clickable zones within an image, commonly referred to as *hotspots*.

Creating an Image Map

In a client-side image map, a *hotspot* is defined by two characteristics:

- *shape* of the hotspot region

- *coordinates* of its position within the image relative to the upper-left corner

Hotspot Shapes

Hotspot shapes can be:

- circular

- rectangular

- polygonal

Hotspot Coordinates

Image map hotspot coordinates refer to the position of the shape within the image. These coordinates are calculated from the upper-left corner of the graphic, starting at 0,0. The first number represents the number of pixels across (horizontally); the second number represents the number of pixels down (vertically).

In FrontPage 2000, you can define the areas for a hotspot using the built-in graphics editor. When editing a page with an image, the Graphics toolbar will appear once the image is selected, as shown in Figure 9-11.

Figure 9-11: FrontPage 2000 Graphics toolbar

You can use the shapes shown in Figure 9-12 below to define hotspot areas on the image.

Figure 9-12: Hotspot creation and editing tools

Exercise 9-9: Creating an Image Map

In this exercise, you will create a basic image map using FrontPage 2000.

You can create image maps using applications other than FrontPage 2000 or by manually scripting the map code. However, if you are creating most of your site using FrontPage, it is typically recommended that you also use FrontPage for image maps.

1. Open STAMPS.HTM. Click the world map graphic.

2. Once the image has been selected, the Graphics toolbar should appear at the bottom of the FrontPage window. (Note: If the Graphics toolbar does not appear at the bottom of the screen, you will need to make the toolbar available by selecting **View** ▶ **Toolbars** ▶ **Pictures**.)

3. Define a rectangular hotspot on the graphic that covers the area of the United States, as shown in Figure 9-13 on the following page, by selecting the **Rectangular Hotspot** button on the toolbar and drawing a rectangle over the area to be linked.

Figure 9-13: Defining a rectangular hotspot

4. After you have drawn the rectangle, the Create Hyperlink dialog box automatically opens.

5. Type **usstamps.htm** in the URL field, as shown in Figure 9-14. You may also select the file from the list of available files shown in the window above.

Figure 9-14: Create Hyperlink dialog box

6. Define a circular hotspot around Australia.

> Note that when you create a rectangular hotspot, the tool will draw from one corner to the other, depending on the direction in which you drag the pointer. However, when you use the circular hotspot tool you must start at the center of the area you are defining and draw outward.

7. Type **foreignstamps.htm** as the URL in the **Create Hyperlink** dialog box.

8. Create hotspots over Europe, Asia, and Africa using the Polygon button on the Graphics toolbar. (Hint: click once to begin defining the area, then again at each corner. You must close the defined area by ending where you began.)

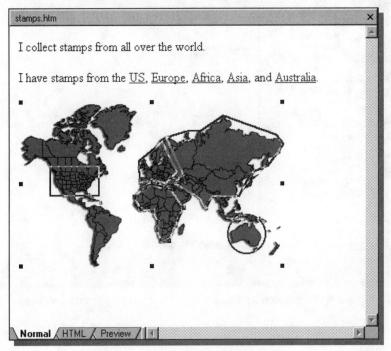

Figure 9-15: Completed image map

9. Use **foreignstamps.htm** as the URL for each of these regions also.

10. Save the file.

11. Preview in your Web browser and test the links by clicking each of them. Use your browser's **Back** button to return to the image map.

12. Save and close the file.

Editing an Image Map

After it is created, you can edit an image map quite easily with FrontPage 2000. When editing the page, simply click on the image and the defined hotspots will appear. However, if the image is detailed and has multiple hotspots, they may be difficult to see.

You can temporarily hide the image and display only the hotspots by clicking on the image and then selecting the Highlight Hotspots tool from the Graphics toolbar, as shown in Figure 9-16. You may also add additional hotspots, or resize or delete existing hotspots.

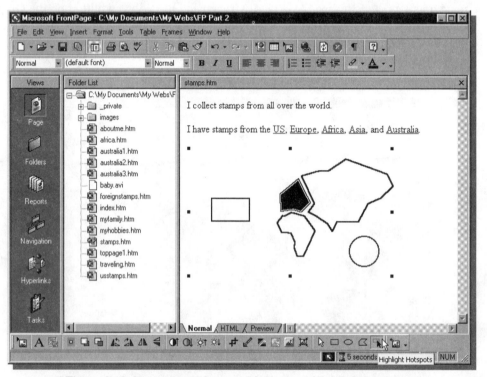

Figure 9-16: Image map shown with Hotspot Highlights selected

Resizing Hotspots

To resize an existing hotspot area, select the hotspot you wish to edit. At each corner point of the hotspot, a small anchor box will appear. You can click and drag these anchors to readjust the size and shape of the hotspot.

Changing Hotspot Hyperlinks

You can change the hyperlink for a given hotspot by right-clicking within the hotspot and choosing **Picture Hotspot Properties** or **Hyperlink**. (You may also double-click the hotspot as a short cut.)

Lesson Summary

▶ The first thing you should do when planning a web site is to define who your target audience is and what the goal of the site will be.

▶ Web site structures are usually either linear or hierarchical, and may be a combination of the two.

▶ A navigation scheme for a site should be chosen after determining the site's structure and size.

▶ FrontPage 2000 aids in the creation of a navigation scheme by providing navigation components such as table of contents, navigation bars, and shared borders. Other navigation schemes, such as site maps and image maps, can also be created in FrontPage 2000.

▶ FrontPage's navigation schemes are generated based on your Web's structure, as defined in **Navigation View**.

▶ You must update **Navigation View** as you add pages to your site, or your navigation tools will not be accurate.

▶ The table of contents component generates a list of hyperlinks to pages within your FrontPage Web. A site map can also be created using the table of contents component.

▶ Navigation bars are buttons or text hyperlinks to pages within your FrontPage Web. They are used to direct users through your site.

▶ An image map is a graphic with one or more hotspots, which are hyperlinks to other pages in your site. A hotspot can be rectangular, circular, or polygonal.

▶ Once created, you can edit the size, shape, and number of hotspots within an image map, as well as the hyperlink to which the hotspot points.

Lesson Review

Matching

___ 1. List of hyperlinks used to display the structure of the site

a. Navigation bar

___ 2. Set of text or button hyperlinks

b. Image map

___ 3. View from which navigation schemes are generated

c. Site map

___ 4. Simple list of hyperlinks to other pages in the site

d. Table of contents

___ 5. Graphic containing hyperlinks

e. Navigation View

Fill in the Blank

6. _____ and _____ are two types of site structure.

7. _____ are areas of an image map that contain hyperlinks.

8. Hotspot shapes are _____, _____, and _____ .

9. Two things you should define before you start to build your web site are _____ and _____ .

10. A Child-Level page is _____ .

True or False?

T / F 11. Changes made to **Navigation View** are saved automatically.

T / F 12. A navigation bar can only be placed on the home page.

T / F 13. A table of contents works best for a site with a linear structure.

T / F 14. A Same-Level page is the same as a Child-Level page.

T / F 15. Any time changes are made to the navigation structure of a site, you must always recompute the table of contents.

Lesson 10
Shared Borders &
Frames

Lesson Topics

► Shared Borders

► Frames

► Frames Page Structure

► Frames Pages in FrontPage

► Important Warnings Regarding Frames

► Lesson Summary

Shared Borders

FrontPage 2000 offers a unique feature called *shared borders*. A shared border is a region that is common to one or more pages within your web site. The shared border may be at the top of each page, at the bottom, at the left, or at the right. Shared borders may also be used in a combination of any of the regions mentioned.

An advantage to using shared borders is that when content is entered or edited within the shared border, it is automatically updated on all pages within the site that are using the shared borders.

From a design point-of-view, although having a shared border on the right-hand side of the page is possible, it usually does not work very well. Depending on the size of the browser window, the shared border may be beyond the edge of the screen, requiring users to scroll over to see the shared border.

Applying a Shared Border

Shared borders may be applied across the entire site or on selected pages. Though the default shared borders contain only navigation bars, they may include any elements that you would find in any Web page. Other uses might be for a company logo or copyright notice.

The files used to generate a shared border are kept in a directory called _BORDERS. This is a hidden directory, since you will not need to edit the files within it directly. Hidden directories are discussed in further detail in *Part 3* of this course.

Figure 10-1 shows the **Shared Borders** dialog box that appears when applying shared borders. Choose **Format ▶ Shared Borders** to open this dialog box.

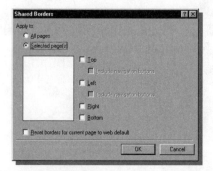

Figure 10-1: Shared Borders dialog box

DDC Publishing • www.ddcpub.com

Exercise 10-1: Applying a Shared Border to the Entire Site

1. In **Navigation View**, choose **Format ▶ Shared Borders**.

2. Choose **Apply to All** pages.

3. Choose **Top** and **Bottom**. Do not include navigation buttons at this time.

4. Click **OK**.

5. Double-click the Home Page, as shown in Figure 10-2.

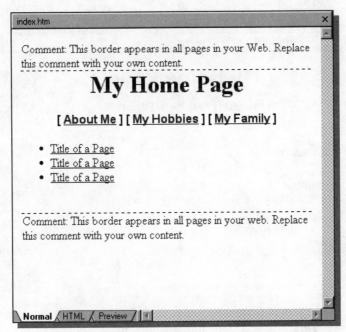

Figure 10-2: Shared borders applied to top and bottom

6. In the top border, delete the text "Comment: This border appears in all pages of your web. Replace this comment with your own content."

7. In the top border, insert the text **(your name)'s Home Page**.

8. In the bottom border, delete the default text as in step 6 above.

9. In the bottom border, insert the text © **2000 by (your name)**. **All rights reserved. Contact me at (your e-mail address)**. Create a link to your e-mail address. (To insert the Copyright symbol, use the Symbol table found under the Insert menu.)

10. Save the file. Preview in your Web browser.

11. When previewed in your browser, your finished page should resemble Figure 10-3.

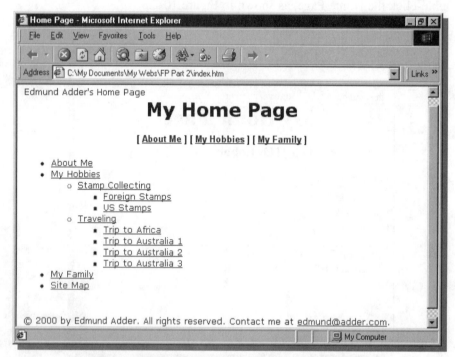

Figure 10-3: Shared borders with custom content

Exercise 10-2: Deleting a Shared Border from the Entire Site

1. In **Navigation View**, choose **Format ▶ Shared Borders**.

2. Choose **Apply to All pages**.

3. Deselect the **Top** checkbox.

4. Click **OK**.

Exercise 10-3: Applying a Shared Border with a Navigation Bar

1. In **Folders View**, select AUSTRALIA1.HTM, AUSTRALIA2.HTM and AUSTRALIA3.HTM. (<u>Hint</u>: To select multiple files, press <CTRL> when selecting.)

2. Choose **Format ▶ Shared Borders**.

3. Choose **Apply to Selected Pages**.

4. Choose **Left** and click **OK**.

5. Double-click AUSTRALIA1.HTM. to open it in the **Page View**.

6. There is now a left-hand border that displays the text *[Edit the properties for this Navigation Bar to display hyperlinks here]*, as shown in Figure 10-4.

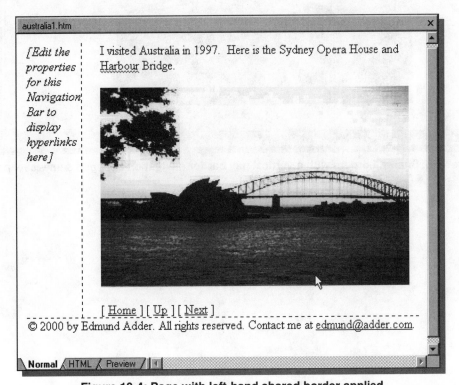

Figure 10-4: Page with left-hand shared border applied

7. Right-click the text and choose **Navigation Bar Properties**.

8. Choose **Back and next**, **Home page**, and **Parent page**.

9. **Orientation and appearance** should be **Vertical** and **Text**.

10. Click **OK**.

11. Because you now have the navigation bar in the shared border at left, you can remove the horizontal nav bar created in Exercise 9-6. Click once on the old nav bar to highlight and press <DELETE>.

12. Save the file and preview it in your browser, as shown in Figure 10-5.

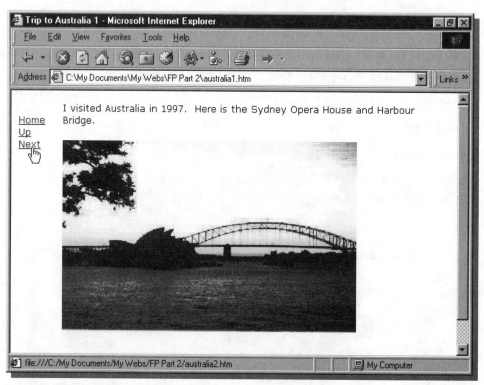

Figure 10-5: Shared borders with a vertical nav bar for navigation between same-level pages

Frames

As discussed in the previous lesson, one of the first decisions a Webmaster must make when planning a Web site is the structure and style that a user encounters when navigating through the site. One method used to aid navigation and structure is *frames*. Frames enable multiple pages to be viewed simultaneously in different areas of the browser window as defined by a *frameset*.

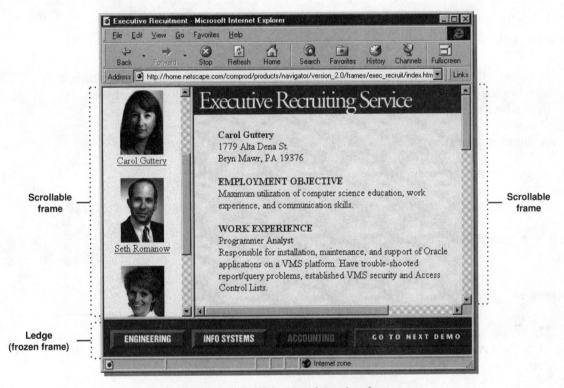

Figure 10-6: Web page featuring frames

 The Web pages displayed in Figure 10-6 has three frames. The bottom frame acts as a navigation bar for the entire Web site. The left frame acts as a nav bar for only one portion of the site (Accounting). The right, largest frame changes when a link in the left frame is clicked. Thus, the right frame acts as a *target* for the left frame.

Frames Page Structure

From the end-user perspective, a page built using frames may appear to be just that, a single page. However, from a technical perspective, that same page actually contains two distinct elements:

- frames

- framesets

Framesets

A layout utilizing frames first requires a *frameset*. A frameset is a page which defines: 1) how the browser window will be divided up into frames, 2) the properties of each particular frame, and 3) the source of the content to be displayed in the frame.

A frameset determines:

- the number of frames

- the size of each frame, either as a percentage of the whole or a fixed pixel size

- the initial page that will be displayed in each frame

Frames

The frames that compose a frameset have several attributes, all of which you must define using the **Frame Properties** dialog box, shown in Figure 10-7. Descriptions of **Frame Properties** are provided in Table 10-1 on the following page.

Figure 10-7: Frame Properties dialog box

Frame Properties	Description
Name	The name of a frame. Each frame in a frameset must have a unique name. The name should be simple, as this will be important when you create links that change the content in a separate frame.
Initial page	First page to appear in the frame when the frameset is loaded.
Width & Row Height	Options: pixels, percent, or relative. Sets size of the frame.
Margins	Area around the inside of each frame border, as measured in pixels.
Resizable in Browser	Ability of end users to resize a frame relative to the other frames in a frameset. If you choose **No Resize** for any frame in a frameset, the other frames that border that frame may also be affected (depending on the layout of the page).
Show Scrollbars	Options: always, never, and if needed. Determines whether users will be able to use the scroll bar to view content in the frame.

Table 10-1: Frame Properties descriptions

If you choose to set a frame's scrollbars to never and not allow resizing, be sure that the content displayed within the frame will be viewable in most browser circumstances.

If these options are turned off and the content is too large for the frame, portions of the content may be *hidden from the user*.

Target Frames

Hyperlinks within frames must specify a *target frame*. The *target* is the *name* of the frame into which the linked file will open when the hyperlink is clicked.

If you are using one of the pre-defined frames pages provided by FrontPage, the target for your hyperlinks is already set (based on the descriptions provided in Table 10-2 in the following section). For example, if you use the pre-designed layout **Contents**—which consists of a content frame on the left and a main frame on the right—the *default target* frame will be the main frame on the right. Clicking hyperlinks in the content frame (on the left) will open files in the main frame (on the right).

Figure 10-8 and Figure 10-9 show the **Edit Hyperlink** and **Target Frame** dialog boxes, respectively. These dialog boxes are opened when you insert hyperlinks.

You can modify the target frame for a given hyperlink by right-clicking the hyperlink and choosing **Hyperlink Properties**. The **Edit Hyperlink** dialog box, which has the same appearance and options as the **Create Hyperlink** dialog box, opens.

Figure 10-8: Edit Hyperlink dialog box

To specify a different target frame, click the pencil icon in the lower right corner of the **Edit Hyperlink** dialog box (as shown above). The **Target Frame** dialog box appears, as shown in Figure 10-9.

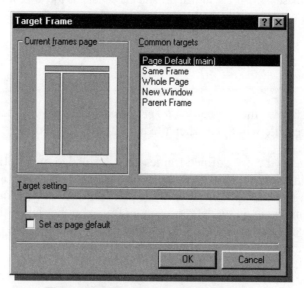

Figure 10-9: Target Frame dialog box

Using the **Target Frame** dialog box, you may change the target frame by:

- selecting from the **Common targets** listed on the right side of the dialog box

- clicking the new target frame of your choice in the **Current frames page** diagram on the left.

The diagram is only available when you are working within the frameset. If you are working on the framed pages individually you will need to enter the name of the desired frame manually.

Problem: Embedded Framesets

A common problem with frames pages is that they can become inadvertently embedded in themselves. This occurs when a hyperlink to a page that contains a frameset is opened within a frame in the current frameset. Continually following the link to the frameset will create an infinite number of framesets within framesets, with no escape for the user.

The Solution

The solution to the problem of embedded framesets is to verify that all hyperlinks to the new frames feature **Whole Page** as their target frame. This instructs the browser to open the next page within the entire browser window and ignore the current frames.

"[FrontPage 2000 is] the one package that builds complex and professional-looking Web sites with minimal effort and maximal results."

— Edward Mendelson, PC Magazine Online, 1999

Frames Pages in FrontPage

You can create a frames page in FrontPage using one of the pre-defined layouts. You can modify each of these layouts further to better suit your needs. The full installation of FrontPage 2000 includes ten different frames page layouts, as detailed in Table 10-2.

Frame Layout	Description
Banner and Contents	Creates a banner frame at the top, with a contents and main frame. Hyperlinks in the banner change the contents frame; hyperlinks in the contents frame change the main frame.
Contents	Creates a contents page on the left containing hyperlinks that change the main page on the right.
Footer	Creates a main frame with a footer underneath. Hyperlinks in the footer change the main frame.
Footnotes	Creates a main frame with footnotes underneath. Hyperlinks in the main frame refer to the footnotes.
Header	Creates a navigation header and a main frame underneath. Hyperlinks in the header change the main frame.
Header, Footer, and Contents	Creates header and footer frames for navigation. Hyperlinks in the header and footer change the contents frame; hyperlinks in the contents frame change the main frame.
Horizontal Split	Creates independent top and bottom frames.
Nested Hierarchy	Creates a nested information hierarchy. General hyperlinks on the left change the more specific frame on the right top.
Top-Down Hierarchy	Creates a top-down information hierarchy. General hyperlinks at the top change the more specific middle frame.
Vertical Split	Creates independent right and left frames.

Table 10-2: Pre-defined Frame Page layouts

You can create the frames pages of a frameset after you have created the frameset, or you can use pages that you had created previously.

If you want to use a layout for your frames that is not one of the pre-defined layouts that FrontPage provides, you can start with a simple pre-defined frame layout and adjust or split frames after the initial set is created.

Exercise 10-4: Creating a Frames Page

1. In **Page View**, select **File ▶ New ▶ Page** and select the **Frames Pages** tab, as shown in Figure 10-10.

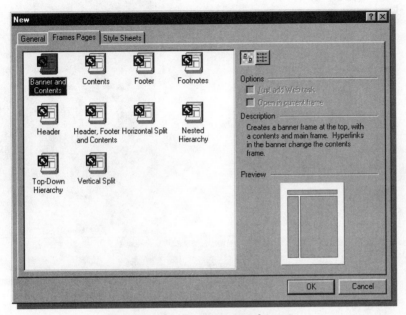

Figure 10-10: Frames page layouts

2. Choose the **Contents** layout from the choices shown in Figure 10-10. This creates a contents frame on the left and a main frame on the right. Hyperlinks in the contents frame (left) change the main frame (right).

3. Click **OK**.

4. In the left frame, choose New Page. Center the title **My Favorite Cars** in the frame. Adjust the width of the frame as necessary, by placing the mouse pointer on the border between the frames, clicking, and dragging to the desired size, as shown in Figure 10-11, on the following page.

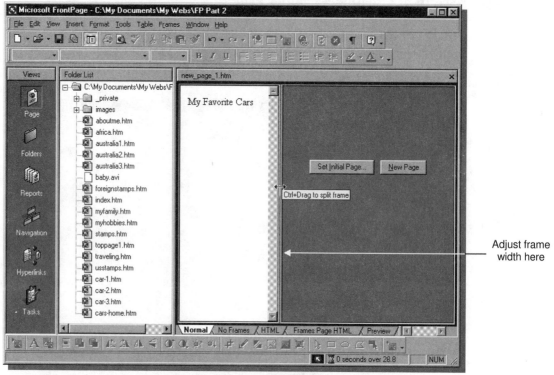

Figure 10-11: Adjusting the relative size of a frame

5. Directly under "My Favorite Cars," insert a one-column, three-row table.

6. Use the following titles and corresponding pages to create hyperlinks in each of the three rows of the table:

    ▪ Corvette (CAR-1.HTM)

    ▪ Mustang (CAR-2.HTM)

    ▪ Vintage Race Car (CAR-3.HTM)

7. Create hyperlinks to each page. The target frame should be the page default, which is the main frame (right).

8. Right click within the left frame and choose **Frame Properties**.

9. Deselect the checkbox for **Resizable in browser**.

10. Click **OK**.

11. In the main frame (right), click **Set Initial Page**. Set the initial page as
    http://www.msn.com/**cars-home.htm**.

Figure 10-12: Completed frameset

12. Save frameset as `CARS.HTM`. You will be prompted to save the contents of each frame and then the frameset, as shown in Figure 10-13.

13. Save the left frame as `CARS-INDEX.HTM`.

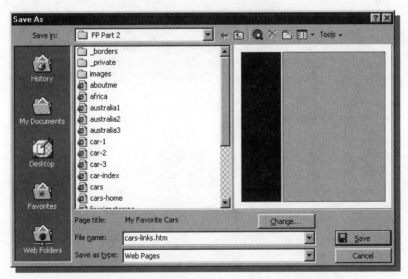

Figure 10-13: Saving the contents of a new frameset

14. Add CARS.HTM to **Navigation View** as a child of *Home Page*.

15. Rename this file FAVORITE CARS.HTM.

16. Right-click the navigation scheme background and select **Apply Changes**.

17. Change to **Page View** and select **File ▶ Preview in Browser**.

18. Save and close the file.

Important Warnings Regarding Frames

It is important to use care when designing frames pages. Remember these important rules when creating frames:

- Ensure that hyperlinks point to the correct target frame.

- If you choose to disallow resizing windows or scrolling, great care is required to ensure that all of the information you need will be viewable.

Although all of the most popular browsers in use today support frames, there are still a few older versions in use that do not. It is important to provide an alternative means of viewing your site's content for users of such browsers. FrontPage 2000 makes this easy by providing a **No Frames** tab in **Page View**. The content shown in the No Frames tab is what a user will see when the browser can not interpret the frameset.

By default, the text in the **No Frames** page in FrontPage 2000 is as follows:

This page uses frames, but your browser doesn't support them.

To edit this text, open your frames page in **Page View** and switch to the **No Frames** tab. After editing the text, save the file.

There is such a thing as too many frames! Adding frames should make it easier to navigate your site, not more difficult. Do not use frames in your site simply because you know how.

Lesson Summary

▶ Shared borders can be placed on the top, bottom, and/or both sides of a page.

▶ Shared borders frequently contain navigation bars, but can contain any element that can appear on a regular page, such as a logo or copyright statement.

▶ Frames are similar to shared borders in that they allow content or links to stay on the screen while changing the content in another area of the screen.

▶ Frames pages divide the browser window into regions in which different files can be viewed simultaneously.

▶ A frameset defines the layout of a frames page, including location and relative size of each frame.

▶ The target attribute of a hyperlink specifies the frame into which the file that is called will open.

▶ FrontPage 2000 allows for the easy creation of frames pages with several pre-defined frames layouts.

▶ Several options can be set for each frame, including whether or not to allow scrolling or resizing.

▶ When enabling the **noresize** or **scrolling=no** options, it is important to allot sufficient space for the frame.

▶ When creating a frameset page in FrontPage 2000, you can use existing files, or you can build the frames pages as you go.

▶ Frames pages can become embedded in themselves if the page that defines a new frameset is called from a hyperlink within an existing frameset. To prevent this, be sure to set the target to **Whole Page** for all hyperlinks that point to a new frameset.

Lesson Review

Matching

____ 1. Area of a page shared by other pages   a. Frameset

____ 2. Defines the layout of frames pages   b. Shared border

____ 3. Prevents users from changing the frame size   c. Target

____ 4. Hyperlink attribute that specifies in which frame a link will open   d. Noresize

____ 5. Unique identifier for a frame   e. Name

Fill in the Blank

6. The top and left shared borders by default contain _____ _____ .

7. _____ allow multiple pages to be viewed in different areas of the browser window.

8. A hyperlink in one frame can refer to another web page in a different frame. The instructions for defining the referenced frame is called a _____ .

9. The _____ frame property prevents the user from adjusting the frame borders.

10. When the page that defines the frameset is called from a link within a frames page, the target needs to be set to _____ .

True or False?

T / F   11. Shared borders cannot be applied to the right-hand side of the page.

T / F   12. You can never have too many frames on a page.

T / F   13. The shared borders dialog box allows you to apply shared borders to the entire site.

T / F   14. You are limited to the pre-defined frames page layouts.

T / F   15. When applying frames, use the theory "less is more."

Lesson 11
Style Sheets

Lesson Topics

► What are Style Sheets?

► External Style Sheets

► Embedded Style Sheets

► Inline Styles

► Style Sheets & Browser Compatibility

► Lesson Summary

What are Style Sheets?

It is often difficult to apply a consistent style across all of your Web pages using standard HTML. Thus, *style sheets*—often called *cascading style sheets*, or simply *CSS*—were introduced to increase presentation options for Web designers. Just like all other HTML code, style sheets can be written using a basic text editor, such as Windows Notepad. FrontPage provides a user-friendly interface for working with style sheets.

Style Sheet Components

 A style sheet is a configuration file that specifies the details of a Web page's appearance.

A style sheet contains rules for elements of a Web page (i.e., its header, body, paragraph, etc.) that determine precisely how each element will be displayed by a user's Web browser.

A CSS rule has two main parts:

- selector

- declaration

 In the rule **H1 { color: red }**, "H1" is the selector. It is the element whose appearance is determined by the declaration **color: red**. If this rule is applied to a Web page, all H1 headers on that page will be shown in red.

There are three types of style sheets:

- external

- embedded

- inline

 "Advanced features once available only in rival products are now built into FrontPage. Pixel-precise positioning of graphic elements is supported through Cascading Style Sheet (CSS) positioning…"

— *Edward Mendelson, PC Magazine Online, 1999*

External Style Sheets

An external style sheet is a file that can be linked to by multiple pages. The file name of an external style sheet uses the .CSS extension. Using an external style sheet is the easiest way to create a consistent look among all the pages of your site.

Creating an External Style Sheet

FrontPage provides several preformatted external style sheets, as seen in Figure 11-1. This dialog box is opened by selecting **File ▶ New ▶ Page ▶ Style Sheets** tab.

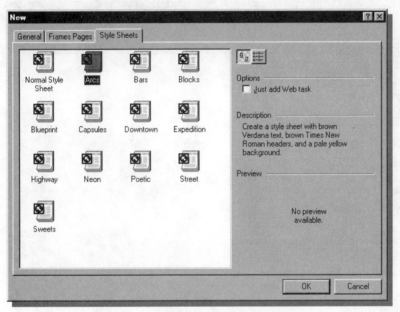

Figure 11-1: Preformatted style sheets

You can use these templates as they are, modify them, or create your own external style sheet from a blank template.

Exercise 11-1: Creating an External Style Sheet from a Preformatted Template

1. From **Page View**, select **File** ▶ **New** ▶ **Page**.

2. Click the **Style Sheets** tab.

3. Select **Neon**.

4. Click **OK**.

5. Save the file (shown in Figure 11-2) as NEON.CSS.

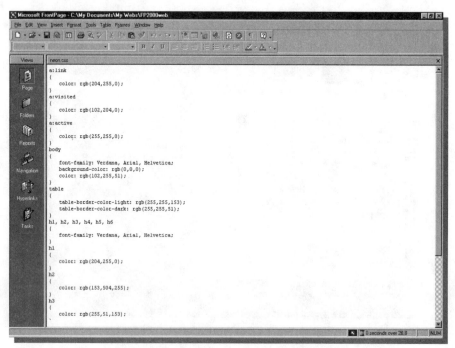

Figure 11-2: Page View of NEON.CSS

DDC Publishing • www.ddcpub.com

Linking and Unlinking Pages to an External Style Sheet

To apply an external style sheet to any or all of the pages of your Web site, you create a link to that style sheet file within the <HEAD> tags.

Exercise 11-2: Linking All Pages to an External Style Sheet

1. Open INDEX.HTM.
2. Select **Format ▶ Style Sheet Links**.
3. Select **All pages**.
4. Click **Add**.
5. Select NEON.CSS.
6. Click **OK**.
7. Click **OK** again.
8. Save the file. Preview this page in your browser. Note the changes in the page's appearance.

Exercise 11-3: Unlinking Pages from an External Style Sheet

1. Open INDEX.HTM.
2. Select **Format ▶ Style Sheet Links**.
3. Select **All pages**.
4. Select NEON.CSS.
5. Click **Remove**.
6. Click **OK**.
7. Save the file and preview in your browser.

Embedded Style Sheets

An embedded style sheet is one that is completely contained within the <HEAD> tags of a Web page. Its styles will only apply to that page.

Exercise 11-4: Creating an Embedded Style Sheet

1. Open INDEX.HTM.

2. Select **Format** ▶ **Style**.

3. Select **H2** from the **Styles** list and click **Modify**.

4. Click **Format**, then select **Font**.

5. For **Font**, select **Arial**.

6. For **Font style**, select **Bold**.

7. For **Size**, select **24pt**.

8. For **Color**, select **red**.

9. Click **OK**.

10. Click **Format** and select **Paragraph**.

11. For **Alignment**, select **Left**.

12. Click **OK** (three times).

13. Save the file.

If you examine the contents of the **HTML** tab, you will see:

```
<style>
<!--
h2   { font-family: Arial; font-size: 24pt;
color: #FF0000; font-weight: bold; text-align:
Left;}
-->
</style>
```

Inline Styles

An inline style is applied only to one particular element on the page. For example, you can apply an inline style to a table.

Exercise 11-5: Applying an Inline Style to a Table

1. Open CARS.HTM.
2. Right-click the table and select **Table Properties**.
3. Click **Style**.
4. Click **Format** and select **Font**.
5. For **Font**, select **Arial**.
6. For **Size**, select **14pt**.
7. Click **OK**.
8. Click **OK** again.
9. Click **Apply**, then click **OK**.
10. Save the file and preview it in your browser.

 The table's inline style is defined within the <TABLE> tag:

```
<table border="1" width="100%"
style="font-family: Arial; font-size:
14pt">
```

Style Sheets & Browser Compatibility

Just as there are several versions of HTML, there are also several versions of CSS.

- CSS 1.0 provided for basic formatting elements.

- CSS 2.0 has added positioning functionality.

As shown in Table 11-1, older browsers do not support all versions of CSS.

Browser	CSS 1.0	CSS 2.0
Internet Explorer 5.x	✓	✓
Internet Explorer 4.x	✓	✓
Internet Explorer 3.x	✓	⊘
Netscape Navigator 4.x	✓	✓
Netscape Navigator 3.x	⊘	⊘

Table 11-1: CSS Web browser compatibility

Remember your audience when considering the use of style sheets. Standards and browser compatibility are addressed in greater detail in *Part 3*.

Lesson Summary

▶ A style sheet is a configuration file that specifies the details of a Web page's appearance.

▶ Style sheets allow you to control font, color, positioning, and other aspects of a Web page.

▶ There are three types of style sheets: external, embedded, and inline.

▶ An external style sheet is a file (with a CSS extension) that is linked to and from the page.

▶ FrontPage provides several preformatted external style sheets. You can also create your own.

▶ When a Web page has style sheet language contained within its headers, it is called an embedded style sheet. This style affects only that page.

▶ Inline styles are specifications that affect only specific elements of a page.

▶ Not all browsers support the latest version CSS. You must consider the needs of your users when choosing to implement style sheets.

Lesson Review

Matching

___ 1. Style defined for one particular element within a page

___ 2. Style sheets that are linked to by one or many pages

___ 3. Styles defined within the header of a page

___ 4. Provides positioning functions

___ 5. Part of a CSS rule

a. External style sheets

b. Embedded style sheets

c. Inline styles

d. Declaration

e. Cascading Style Sheets 2.0

Fill in the Blank

6. FrontPage 2000 supports versions 1.0 and 2.0 of _____ _____ _____.

7. There are three types of style sheets: _____, _____, and _____.

8. _____ style sheets are applied by creating links from your pages.

9. An _____ style sheet is contained within the <HEAD> tags of a web page.

True or False?

T / F   10. Style sheet files end with the `.SSF` extension.

T / F   11. There are several style sheet languages.

T / F   12. External style sheets are written in HTML.

T / F   13. Embedded style sheets can define the font for multiple pages.

T / F   14. The declaration part of a CSS rule declares the element to be affected

Lesson 12
Web Page
Interactivity

Lesson Topics

► Collecting User Feedback & Data

► Creating a Guest Book

► Form Elements

► Form Handlers & Properties

► Making Your Site Searchable

► Lesson Summary

Collecting User Feedback & Data

Most data collection on the Web is accomplished through the use of *forms*. Users can input information into form fields, which can then:

- be sent to any receiving address via e-mail

- be sent to and stored in a database

- execute a query on a database or index and return information to the user (based on the information they uploaded)

Form Page Templates

FrontPage 2000 makes it easy to create a form for collecting user input. FrontPage 2000 comes with four standard form page templates:

- Feedback Form

- Guest Book

- Search Form

- User Registration

There is also a Form Page Wizard, which you can use to help develop custom forms.

Form Elements

Forms use the following elements for data input:

- One-Line Text Box

- Scrolling Text Box

- Check Box

- Radio Button

- Drop Down Menu

- Push Button

In this lesson, you will create a Guest Book and a Search Form using FrontPage templates. You will also create a custom form for collecting user feedback.

Creating a Guest Book

A *guest book* can be used to collect and display user feedback on your site. Visitors can submit their comments, which are then written to a separate page (a log). Users can view that page to see what other users had to say about your site. You can customize both the page on which users submit their comments and the page that displays all of the comments.

Exercise 12-1: Creating a Guest Book

1. In **Page View**, **Normal** tab, select **File ▶ New ▶ Page**.

2. Choose **Guest Book** from the list of General Templates.

3. Click **OK**.

 Your result should look like Figure 12-1. Note that there is only one field in which users can enter information. In the next part of the exercise, you will add an additional field.

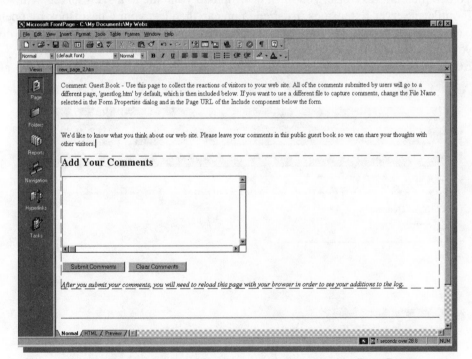

Figure 12-1: Basic Guest Book entry page created in FrontPage

4. Insert your cursor after **Add Your Comments** and press <ENTER>.

5. Type **Name:**

6. Select **Insert ▶ Form ▶ One-Line Text Box**.

7. Delete the **Author Information** section near the bottom of the page.

8. Select **File ▶ Properties** and set the page title to **Guestbook**.

9. Save the file as GUESTBOOK.HTM.

 By default, FrontPage names the page on which the guest book entries are displayed GUESTLOG.HTM and displays this page below the submission form (similar to a shared border).

 If you do not have access to a server with FrontPage Server Extensions enabled, you will not be able to complete the remainder of this exercise.

10. To complete this exercise, you must now upload your site to a Web server with FrontPage Server Extensions installed. You can then test your Guest Book by opening the page *from your published Web site*, as shown in Figure 12-2. (Hint: open your web in your browser and select **Guestbook** from the TOC or specify **http://yourwebsite/guestbook.htm** as the URL in your Web browser).

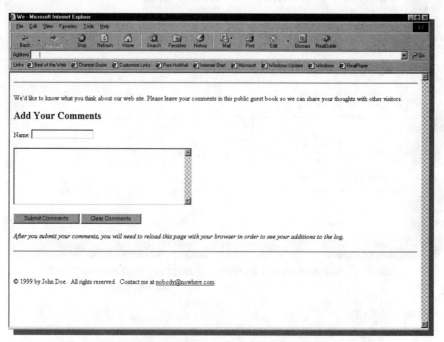

Figure 12-2: Published Guest Book previewed in browser

11. With your published Guest Book open in your browser, type your name and the comments of your choice where indicated, as shown in Figure 12-3.

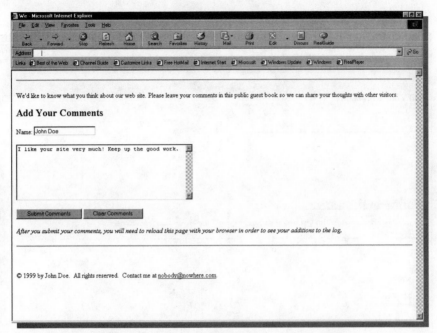

Figure 12-3: Entering comments in the Guest Book

12. Click **Submit Comments**. A confirmation screen will appear, as shown in Figure 12-4.

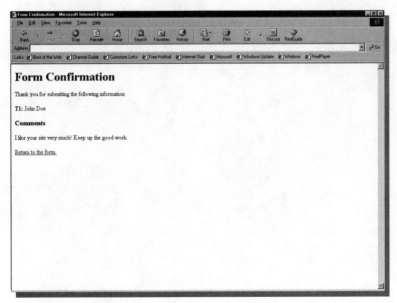

Figure 12-4: Confirmation of Guest Book submission page

13. Clicking **Return to the form** on the confirmation screen takes you back to the Guest Book page. Refresh the page to view the comments that you added, as shown in Figure 12-5.

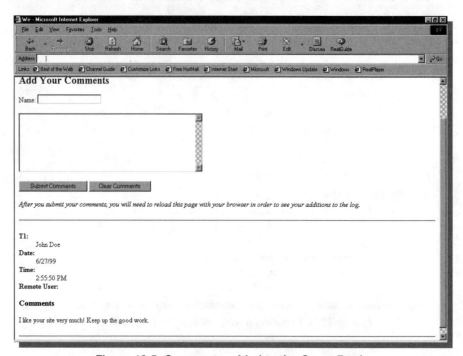

Figure 12-5: Comments added to the Guest Book

 In the next part of this lesson, you will learn how to create custom forms. You can apply any of these customizations to the Guest Book as well.

Form Elements

Form elements are fields used to gather information from users visiting your site.

There are six basic form elements, as shown below.

- One-Line Text Box

- Scrolling Text Box

- Check Box

- Radio Button

- Pull-Down Menu

- Push Button

One-Line Text Boxes

The most common form element, the One-Line Text Box, collects user input data, such as name, addresses, etc. To insert a One-Line Text Box within a form, choose **Insert ▶ Form ▶ One-Line Text Box**. To edit a form field, right-click the box and choose **Form Field Properties**.

FrontPage enables you to control many attributes of a One-Line Text Box using the Text Box Properties dialog box, as shown in Figure 12-6.

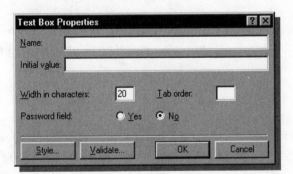

Figure 12-6: Text Box Properties dialog box

Name

The name attribute specifies the name of a field. You should give your fields unique, descriptive names to make identifying results from a particular form field easier. Form handlers interpret the form based on the **Name** of each form field.

In Exercise 12-1, you may have noticed that the **Name** field was labeled **T1**, which is the default label for the first one-line text box field in a form. The second would be **T2**, and so on, unless you specify a different property for **Name** in the **Text Box Properties** dialog box.

When choosing labels for your fields, be sure to use only ASCII characters in the names. Spaces are not permitted. Some form handling scripts cannot process spaces and other non-ASCII characters. FrontPage will generate an error as shown in Figure 12-7 if you try to use an illegal character.

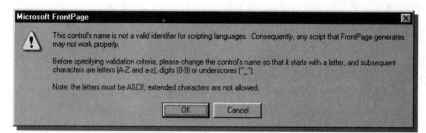

Figure 12-7: Error message generated if an illegal character is used

FrontPage 2000 does not require that each field in a form have a unique name. However, it is recommended that you make each field name unique because some form handlers may require that each field have a distinct name.

Initial value

The **Initial value** of a form field is what appears in that field by default when the form is first displayed in the browser or if its values are reset. Users then have the option of keeping the **Initial value** or replacing it with their own preference. In most cases, this field is left blank.

Width in characters

This attribute specifies the horizontal length of the field. This value can be set to a particular number, or it can be adjusted by clicking and dragging with the mouse to resize the field.

Tab order

Normally, when a user moves through a form using the <TAB> key, the order in which the fields are navigated is the order in which they appear on the screen, from top to bottom. However, if you wish to change the tab order, you can do so.

Specifying the **Tab order** works only for visitors using Microsoft's Internet Explorer to browse your site. Netscape does not recognize this attribute of the form field element.

Password field

You can specify any One-Line Text Box field as a **Password field**. With **Password fields**, text entered by the user will appear on the screen as asterisks (*). You should use **Password fields** for any type of information that would be submitted by a user that requires security, such as Social Security or credit card numbers. IN the instance where a person is looking over the shoulder of the user typing confidential information into a password field, the "spy" will see nothing only asterisks.

Making a field a **Password field** does *not* encrypt the data typed into that field. It only appears as asterisks on the screen of the user entering data in that field. Do not use this option for submission of secure data via e-mail. If the data is obtained by an unauthorized third party, it offers no security and can be read.

Validation

You can limit the range of acceptable input in a text box, as shown in Figure 12-8.

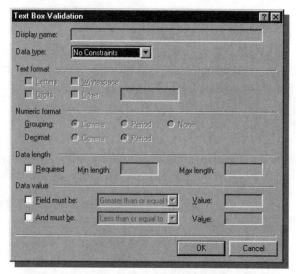

Figure 12-8: Text Box Validation dialog box

By default, no constraints are put on the type of data a user may input in a given One-Line Text Box. You can choose to limit your users to **Text**, **Integer**, or **Number**.

- <u>Text</u>: choosing this option allows you to specify what types of characters your users may enter. This activates the check boxes under **Text format**, through which you can allow **Letters**, **Digits**, **White space**, or **Other**. The **Other** characters would be non-alphanumeric symbols, such as @, #, $, etc.

- <u>Integer</u>: choosing this option limits users to entering whole numbers in a given field. This activates the radio buttons under **Grouping**, through which you can specify whether to group numbers according to American (1,234,567) or European (1.234.567) standards, or not to group them at all (1234567).

- <u>Number</u>: choosing this option allows users to enter non-integer numbers, including decimals. Both the **Grouping** and **Decimal** radio buttons are activated. You can again choose to group numbers according to American (1,234.56) or European (1.234,56) standards. Whereas with **Integers** there is an option for **No Grouping**, there is no option with the **Number** data type to disallow decimals.

If you choose to constrain your users to text, integers, or numbers, you must specify the kind of text that can be entered. If you do not specify this, FrontPage will automatically change back to **No Constraints**.

Data Length & Required Fields

The **Validation** dialog box also allows you to set a minimum and maximum length for the user's entry, whether or not you choose to specify a Data Type. Users will, therefore, not be permitted to enter too few or too many characters. You can also designate a particular field as a **Required** field. Users must make an entry in a required field or they will not be able to submit the form.

 It is always a good idea to alert your users to any constraints you have placed on your fields. You should always indicate required fields as such. Users will get very frustrated (and may not come back to your site again) if your form instructions are unclear.

Data Value

You can specify a range of values for your data. The choices are:

- greater than

- less than

- greater than or equal to

- less than or equal to

- equal to

- not equal to

With numbers and integers, values are compared arithmetically. Text data is compared alphabetically.

Display Name

This is the name of the field as shown to the user in error messages. Unlike the actual **Name** attribute of the form field, it is not limited to alphanumeric characters.

 If you have a form field for users to enter their ZIP code, and in your form that field has the name **ZCode**, you can designate a display name of **ZIP Code**. If users made an invalid entry (six digits, for example), the error would tell them to correct the field **ZIP Code** rather than **ZCode**. In Exercise 12-2 and Exercise 12-3, you will create several such fields.

Exercise 12-2: Creating a Custom Form with One-Line Text Boxes

1. Open the file ABOUTME.HTM.

2. Insert a horizontal line below the text **This page is under construction**.

3. Select **Insert ▶ Form ▶ Form**.

4. At the top of the form, center the title `Tell Me About You` in Heading 2.

5. Insert the text `Name:` and a One-Line Text Box on the next line by selecting **Insert ▶ Form ▶ One-Line Text Box**.

6. On the next line, insert the text `Address:` and a One-Line Text Box.

7. On the next line, insert the text `City:`, `State:`, and `ZIP:`. Insert One-Line Text Boxes after each name.

8. On each of the next two lines, add One-Line Text Boxes labeled `E-mail Address:` and `Age:`.

9. Save the file.

Exercise 12-3: Editing One-Line Text Box Properties

To edit the properties of a One-Line Text Box, right click the One-Line Text Box and choose **Form Field Properties**. Click **OK** to close dialog boxes when finished editing.

1. For **Name:**
   - Change the attribute **Name** to `Name`.
   - Under **Validate**, set the required **Data type** to `Text`. Allow **Letters, White Space**, and **Other**. Next to **Other**, specify the hyphen (-).
   - Make this a **Required** field. Leave the **Min length** or **Max length** fields blank.

2. For **Address:**
   - Change the attribute **Name** to `Address`.
   - Change the attribute **Width in characters** to `40`.

3. For **City:**
   - Change the attribute **Name** to `City`.

4. For **State:**
   - Change the attribute **Name** to `State`.
   - Change the attribute **Width in characters** to `2`.
   - Under **Validate**, set the required **Data type** to `Text`. Allow **Letters** only.

5. For **ZIP**:

   ▪ Change the attribute **Name** to **ZIP**.

   ▪ Change the attribute **Width in characters** to **10**.

   ▪ Under **Validate**, set the required **Data type** to **Text**. Allow **Digits** and **Other**. Next to **Other**, specify the hyphen (-).

   ▪ Make this field **Required** with a **Min length** of **5**. Leave **Max length** blank.

6. For **E-mail Address:**

   ▪ Change the attribute **Name** to **Email**.

7. For **Age:**

   ▪ Change the attribute **Name** to **Age**.

   ▪ Change the attribute **Width in characters** to **2**.

   ▪ Under **Validate**, set the required **Data type** to **Integer**. Set the acceptable range of data values **Greater than or equal to 1** and **Less than or equal to 99.**

8. Save the file and preview in your browser. An alert box appears that warns you that the page contains elements that may need to be saved or published to preview correctly.

9. Click **OK**. You can preview the file in your browser, but attempts to test the unpublished form will result in a FrontPage run-time component error. The published form will function properly when accessed from a Web server with FrontPage Server Extensions installed.

 The completed form layout is shown in Figure 12-9.

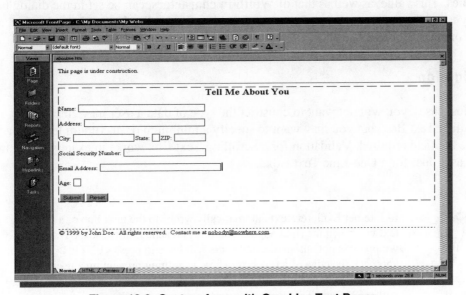

Figure 12-9: Custom form with One-Line Text Boxes

Scrolling Text Boxes

Scrolling Text Boxes are similar to One-Line Text Boxes, except that multiple lines of data may be entered. You can resize the text area both vertically and horizontally by performing a drag and drop with your mouse.

To insert a Scrolling Text Box within your form, choose **Insert ▶ Form ▶ Scrolling Text Box**. To edit the Scrolling Text Box, right-click it and choose **Form Field Properties**. FrontPage enables you to specify the attributes of a Scrolling Text Box using the Scrolling Text Box Properties dialog box, as shown in Figure 12-10.

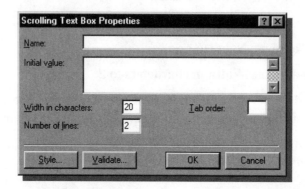

Figure 12-10: Scrolling Text Box Properties dialog box

Scrolling Text Box Properties

Most attributes of the Scrolling Text Box are analogous to those of the One-Line Text Box, with a few notable exceptions. You cannot, for example, make a Scrolling Text Box into a **Password Field**. You can also, with the Scrolling Text Box, specify the **Number of lines**. This value, as well as that of **Width in characters**, can be set in the dialog box or by using the mouse to resize the box to the desired size. The **Name**, **Initial value**, and **Tab order** attributes are functionally identical to those of a One-Line Text Box.

Validation

In most cases, you will not want to constrict the type of data a user may enter in a Scrolling Text Box, but you may want to specify a minimum or maximum length, or make the field required. Validation for a Scrolling Text Box works in exactly the same way as it does for a One-Line Text Box.

In Internet Explorer, text automatically wraps to the next line of a scrolling text box when the right edge of the box is reached. In Netscape Navigator, wrapping is not automatic, and users will have to press <ENTER> when they approach the edge of a text box. There is nothing preventing a user from entering text beyond the edge of the box, as scroll bars automatically appear with a Scrolling Text Box.

Exercise 12-4: Adding a Scrolling Text Box to Your Form

1. Open `ABOUTME.HTM` (the form you created in Exercise 12-2).

2. Beneath the last of your One-Line Text Boxes, type the text **Additional Comments:** and insert a Scrolling Text Box.

3. By clicking and dragging with your mouse, resize the width of the box so that it is approximately even on the right-hand side with the other boxes.

4. Right-click the Scrolling Text Box and choose **Form Field Properties**.

5. Change the **Name** attribute to **Comments** and the **Number of lines** to **5**.

6. Click **OK** to close the **Scrolling Text Box Properties** dialog box.

7. Save the file.

 The updated form layout is shown in Figure 12-11.

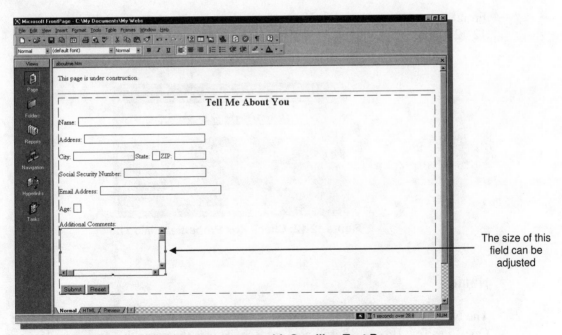

The size of this field can be adjusted

Figure 12-11: Updated form layout with Scrolling Text Box

Check Boxes

Check boxes are most effective for input in which there are only two logical choices, such as:

- Yes/No

- True/False

Check boxes are a *Boolean* data type form field.

The term *Boolean*, often encountered when doing searches on the Web, refers to a system of logical thought developed by the English mathematician and computer pioneer, George Boole (1815-64). Boolean logic is used most frequently to indicate True or False, Yes or No, and On or Off.

To insert a Check Box within your form, choose **Insert ▶ Form ▶ Check Box**. Right-click the box and choose **Form Field Properties** to edit.

FrontPage enables you to specify the attributes of a Check Box, as shown in Figure 12-12.

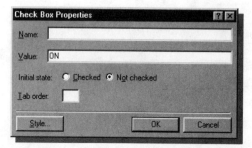

Figure 12-12: Check Box Properties dialog box

Name

The **Name** attribute of a Check Box is identical in function to the **Name** attribute of a One-Line Text Box or a Scrolling Text Box. This is the name that form handlers give to the field when interpreting the form. As with all fields, each Check Box should have a unique name.

Value

This is the value that is submitted to the form handler when the box is checked. By default, when a Check Box is selected, the **Value** that is passed is **ON**. You can specify any value for this field. This attribute is also required.

Even if you have multiple Check Boxes in a form, each Check Box functions independently of the others. While each field in a form should have a unique **Name** attribute, you may want to give all of the Check Boxes in a related series the same **Name**, and specify a different **Value** for each. If you do so, make sure your form handler can process multiple fields with the same **Name**.

Initial state

This determines whether a given Check Box is checked or unchecked by default. By default, FrontPage sets all Check Boxes to an **Initial value** of unchecked.

Tab order

The **Tab order** attribute functions in the same way for Check Box fields as for the One-Line Text Box and Scrolling Text Box fields.

Validation

There is no validation option for a Check Box field. You cannot specify a Data type, as the only choices are checked and unchecked. Likewise, you cannot make a Check Box field required, as that disallows the option of leaving the box unchecked.

"FrontPage 2000 makes collecting and viewing data via your Web site easy and straightforward."

— *Lance Ulanoff, Windows Magazine, 1999*

Exercise 12-5: Adding a Check Box to Your Form

1. Open `ABOUTME.HTM` (the form you created in Exercise 12-2).

2. Beneath the last of your One-Line Text Boxes, insert the text **Check here if you collect stamps:** and add a Check Box.

3. Right-click the Check Box and select **Form Field Properties**.

4. Change the **Name** attribute to **Stamp** and the **Value** to **Yes**.

5. Click **OK** to close the **Check Box Properties** dialog box.

6. Save the file.

 The updated form layout is shown in Figure 12-13.

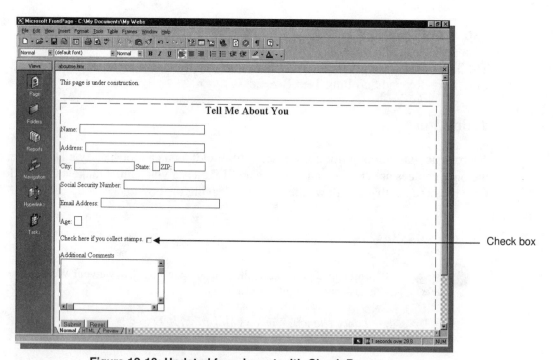

Figure 12-13: Updated form layout with Check Box

Radio Buttons

Like Check Boxes, Radio Buttons allow users to make a selection by pointing and clicking with the mouse, as opposed to One-Line Text Boxes and Scrolling Text Boxes, which accept input from the keyboard. Unlike a Check Box, however, a Radio Button can include two or more choices, and can be grouped.

When grouped, only one Radio Button in the given group may be selected. If you want to give users the option of selecting more than one choice, you should use Check Boxes.

Although it is possible to have a single Radio Button in a form, normally, if there is only one choice, you would use a Check Box. If you have multiple choices, and want users to select only one, you would use Radio Buttons.

To insert a set of Radio Buttons within your form, choose **Insert ▶ Form ▶ Radio Button**. Right-click the box and choose **Form Field Properties** to edit.

FrontPage enables you to specify the attributes of a Radio Button, as shown in Figure 12-14.

Figure 12-14: Radio Button Properties dialog box

Group name

The first thing you will notice about the **Radio Button Properties** dialog box that differs from those for the One-Line Text Box, the Scrolling Text Box, and the Check Box is that instead of a **Name** attribute, the Radio Button has a **Group name**. It functions analogously to the **Name** attribute in these other form elements. To associate Radio Buttons with one another (and thereby make the selection thereof mutually exclusive), give them the same **Group name**. This attribute is required.

Value

This is the value that is submitted to the form handler when the Radio Button is selected. You can specify any value for this field. This attribute is also required.

Initial state

This determines whether a given Radio Button is selected or unselected by default. Remember, only one Radio Button in a given group can be selected. Setting an **Initial state** for any one Radio Button in a group will automatically make all of the others unselected by default.

Tab order

The **Tab order** attribute functions in the same way for Radio Button fields as for the other form elements you have seen.

Validation

As shown in Figure 12-15, you can require that users select one of the Radio Buttons in a given group. You need set this for only one of the Radio Buttons in a given group to make the selection of any one of them required.

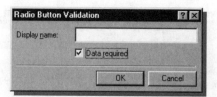

Figure 12-15: Radio Button Validation dialog box

For example, if you want users to indicate their gender on your form, you would group two Radio Buttons together, thus eliminating the possibility of a user accidentally (or otherwise) indicating that they are both male and female.

If, on the other hand, you wanted users to indicate all of the choices in a given set that apply to them, such as ethnic background, you would use Check Boxes.

Exercise 12-6: Adding Radio Buttons to Your Form

In this exercise, you will add Radio Buttons to your form and group the buttons.

1. Open ABOUTME.HTM (the form you created in Exercise 12-2).

2. On the same line as **Age**, insert the text **Gender:** and two Radio Buttons. To the right of the first, add the text **Male**; to the right of the second, add the text **Female**.

3. Right-click the first Radio Button and select **Form Field Properties**.

4. Change the attribute **Group name** to **Gender** and the **Value** to **Male**. Make the field **Not selected** by default.

5. Click **OK** to close the **Radio Button Properties** dialog box.

6. Right-click the second Radio Button and select **Form Field Properties**. Change the attribute **Group name** to **Gender** and the **Value** to **Female**. Make the field **Not selected** by default.

7. Click **OK** to close the **Radio Button Properties** dialog box.

8. Save the file.

 The updated form layout is shown in Figure 12-16.

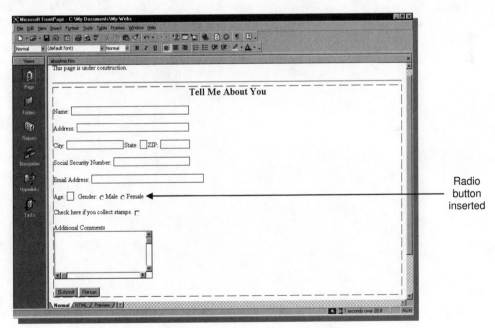

Figure 12-16: Updated form layout with radio buttons

Drop-Down Menus

Drop-Down Menus allow users to select one or more choices from among a number of options, similar to Check Boxes or Radio Buttons. You can define whether to allow users to select multiple items from the list, or to limit their selection to one. You can also define how much of given Drop-Down Menu is visible to a user at any time.

To insert a Drop-Down Menu within your form, choose **Insert ▶ Form ▶ Drop-Down Menu**. Right-click the box and choose **Form Field Properties** to edit. FrontPage enables you to specify the attributes of a Drop-Down Menu, as shown in Figure 12-17.

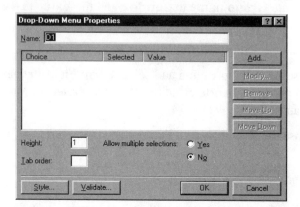

Figure 12-17: Drop-Down Menu Properties dialog box

Name

This attribute functions in the same way for a Drop-Down Menu as it does for the other form field elements you have seen.

Choice

Each of the items that will appear in the Drop-Down Menu is a **Choice**. To add choices, click the **Add** button. This opens the **Add Choice** dialog box, shown in Figure 12-18 on the following page.

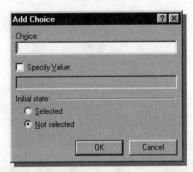

Figure 12-18: Add Choice dialog box

Each Drop-Down Menu must have at least one **Choice**. For each, you must specify the **Choice** itself, which will appear in the Drop-Down Menu. If you want the value passed to your form handler to be different from that which appears in the Drop-Down Menu itself, check **Specify value** and indicate the value that should be passed to the form handler. You can also define the **Initial state** for a **Choice**, determining whether the **Choice** is, by default, selected.

You can also **Modify** or **Delete** items from the list of choices using the respective buttons on the **Drop-Down Menu Properties** dialog box. You can also change the order of the choices by using the **Move Up** and **Move Down** buttons. To do so, highlight the list item you want to move, and click the appropriate button for up or down.

Height

This attribute defines the size of the Drop-Down Menu as it appears on the form. By default, FrontPage sets the **Height** attribute at 1, meaning that only one choice appears in the form unless a user selects the menu, causing it to "drop down", as shown in Figure 12-19. If you use a number greater than one for the **Height** attribute, the Drop-Down Menu becomes a stationary list with a vertical scroll bar, as shown in Figure 12-20. If there are fewer items in the list than the value of the **Height** attribute, then no scroll bar will appear.

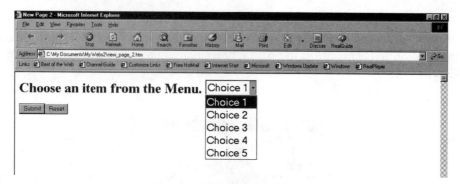

Figure 12-19: Drop-Down Menu with a height of 1

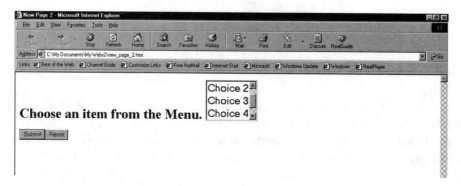

Figure 12-20: Drop-Down Menu with a height of 3

 You cannot specify the width of a Drop-Down Menu field. The width of the field is determined by the length of the longest text string among the items in the menu.

Allow Multiple Selections

This attribute allows users to make more than one selection from the items on the Drop-Down Menu.

Tab order

The **Tab order** attribute functions in the same way for Drop Down Menu as for the other form elements you have seen.

Validation

The validation of data in a Drop-Down Menu is in part dependent on whether or not you have chosen to allow multiple selections. If more than one selection is allowed, you can define a **Maximum** and **Minimum** number of items to be selected, as shown in Figure 12-21.

You can also specify a given Drop-Down Menu field as required. You can also make a Drop-Down Menu field that allows only one selection required, as shown in Figure 12-22.

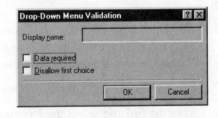

Figure 12-21: Drop-Down Menu Validation dialog box (multiple selections allowed)

Figure 12-22: Drop Down Menu Validation dialog box (multiple selections not allowed)

You may have noticed an option in both dialog boxes for **Disallow first choice**. In instances where you want the first choice to read "Select an item from the list below," you can use the **Disallow first choice** option to prevent users from selecting that instructional message as their choice.

Exercise 12-7: Adding Drop-Down Menus to Your Form

In this exercise you will add a Drop-Down Menu to your form.

1. Open ABOUTME.HTM (the form you created in Exercise 12-2).

2. Below the **Age** and **Gender** line, insert the text **Annual Household Income:** and a Drop-Down Menu.

3. Right-click the Drop-Down Menu and select **Form Field Properties**.

4. Change the **Name** attribute to **Income**.

5. Click **Add** to add the following items to the list:

   - less than 20,000

   - 20,000-29,999

   - 30,000-39,999

   - 40,000-49,999

   - more than 50,000

6. Add an additional choice of **Choose a range from the options below**. Select this choice and move it to the top of the list by selecting the item in the list and clicking **Move Up** until it is in the proper position.

7. Click **Validate** and select **Disallow first choice**. Click **OK** (twice).

8. Save the file and select the **Preview** tab.

When extended, the Drop-Down Menu appears similar to Figure 12-23.

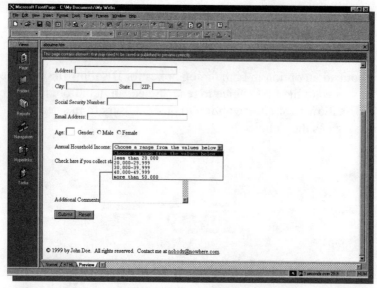

Figure 12-23: Drop-down menu as displayed on the Preview tab

9. Return to **Normal** tab.

10. Below "Annual Household Income," insert the text **Where would you like to travel? (Choose up to three)** and another Drop-Down Menu.

11. Right-click the Drop-Down Menu and select **Form Field Properties**.

12. Change the **Name** attribute for **Travel**. Change the **Height** to **3** and choose **Allow multiple selections**.

13. Add the following travel destinations to the list:

   - Dallas, Texas

   - Kansas City, Missouri

   - Maple Ridge, British Columbia

   - Sandusky, Ohio

   - Purcellville, Virginia

   - Banff, Alberta

14. Click **Validate**. Make the maximum number of allowable items equal to **3** and click **OK**.

15. Click **OK** to close the **Drop-Down Menu Properties** dialog box.

16. Save the file and select the **Preview** tab.

 Your updated form should appear, as shown in Figure 12-24.

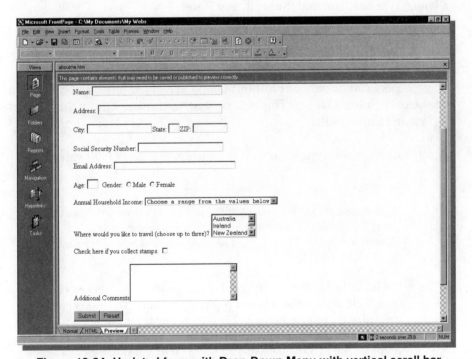

Figure 12-24: Updated form with Drop-Down Menu with vertical scroll bar

Push Buttons

Whereas the other form field elements accept user input, Push Buttons are strictly operational. They are used for form submission and resetting and are automatically added when you create a form.

To insert a Push Button within your form, choose **Insert ▶ Form ▶ Push Button**. Right-click the box and choose **Form Field Properties** to edit. FrontPage enables you to specify all attributes of a Push Button, as shown in Figure 12-25.

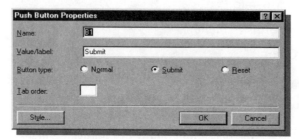

Figure 12-25: Push Button Properties dialog box

The **Name** and **Tab order** attributes function for Push Buttons function similarly to other form elements. The **Value/label** is the text that is displayed on the Push Button.

Button Types

The three button types are **Normal**, **Submit**, and **Reset**.

- Normal: buttons of this type have no built-in function and must be associated with a script in order to provide functionality.

- Submit: there can be only one **Submit** button in a given form, and every form must have a **Submit** button. This button passes information from the completed form to the form handler.

- Reset: buttons of this type restore all form fields to their default values.

You should always put some kind of label next to every field so that users know what to enter in the field. Though there is no such association possible in HTML, FrontPage enables you to associate a label with a form field.

To do so, highlight both the text that you want as your label and the form field itself. Choose **Insert ▶ Form ▶ Label**. The text is now related to the form field itself. The only advantage to doing so is that, for Check Box and Radio Button fields, users of Internet Explorer 4.0 or 5.0 can make their selection by clicking the label rather than the box itself.

Form Handlers & Properties

Once you have created your form, you will need somewhere for user-entered data to go. This is accomplished through form handlers. There are four basic choices for handling of a submitted form:

- send completed form via e-mail to a specified recipient

- save completed form to a file

- add completed form to a database

- parse results through a script

Setting Form Properties

Form Properties are set using the **Form Properties** dialog box, shown in Figure 12-26. To access the **Form Properties** dialog box, right-click anywhere within the borders of the form and select **Form Properties**.

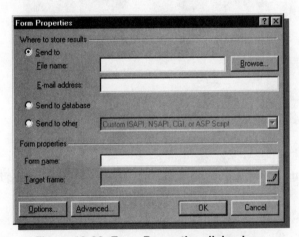

Figure 12-26: Form Properties dialog box

- To save the form data to a file, choose **Send to File name** and specify the name of the file to which the form results will be written.

- To send the form data via e-mail, choose **Send to E-mail address** and specify the address to which the form results should be sent.

- It is possible to save the completed form to a file *and* send it via e-mail.

Form Properties Options

You will notice a button on the **Form Properties** dialog box in Figure 12-26 that reads **Options**. Clicking this button enables you to set additional form properties.

File Results

As shown in Figure 12-27, the **File Results** tab allows you to specify both the name and format of the file to which the form results are written. You can also specify whether or not to include the field names, and whether the latest results would go at the top or bottom of the file. You also have the option of specifying a second file to which results will be written, which can be of a different format than the first.

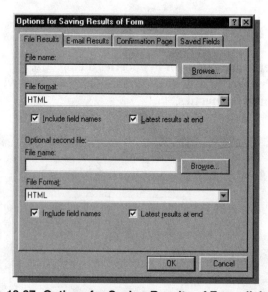

Figure 12-27: Options for Saving Results of Form dialog box

 When saving the results of a form to a file, the user submitting the form must have write permissions to the file to which the form data is being written. Permissions is covered in *Part 3*.

E-mail Results

The **E-mail Results** tab, shown in Figure 12-28, allows you to specify a receiving address and indicate the format in which form messages are sent. You can give the e-mail message a subject line and a reply-to field. One or both of these fields can be passed from the form by selecting the **Form field name** check box and specifying the name of the field to be used.

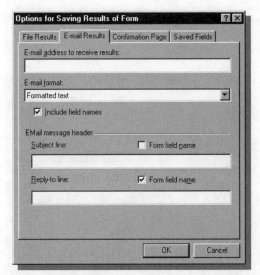

Figure 12-28: Sending form results via e-mail

Confirmation Page

As shown in Figure 12-29, you can set a confirmation page that will be sent to users when a form is successfully submitted. Alternatively, you can create a validation failure page to which users will be directed if they enter invalid data in one or more fields.

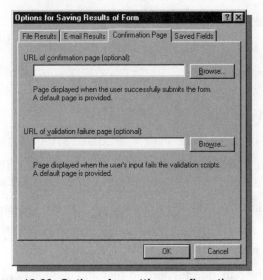

Figure 12-29: Options for setting confirmation pages

Saved Fields

Figure 12-30 shows the options for specifying which form fields to save. You can save all of the fields from the form or you can specify particular fields to be saved. You can also tag each submission with the date and time, as well as the name of the remote computer that completes the form, the type of browser used to do so, and the user's username (if available).

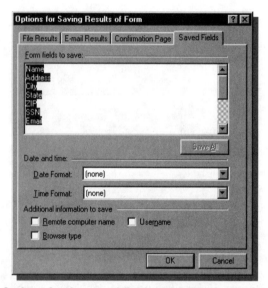

Figure 12-30: Options for the saved fields submitted with a completed form

Exercise 12-8: Setting Form Properties

In this exercise, you will set form properties so that the results from the completed form you have just created will be saved to a text file, saved as an HTML file, and emailed to you.

1. Open the ABOUTME.HTM form you created in Exercise 12-2.

2. Right-click within the form and choose **Form Properties**.

3. Send the form results to the file _PRIVATE/FORM_RESULTS.TXT and to your e-mail address.

4. Click **Options** and select the **File Results** tab.

5. Set the file format of _PRIVATE/FORM_RESULTS.TXT as **formatted text**.

6. Set a second file to which the results will be written. Call this file _PRIVATE/RESULTS.HTM. Set the format of this file as HTML.

7. Include the field names in both files. Choose not to have the latest results at the end of the second file.

8. Select the **E-Mail Results** tab.

9. Set the format of the e-mail to **formatted text** and include field names.

10. Define the **Subject** of the message as `Completed Form`.

11. Define the **Reply-to** line as the Form field **Email**.

12. Select the **Saved Fields** tab. Choose to add the date and time to the submitted form in the format of your choice.

13. Choose to save the browser type with the form results as well.

14. Click **OK**.

15. Click **OK** to close the **Form Properties** dialog box.

 You may get an error message at this point, indicating that this form is being created on a disk-based web or that you do not have FrontPage Server Extensions enabled, and asking if you want to remove the e-mail recipient. Do not agree to do so by clicking **NO**.

16. Delete **This page is under construction** from the top of the page and save the file.

 If you do not have access to a server with FrontPage Server Extensions enabled, you will not be able to complete the rest of this exercise.

17. At this point you will need to publish your site to a web server that supports FrontPage Server Extensions.

18. View the published form on your Web site in your browser. Complete the form (as shown in Figure 12-31) and submit it.

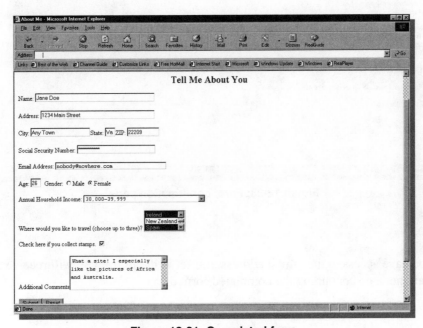

Figure 12-31: Completed form

Pop-up error messages, such as the one shown in Figure 12-32, will appear if invalid entries are made in any of the form fields.

Figure 12-32: Error message for invalid entry

19. If the form is accepted successfully, you will be taken to the confirmation page, as shown in Figure 12-33.

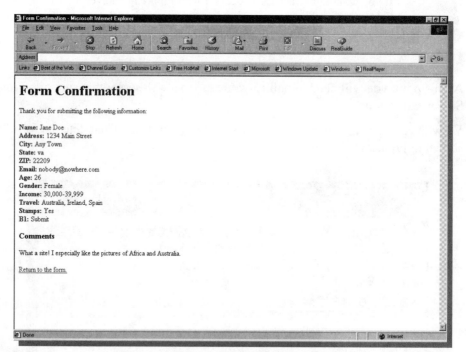

Figure 12-33: Form confirmation page

20. If you have access to the e-mail address you set in the Form, you will receive an e-mail message containing the completed form data.

Making Your Site Searchable

If you have a large Web site, you may want to provide your site visitors with a tool for searching your site. Keyword searches allow users to locate precise information on your site. Searching is also known a *querying*. A search is accomplished when a user submits a keyword (or several keywords) to a form on your site.

Enabling Keyword Searching

With FrontPage 2000, there are two ways to create a keyword search:

- Use the pre-formatted Search Form Page.

  Choose **File ▶ New ▶ Page** and select **Search Form** from the **General** tab as shown in Figure 12-34.

- Insert a Search Component on any page in your web.

  Choose **Insert ▶ Component ▶ Search Form** at the location on your page where you wish to add the form.

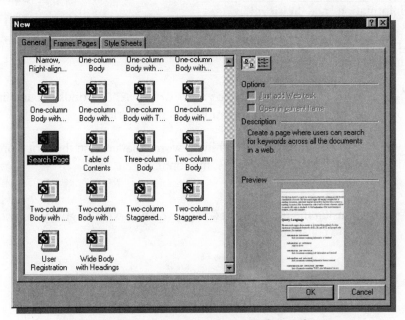

Figure 12-34: Using the pre-formatted search page

The pre-formatted page includes the Search Form Component, as well as an explanation of the query language to assist your users in defining their search criteria.

Query Language

The instructions included on the pre-formatted searching page provided to your users by FrontPage are listed below.

The text search engine allows queries to be formed using Boolean logic. Boolean logic involves operators, the most popular of which are AND, OR, and NOT.

Boolean operators can be grouped with parentheses to create more exact and powerful query terms. These are called *Boolean parenthetical phrases*.[6]

For example:

- `information retrieval`: finds documents containing "information" <u>or</u> "retrieval"

- `information or retrieval`: same as above

- `information and retrieval`: finds documents containing <u>both</u> "information" and "retrieval"

- `information not retrieval`: finds documents containing "information" but not "retrieval"

- `(information not retrieval) and WAIS`: finds documents containing "WAIS" and "information" but not "retrieval"

- `hydro*`: finds documents containing words that contain the root word hydro, such as hydrodynamic, hydrolysis, hydroponics, etc.

Even if you are not using the pre-formatted page, you will want to give your users some instructions on how to construct queries.

---

[6] For more information regarding Boolean logic, see DDC's *Conducting Internet Research* and *Advanced Internet Research*.

Search Form Properties

The Search Form component is included in the FrontPage pre-formatted Search Form page. It can also be added to any page of your site.

To modify Search Form properties, right click within the borders of the form and select **Search Form Properties**. The **Search Form Properties** dialog box will appear, as shown in Figure 12-35.

Figure 12-35: Search Form Properties dialog box

- Label for input: the label that appears to prompt users to enter a query.

- Width in characters: the familiar **Width in characters** attribute of the One-Line Text Box. This can be set here or by editing the **Form Field Properties** of the One-Line Text Box.

- Label for "Start Search" button: text that appears on the Push Button to execute the query. This can be set here or by editing the Push Button **Form Field Properties**.

- Label for "Clear" button: text that appears on the Push Button and resets the query form. This can be set here or by editing the Push Button **Form Field Properties**.

You can edit the properties of either the Push Buttons or the One-Line Text box in the same manner you would for any form field element. You should *not*, however, modify the **Name** attribute of any of these, because they are what the Search Form handler requires to execute the query.

Search Results

To modify **Search Form Properties**, select the **Search Results** tab of the **Search Form Properties** dialog box, as shown in Figure 12-36.

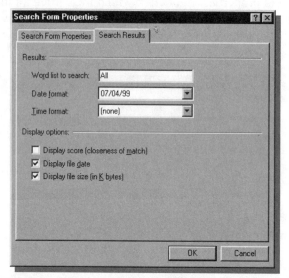

Figure 12-36: Search Form Properties Search Results tab

- <u>Word list to search</u>: defines the scope of your search. By default, the Search Form component searches **All**, meaning your entire site excluding files that are within the directories that begin with an underscore ("_"). If you have a large site with subwebs, you can narrow the scope of the search.

- <u>Date format</u>: defines the format of the date displayed with the query results (which is the date the file was last modified).

- <u>Time format</u>: defines the format of the time displayed with the query results (which is the time the file was last modified).

- <u>Display score (relevancy of search)</u>: if selected, displays a relevancy rating.

- <u>Display file date</u>: if selected, **Date** and **Time** are displayed with search results.

- <u>Display file size (in K bytes)</u>: if selected, displays the size of the file in kilobytes.

 The site index catalog should automatically be updated every time you make an addition to your site, but frequently this is not the case. To re-index the site, choose **Tools ▶ Recalculate Hyperlinks**.

Exercise 12-9: Creating a Search Form

In this exercise, you will create a search form for your Web site.

1. In **Page View**, **Normal** tab, select **File ▶ New ▶ Page**.

2. Select **Search Page** from the **General** tab. Click **OK**.

3. Right-click within the search form and choose **Search Form Properties**.

4. Change the **Width in characters** to **40**.

5. In the **Search Results** tab, change the **Date format** so that it displays the day of the week along with the date. Select **[none]** for **Time format**.

6. Select **Display score** and **Display file date**. Deselect **Display file size (in K bytes)**.

7. Click **OK**.

8. Change the title of the page to *Search Page* and save the file as SEARCH.HTM. Publish your web, selecting **Publish changed pages only**.

 If you do not have access to a server with FrontPage Server Extensions enabled, you will not be able to complete the rest of this exercise.

9. Open SEARCH.HTM from your Web site in your browser.

10. In the **Search for:** field, type **Australia**. Figure 12-37 displays the results.

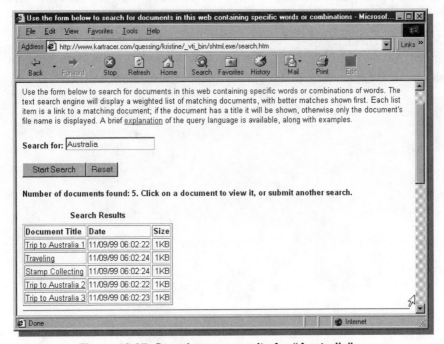

Figure 12-37: Search query results for "Australia"

Lesson Summary

▶ Forms make your Web site interactive.

▶ Form data can be processed in several ways. The results can be sent via e-mail or written to a text file or database.

▶ FrontPage has four standard form page templates: Feedback Form, Guest Book, Search Form, and User Registration.

▶ You can develop your own forms using the Form Page Wizard or by creating a custom form.

▶ There are six basic form elements: One-Line Text Box, Scrolling Text Box, Check Box, Radio Button, Drop-Down Menu, and Push Button.

▶ A One-Line Text Box is the most commonly-used form element. It is used to collect user input such as names, addresses, etc. One-Line Text Boxes can be set as password fields so that the information typed appears as asterisks (*).

▶ A Scrolling Text Box allows users to submit multiple lines of data, such as comments.

▶ Check Boxes are used to indicate whether something is true or false. Check Boxes cannot be grouped or validated.

▶ Radio Buttons are similar to Check Boxes, except that they can be grouped. When grouped, only one Radio Button in a given group can be chosen.

▶ Drop-Down Menus allow users to select one or more options from a list.

▶ Push Buttons are required to submit a form. They are automatically added when a form is created.

▶ For most form field elements, you can validate data entered or make the field required.

▶ You can create a Search form that will allow people to search your site.

Lesson Review

Matching

___ 1. Page of comments submitted by site visitors

___ 2. Allows users to submit multiple lines of text

___ 3. Required form element

___ 4. Tool for visitors to search your site

___ 5. Allows more than one choice

a. Push Button

b. Guest Book

c. Radio Button

d. Scrolling Text Box

e. Search Form

Fill in the Blank

6. There are two types of text box: _____ - _____ and _____ .

7. _____ _____ are automatically added when a form is created.

8. There are _____ standard form page templates available in FrontPage.

9. Search queries are formed using _____ expressions.

10. The _____ shows how closely a given document matches the search criteria.

True or False?

T / F 11. Drop-Down Menus should be used for True/False data.

T / F 12. Radio buttons can be grouped.

T / F 13. If you use a One-Line Text Box in a form, you cannot also use a Scrolling Text Box.

T / F 14. Using "All" in the Search Results Properties will allow searches of all the files and directories in your web.

T / F 15. Form results can be sent to a file or email address, but never both from the same form.

Lesson 13 Discussion Groups

Lesson Topics

▶ About Discussion Groups

▶ Creating a Discussion Group

▶ Modifying Discussion Group Properties

▶ Posting & Replying to Discussion Articles

▶ Managing the Discussion Group

▶ Lesson Summary

About Discussion Groups

The Web is a medium of communication. At the most basic level, a Web site presents information to the user. But the Web also provides the ability for users to interact with the site itself, with its creators, and with other users.

Discussion Groups

A discussion group provides a forum for users of your site to write about topics of interest to them. They can read articles that have been posted by other users, reply to these articles, and post new ones. You can design your discussion group to include the following:

- table of contents

- search form

- submission form

- confirmation form

- registration form

Degree of Interactivity

A discussion group is not the same as a chat room. Unlike chat rooms, users do not engage in real-time text-based communications. Instead, discussion groups are more analogous to message boards. If you are familiar with Usenet newsgroups, or have ever searched a newsgroup/mailing list database (such as Deja.com), you will recognize the similarity between these forums and your FrontPage discussion group.

You are the Moderator

However, unlike most Usenet newsgroups, your discussion group will be moderated. You, as the Web site creator/editor, maintain complete control. You can edit posts (for offensive language or other undesirable content) or completely remove posts. The discussion group belongs to your Web site and you determine how it is used.

 "[FrontPage 2000 has the] best Web site production wizards of any product in its class."

— *Lance Ulanoff, Windows Magazine, 1999*

Creating a Discussion Group

A discussion group can be created in two forms:

- as a sub-web of your main site

- as a separate FrontPage Web

You will use the Discussion Web Wizard to create the discussion group. You can also modify certain aspects of the discussion group once the Wizard is finished.

Discussion Web Wizard

To build your discussion group, you will create a new FrontPage Web, selecting **Discussion Web Wizard** as shown in Figure 13-1.

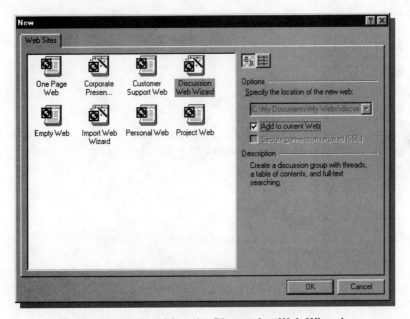

Figure 13-1: Launching the Discussion Web Wizard

You will be prompted to specify the location of the discussion Web, unless you choose to add it to your current Web.

 If you add the discussion Web to your current Web, it will affect your site's navigation elements. Plan carefully if you choose this option.

You can also create a separate Web for your discussion group and link it to your site.

The Discussion Web Wizard is comprised of a series of screens offering opportunities to customize your discussion group. Below is a summary of each screen's options:

- discussion features (submission form, table of contents, search form, threaded replies, confirmation page)

- discussion title and location of discussion folder

- input fields for submission form

- security

- table of contents chronology

- identification of the "home page" for discussion Web

- search results

- application of a theme

- frames and browser compatibility

 Before beginning the exercises in this lesson, you must first publish your main FrontPage web to a Web server with FrontPage Server Extensions installed.

Exercise 13-1: Creating a Discussion Group

In this exercise, you will use the FrontPage Discussion Web Wizard to create the basic structure and files for your discussion group. It will be created as part of your main Web site.

1. Open your published FrontPage web. (Hint: Select **File ▶ Open web** and for the **Folder name**, type `http://yourwebsite` and click **Open**.) After your published web is open, select **File ▶ New ▶ Web**.

2. Click once to highlight the **Discussion Web Wizard**.

3. For the location of the new web, select **Add to current Web**.

4. Click **OK**.

 The Discussion Web Wizard will open.

5. Click **Next**.

6. Select the features for your discussion web. Choose all of the options and click **Next**.

7. When prompted for a descriptive title, enter **Family News**.

8. For the name of the discussion folder, type **_disc** and click **Next**.

9. Choose to include **Subject, Comments** for submission form input fields and click **Next**.

10. Choose **No** when asked if discussion will take place in a protected Web and click **Next**.

11. Choose to sort the list of posted articles from **Oldest to Newest (default)** and click **Next**.

12. Choose **No** when asked if the Table of Contents should be the home page of this Web and click **Next**.

13. For the Search results, select to include **Subject, Size, Date** and click **Next**.

14. For frames choices, select **No frames** and click **Next**.

15. Click **Finish**.

16. When the Wizard has completed, return to **Folders View**.

 Folders View should appear similar to Figure 13-2.

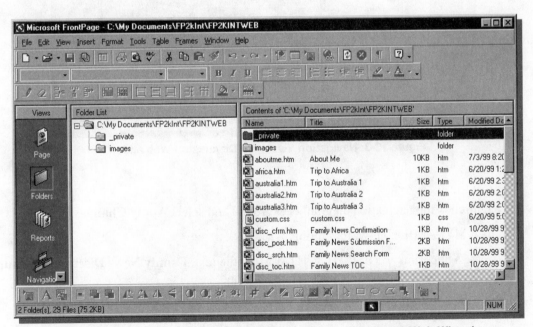

Figure 13-2: Folders View showing files created by Discussion Web Wizard

Exercise 13-2: Linking the Discussion Group to Your Main FrontPage Web

You will want to access your discussion web from within your main Web site. In this exercise, you will do this by modifying the **Navigation View** and manually creating hyperlinks. As in the last exercise, you will be working with your live web.

1. Open your web and select **Navigation View**.

2. Click DISC_TOC.HTM in the Folder List, and drag it over to the navigation schematic, placing it beneath the **My Family** icon, as shown in Figure 13-3.

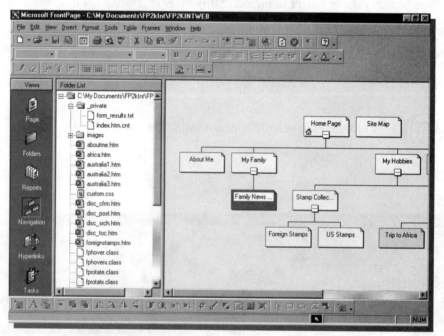

Figure 13-3: Navigation View with Discussion Web added

3. Right-click the navigation diagram background and select **Apply Changes**.

4. Open MYFAMILY.HTM for editing.

5. Create a hyperlink to DISC_TOC.HTM using the text, **Family News Discussion Group**. Delete the text "This page is under Construction."

6. Save and close file.

Modifying Discussion Group Properties

The Discussion Web Wizard cannot offer you every possibility for customizing your discussion group. It creates the basic files, which you can then alter to suit your needs.

Modifying the Submission Form

The Discussion Web Wizard offers three options for the submission of form fields:

- Subject, Comments

- Subject, Category, Comments

- Subject, Product, Comments

To add other fields, you have to modify the form itself. If you want new fields to appear in the table of contents, you must modify the form properties.

Exercise 13-3: Adding a Field to the Article Submission Form

In this exercise, you will add the **E-Mail** field to the **Family News** submission form.

1. Open `DISC_POST.HTM` for editing.

2. Add a One-Line Text Box to the form with the label **E-Mail:**. You can place it between the **From:** text box and the **Comments:** text box.

3. Modify **Form Field Properties** to include the name **EMail** and the width **50**.

4. Open **Form Properties** and select **Options**. Add **EMail** to the **Form fields** box under **Table of contents layout** after Subject and From. Click **OK**.

5. Click **OK** again to close the **Form Properties** dialog box.

6. Save the file.

   The `DISC_POST.HTM` file should resemble Figure 13-4.

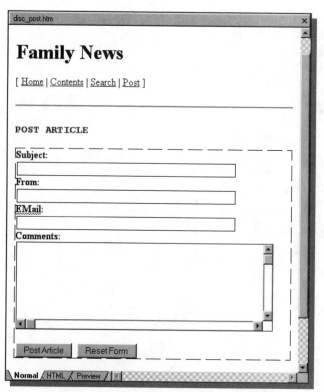

Figure 13-4: Modified submission form

Modifying Other Discussion Pages

The default confirmation page, `DISC_CFRM.HTM`, created by the Discussion Web Wizard, is shown in Figure 13-5.

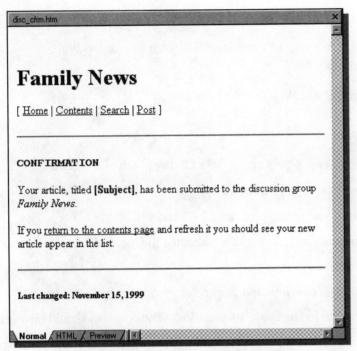

Figure 13-5: Default confirmation page

Like the other default pages, the confirmation page does not have much personality. The Discussion Web Wizard takes care of the basics, and it is up to you to tailor the pages to your design needs. You can apply themes and use style sheets to unify the look of your discussion Web with your main web.

You can modify features in addition to appearance. In Exercise 13-3, the submission form was altered to retrieve more data for each post. You can use the skills you learned in Lesson 12: *Web Page Interactivity*, to add functionality to your discussion Web.

Posting & Replying to Discussion Articles

Visitors to your discussion Web can read articles, post new articles, or reply to previous articles.

Exercise 13-4: Posting a New Article to a Discussion Group

In this exercise, you will post a new article to your discussion Web.

1. Open the discussion Web in your browser
   (HTTP://YOURWEBSITE/DISC_TOC.HTM).

2. Click **Post**.

3. In the **Subject** box, type **Happy Birthday, Uncle Mike**!

4. In the **From** box, type your name.

5. In the **E-Mail** box, type your e-mail address.

6. In the **Comments** box, type a short message to Uncle Mike.

7. Click **Post article**.

8. You should see a confirmation page resembling Figure 13-6.

9. Click the **return to the contents page** link. The contents should now resemble Figure 13-7 on the following page.

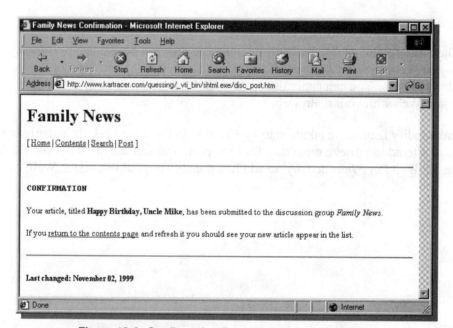

Figure 13-6: Confirmation Page after article is posted

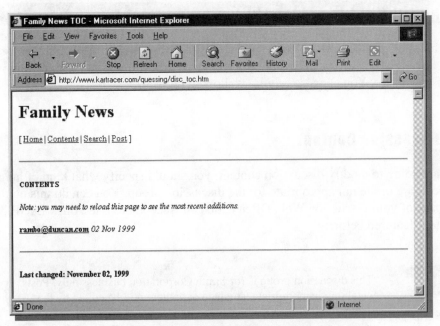

Figure 13-7: Contents page after new article is posted

Exercise 13-5: Replying to a Discussion Group Article

In this exercise you will post a reply to the article posted in Exercise 13-4.

1. In your browser, click the first post (the "`Happy Birthday, Uncle Mike!`" post).

2. Select **Reply**.

3. Pretend to be Mary, Mike's sister. Make up an e-mail address, and wish Mike a happy birthday. Post your article.

4. Click the link to return to the contents page. You will see that your reply has been posted.

Managing the Discussion Group

As Webmaster, you control the content of your site. This also includes your discussion group. Even though you are allowing visitors to post articles, you can alter or remove them if you desire. You can also require visitors to register.

Editing Discussion Content

If you are going to modify discussion content, you should specify what kind of language or subjects are or are not appropriate for the discussion group. You can do this on the home page of your discussion Web. Often called an Acceptable Use Policy (AUP), an example is featured below:

"This discussion group is for Smith Corporation business only. Posts containing inappropriate language or content will be edited by the Webmaster."

You must be connected to your Web server via FrontPage to edit discussion content.

Modify or Delete Articles

In Exercise 13-1, when you created your discussion Web, you specified the folder name _DISC for your articles. In FrontPage, an underscore at the beginning of a folder indicates that it is a *hidden* folder. By default, hidden folders do not appear in **Folders View**.

To modify or delete articles, you first must change your FrontPage settings to show hidden folders. Select **Tools ▶ Web Settings ▶ Advanced** tab, then select **Show documents in hidden directories**. Apply changes and choose to refresh your Web when prompted. Now you will see the _DISC directory in **Folders View**.

Each discussion article is stored as a separate file. FrontPage names these files 0001.HTM, 0002.HTM, 0003.HTM, etc. You can edit or delete any of these files.

You should not delete articles if you are using a threaded discussion. Instead, you can replace the text of offensive or accidental posts with a standard message. This keeps the structure of the discussion intact.

You can use a standard message to replace article text:

 [deleted post]

You might also have accidental or blank posts, which you can also mark with a standard message:

 [blank post]

Exercise 13-6: Removing an Article from a Discussion Group

In this exercise, you will remove a post, but keep the discussion thread intact.

1. In your browser, click the second posted message (Aunt Mary's reply post).
2. Click **Reply**.
3. Post a blank, anonymous message.
4. Click **return to contents page** link. Refresh the page.
5. Be sure that you are connected to your live discussion Web via FrontPage.
6. Select **Tools ▶ Web Settings ▶ Advanced** tab.
7. Select **Show documents in hidden directories** and click **Apply**.
8. Click **Yes** to refresh the web. Click **OK**.
9. In **Folders View**, open the _DISC directory.
10. Open the discussion article files and find the blank, anonymous message that needs to be modified.
11. Write a message to show that this was a blank post. You can use the example above, or create your own statement.
12. Save and close the file.
13. In your browser, refresh the contents page. Click the anonymous post. The text of your anonymous post should include your message, as shown in Figure 13-8.

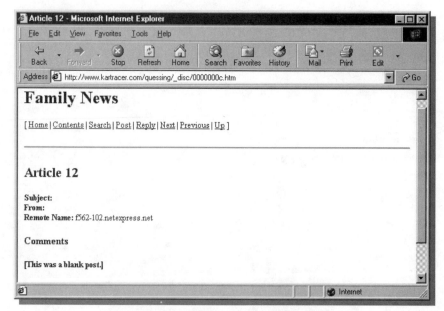

Figure 13-8: Modified discussion article

Lesson Summary

▶ A discussion group allows Web site visitors to interact with the Webmaster and other visitors.

▶ A discussion group is like a message board, where a visitor can post a new message or reply to someone else's message.

▶ A discussion group is not real-time chat.

▶ A discussion group can be added to your main FrontPage Web, or it can be a separate Web linked to from your main site.

▶ The default files created by the Discussion Web Wizard can be modified.

▶ You can edit (or delete) discussion articles.

▶ You should clearly state what you expect from visitors regarding subject matter, language, etc. Documentation of your discussion Web policy is sometimes called an Acceptable Use Policy, or AUP.

▶ If you choose to modify discussion content, you should use a standard message or set of messages that explain your modification.

▶ You should not delete articles if you are using a threaded discussion.

Lesson Review

Matching

___ 1. Person responsible for discussion content   a. Deja.com

___ 2. Discussion group creation shortcut   b. Moderator

___ 3. Real time text-based communications   c. Discussion articles

___ 4. Newsgroup database   d. Chat room

___ 5. Stored as separate files (0001.HTM, etc.)   e. Wizard

Fill in the Blank

6. A FrontPage discussion group can be created in two forms:
   _____ or _____ .

7. The FrontPage Discussion Web Wizard offers three options for the submission of form
   fields: _____ , _____ ,
   _____ .

8. Visitors to your discussion Web site can read new _____ .

9. To modify or delete articles, you first must change your FrontPage settings to
   _____ hidden _____ .

True or False?

T / F   10. The Discussion Web Wizard allows you to easily create discussion
webs, chat rooms, mailing lists, and newsgroups.

T / F   11. A FrontPage discussion web can exist as its own web and be linked to
your main Web site.

T / F   12. If you want new submission form fields to appear in the TOC, you
must modify the form properties and reload the FrontPage Server
Extensions.

T / F   13. You should always delete articles if you are using a threaded
discussion.

Lesson 14
Special Effects

Lesson Topics

► About FrontPage Special Effects

► Hit Counters

► Marquees

► Hover Buttons

► Transitions

► Banner Ads

► Lesson Summary

About FrontPage Special Effects

FrontPage 2000 allows you to easily create several types of special effects. You can use these effects to give your Web site a distinctive flair.

Special effects will work only if your Web server has FrontPage Server Extensions installed. Be sure that your server supports the Extensions before incorporating special effects into your site.

The FrontPage Special Effects covered in this lesson are:

- hit counters

- marquees

- hover buttons

- transitions

- banner ads

Marquees and transitions can only be displayed by Internet Explorer. They are not supported by Netscape or other browsers. The HTML code that generates them does not cause problems, however; is ignored.

"[FrontPage 2000 is] the one package that builds complex and professional-looking Web sites with minimal effort and maximal results."

— *Edward Mendelson, PC Magazine Online, 1999*

Hit Counters

You have worked hard on your Web site, and you will probably want to know how many people are using it. A user's single visit to a site is generally referred to as a *hit*. FrontPage provides a *hit counter* component for your use.

A *hit counter* is a graphic or text display of the number of visits to a Web page.

A hit counter is most effective when placed on your home page, where it can provide a general idea of the number of people visiting the site.

For in-depth site traffic analysis, the hit counter is not a substitute for HTTP logs generated by your Web server. It is only an estimate of the number of visitors, since one user can reload a page several times, increasing the hit counter each time.

Hit Counter Options

FrontPage has several hit counter graphics from which to choose, as shown in Figure 14-1.

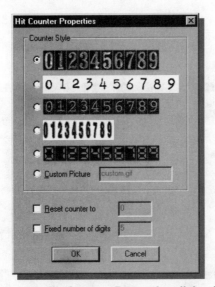

Figure 14-1: Hit Counter Properties dialog box

You can also provide your own custom graphics. To do so, you will need to create a .GIF file containing the numbers 0-9, evenly spaced. Then select the **Custom Picture** option, and enter the name of your custom GIF image.

You must publish your Web to a server with FrontPage Server Extensions installed to complete all the exercises in this lesson.

Exercise 14-1: Adding A Hit Counter To Your Home Page

1. Open `INDEX.HTM` for editing.

2. Insert cursor below the table of contents.

3. Type **Hits to this page:**

4. Select **Insert ▶ Component ▶ Hit Counter**.

5. Select a style.

6. Click **OK** and save file. (Publish your Web if you did not modify it directly on the server.)

7. Open your site in a Web browser.

8. Click **Refresh**. The hit counter should increase by one.

9. Click **Refresh** again.

Your hit counter should resemble Figure 14-2.

Figure 14-2: The hit counter

Resetting the Hit Counter

In Exercise 14-1, you learned how reloading a page increases the hit counter. When you are finished testing your Web site and are ready to "go live," you can reset the hit counter and remove the hits you made during testing. This enables you to better track the number of visitors to the site. Note that you can reset the hit counter at any time.

Exercise 14-2: Resetting The Hit Counter

1. Open your web on your server. Open INDEX.HTM for editing.

2. Double-click [**Hit Counter**].

3. Select **Reset counter to** and enter **0**.

4. Click **OK** and save file. Open your Web site in your browser or refresh the page if it is already open.

If you modify the hit counter properties again later, be sure that the **Reset counter to** option is not checked, unless you want the counter reset.

Using a Fixed Number of Digits

This option allows you to specify how many digits to use for your counter.

A value of **3** for **Fixed number of digits** will cause a single-digit number, such as 7, to appear as 007.

Exercise 14-3: Setting A Fixed Number of Digits

1. Open INDEX.HTM for editing.

2. Double-click [**Hit Counter**].

3. Select **Fixed number of digits** and enter **3**.

4. Click **OK** and save file.

5. Preview the file in your browser.

 Your hit counter should resemble Figure 14-3.

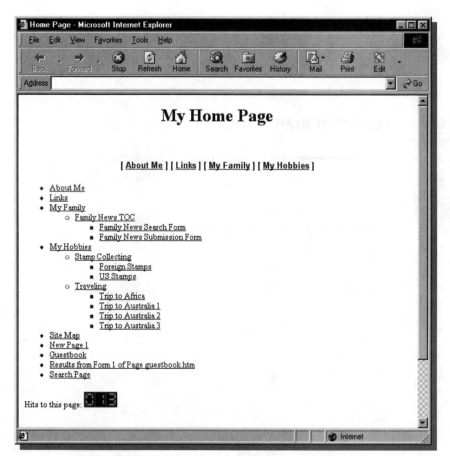

Figure 14-3: Hit Counter with fixed number of digits

Marquees

A marquee is a text message that scrolls horizontally across a Web page. You can modify the formatting of marquee text as you would any other page text.

There are many options for designing a marquee. The text can move left or right, and you can make it scroll, slide, or alternate between the two. You can also choose the speed at which the text moves.

Marquee animation appears in Internet Explorer, but not in Netscape Navigator. In Navigator, the text simply appears without motion effects.

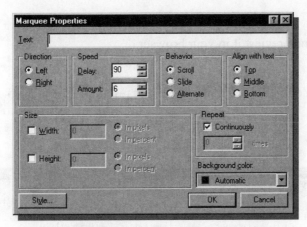

Figure 14-4: Marquee Properties dialog box

Exercise 14-4: Creating a Marquee

In this exercise, you will create a marquee using text already on your home page.

1. Open your web on your server. Open `INDEX.HTM` for editing.
2. Highlight **My Home Page**.
3. Select **Insert ▶ Component ▶ Marquee**.
4. Do not modify the default settings.
5. Click **OK**.
6. Save file and preview it in your browser. Remember: Netscape Navigator does not currently support marquees.

Exercise 14-5: Modifying Marquee Properties

1. Open your web on your server. Open `INDEX.HTM` for editing.

2. Right-click the marquee text and select **Marquee Properties**.

3. Under **Direction**, select **Right**.

4. Under **Behavior**, select **Slide**.

5. Click **OK**.

6. Right-click the marquee text and select **Font**.

7. Under **Font style**, select **Italic**.

8. Click **Apply**.

9. Click **OK**.

10. Save the file and preview it in your browser.

 Your modified marquee should resemble Figure 14-5.

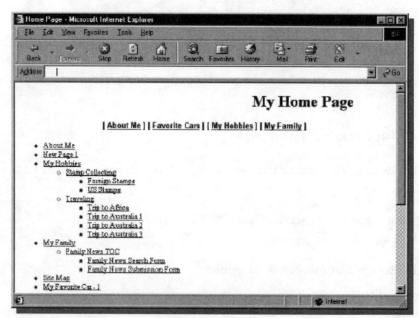

Figure 14-5: Modified marquee (sliding across page)

Hover Buttons

Unlike the regular buttons created by FrontPage themes, hover buttons produce visual and/or sound effects when the cursor "hovers" over them. You set the properties, and FrontPage does the scripting work for you.

 Hover buttons contain hyperlinks. Hover button effects are provided by Java applets.

You can customize the text, visual effects, size, and colors used for hover buttons. You can also add your own custom pictures and sound effects. (Multimedia data is covered in greater detail in Lesson 15.)

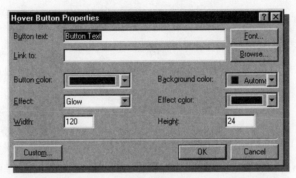

Figure 14-6: Hover Button Properties dialog box

There are several different hover button effects:

- Color fill

- Color average

- Glow

- Reverse glow

- Light glow

- Bevel out

- Bevel in

Exercise 14-6: Creating Hover Buttons

In this exercise, you will create hover buttons for the main page of the stamp collection area of your site.

1. Open your web on your server. Open STAMPS.HTM for editing.

2. Place your mouse cursor to the right of the world map graphic.

3. Press <ENTER> twice to create two blank lines under the map.

4. Select **Insert** ▶ **Component** ▶ **Hover Button**.

5. For **Button text**, type U.S. Stamps.

6. Link the button to USSTAMPS.HTM.

7. For button color, select **Navy blue**.

8. For effect, select **Glow**.

9. Leave **Effect color**, **Background color**, **Width**, and **Height** set to the defaults.

10. Click **OK**.

11. Save the file.

12. Select **Preview** tab. Move your cursor over the hover button to see the effect.

13. Return to **Normal** tab. Place your cursor to the immediate right of the hover button.

14. Press <TAB>.

15. Insert another hover button labeled **Foreign Stamps**.

16. Link the button to FOREIGNSTAMPS.HTM.

17. Select the same properties as the other hover button or specify your own properties.

18. Save file and click **Preview** tab.

19. Move your cursor over the hover button to see the effect.

Transitions

Transitions are special effects that alter the way a page appears in the browser when that page is requested.

Page transitions in FrontPage 2000 are very similar to slide transition effects available in Microsoft PowerPoint.

Just as with marquees, users can view page transitions in Internet Explorer, but not in Netscape Navigator.

Transition Properties

When designing a transition, you will choose the event to trigger the transition, the type of transition, and the duration (in seconds) of the transition. The transition properties box is shown in Figure 14-7.

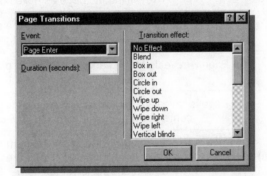

Figure 14-7: Transition Properties dialog box

Transition effects are linked to an event. There are four possible events for FrontPage transitions:

- Page Enter

- Page Exit

- Site Enter

- Site Exit

Transition Effect	Description
Blend	Page images appear in a reverse-fade fashion. If another page is open in the browser when a Blend transition effect page is loaded, the images from the Blend page fade in, gradually replacing the images from the previous page.
Box in or Circle in	Page images are displayed, beginning from the outer edges, forming either a box or a circle that diminishes in size, revealing the page as the box or circle shrinks.
Box out or Circle out	Page images are displayed beginning with a small box or circle shape in the center of the page. The page is revealed as the box or circle expands.
Wipe (up or down)	Effect is similar to a window shade being raised (up) or lowered (down) to reveal the page.
Wipe (right or left)	Similar to Wipe up or down, except the page is revealed from left to right (Wipe right) or right to left (Wipe left).
Vertical blinds	Vertical columns increase in width, revealing the page. This mimics effect of opening vertical blinds.
Horizontal blinds	Similar to Vertical blinds, except horizontal rows increase in height to reveal the page.
Checkerboard across or down	Multiple boxes expand horizontally (across) or vertically (down), revealing the page as boxes expand.
Random dissolve	Page appears at first as tiny spots across the screen; quantity of dots increases to fill and reveal the page.
Split vertical (in or out)	Page is revealed from each side (in) or beginning from the center toward each side (out).
Split horizontal (in or out)	Page is revealed from top and bottom simultaneously (in) or from center toward top and bottom simultaneously (out).
Strips (left or right; down or up)	Page is revealed diagonally, beginning from upper right corner (left down), from lower right corner (left up), from upper left corner (right down), or from lower left corner (right up).
Random bars (horizontal or vertical)	Page is revealed as a series of bars of random height (horizontal) or of random width (vertical), gradually cover the page.
Random	Any of the effects listed in this table may appear.

Table 14-1:Transition effects available

Exercise 14-7: Applying a Transition Effect

In this exercise, you will link a transition effect to the event **Site Enter**.

1. Open your web on your server. Open `INDEX.HTM` for editing.
2. Select **Format ▶ Page Transition**.
3. For **Event**, select **Site Enter**.
4. For **Duration**, type **10**.
5. Choose the **Circle out** transition effect.
6. Click **OK** and save the file.
7. Close any browser sessions you may have open.
8. Launch Internet Explorer and open your site. You should see the transition effect.

Exercise 14-8: Removing a Transition Effect

In this exercise, you will remove the transition effect added in Exercise 14-8.

1. Open `INDEX.HTM` on your web server for editing.
2. Select **Format ▶ Page Transition**.
3. For **Event**, select **Site Enter**.
4. Select **No Effect**.
5. Click **OK** and save the file.

Banner Ads

You have probably seen banner ads on the Web. They are generally used to rotate a series of advertisements. However, you can also use the FrontPage Banner Ad Manager to rotate any pictures of your choice.

 FrontPage banner ads are Java applets.

The Banner Ad Manager Properties box (shown in Figure 14-8) allows you to specify which pictures to use, the size of the ad, transition effects, display duration, and display order.

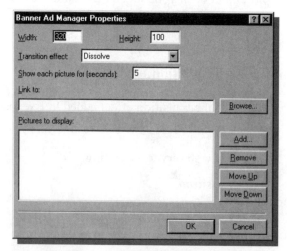

Figure 14-8: Banner Ad Manager Properties dialog box

You can use up to nine different image files in your banner ad. If you decide to change the order of their rotation, you can do that with the Banner Ad Manager Properties box.

Determining Standard Size

Banner ad images should be a standard size. You can determine the size of an image using an image editing application (such as Adobe PhotoShop, Paint Shop Pro, etc.). You can then use the image's resolution data (dimensions) to create your banner ad.

If you have pictures which are not identically sized, you can resize them using the graphics tools provided by FrontPage.

Transition Choices

There are six transition choices for FrontPage banner ads:

- None

- Blinds Horizontal

- Blinds Vertical

- Dissolve

- Box In

- Box Out

The Banner Ad Manager Properties dialog box features a **Link to:** field that allows you to use your banner ad as a hyperlink to a page within your site or to another site.

Exercise 14-9: Creating a Banner Ad

In this exercise, you will use a set of image files to create a banner ad.

1. Open your web on your web server. Open INDEX.HTM for editing.

2. Insert your cursor at the end of the hit counter line. Press <ENTER> twice.

3. Select **Insert ▶ Component ▶ Banner Ad Manager**.

4. For **Width**, enter **100**.

5. For **Height**, enter **57**.

6. For **Transition effect**, choose **Dissolve**.

7. Choose to show each picture for five seconds.

8. Leave the **Link to:** box empty.

9. Click **Add**.

10. The **Add Picture for Banner Ad** box opens. Double-click the IMAGES folder.

11. Click BANNER1.GIF to highlight the filename. Click **OK**.

12. Repeat the process with BANNER2.GIF, BANNER3.GIF, etc., until all eight banner image files have been added.

13. Click **OK**.

14. Save the file and preview in your browser.

Exercise 14-10: Modifying a Banner Ad

In this exercise, you will modify the properties of the banner ad you created in Exercise 14-9.

1. Open your web on your web server. Open INDEX.HTM for editing.
2. Right-click your banner ad. Select **Banner Ad Manager Properties**.
3. Change the transition effect to **Blinds Vertical**.
4. In the **Link to:** field, type **traveling.htm**.
5. Click **OK** (twice).
6. Save file and preview in your browser.
7. Click the banner ad to test the link.

Lesson Summary

► FrontPage special effects include hit counters, marquees, hover buttons, transitions, and banner ads.

► To use FrontPage special effects, FrontPage 2000 Server Extensions must be installed on your Web server.

► Marquees and transitions only function in Internet Explorer.

► A hit counter tracks the number of visits to your Web site.

► There are several pre-designed counters to use, or you can create your own using custom graphics.

► A marquee is a scrolling text message.

► Hover buttons are graphic hyperlinks that produce visual and/or sound effects when a cursor "hovers" over them.

► Transitions are visual effects that alter the appearance of a page when it is requested via a browser.

► There are 25 different transition effects available in FrontPage 2000.

► A banner ad is a rotating series of graphics.

Lesson Review

Matching

___ 1. Scrolling text message   a. Hover button

___ 2. Series of rotating graphics   b. Banner ad

___ 3. Display of number of visits to a site   c. Transition effect

___ 4. Alters appearance of a page when browsed   d. Marquee

___ 5. Hyperlink containing visual and/or sound effects e. Hit counter

Fill in the Blank

6. Transitions and _____ function only in Internet Explorer.

7. There are _____ different hover button effects.

8. _____ and _____ _____ are Java applets.

9. _____ number of digits allows you to specify how many digits are used for your hit counter.

10. You can add a unique look to your hover buttons and hit counter by using _____ _____.

True or False?

T / F   11. A hit counter is a Java applet.

T / F   12. A marquee functions in Netscape, but not in Internet Explorer.

T / F   13. A hit counter can never be reset.

T / F   14. Marquees scroll only text across the page.

T / F   15. Sound can be added to a hover button.

Lesson 15
Multimedia

Lesson Topics

► Web Multimedia Primer

► MIME Types

► Adding Background Audio to Your Site

► Adding Inline Video to Your Site

► Lesson Summary

Web Multimedia Primer

With FrontPage 2000, it is easy to jazz up your site with background sound and inline video. In this lesson you will learn to incorporate multimedia files into your site.

 In the strictest sense, multimedia refers to any means of communication that utilizes more than one method of transferring information. In that sense, any Web page that includes both images and text can be considered multimedia. In practice, however, when one refers to multimedia on the web, one is usually referring to moving pictures (video) or sound (audio).

 Keep your target audience in mind. Older versions of Netscape Navigator and Internet Explorer cannot interpret audio or video without the help of a plug-in. Even older browser versions cannot interpret audio or video whatsoever.

The HTML code that FrontPage 2000 uses to display video or audio is specific to Internet Explorer. Netscape users will not be able to see or hear your multimedia files as FrontPage encodes them. There is a "work-around" for inserting multimedia pages in your files that can be seen by users of Netscape. This work-around will be discussed later in this lesson.

Audio File Formats

There are a variety of different sound file formats available on the Internet. FrontPage supports the following for the creation of background sounds for your site:

- Wave (WAV): Windows standard audio format

- AIFF (AIF, AIFC, AIFF): Macintosh standard audio format

- AU Sound (AU, SND): Sun Microsystems standard audio format

- Real Audio (RA, RAM): Real Networks standard audio format

- Musical Instrument Digital Interface (MIDI): generated by synthesizers

Of these, the AU and MIDI formats are the most cross-platform capable. MIDI files differ from the others noted above. Whereas the other formats record sound samples, also known as *waveform audio*, MIDI files encode the instructions for recreating sound. The difference is subtle but significant. MIDI files are much more limited in what they can contain, but are significantly smaller. While an AU or WAV file is fine for a short sound effect, a lengthy musical composition would be better served in a MIDI format.

Another audio file format that is gaining in popularity is *MP3*. FrontPage does not yet support the incorporation of MP3 files for background sound. More information is available at the MP3 Web site at `www.mp3.com`.

The W3C (World Wide Web Consortium) is the organization responsible for setting standards on the World Wide Web. A major effort is currently underway to make the Web more accessible to persons with disabilities. Developers are encouraged to incorporate sound files in their sites in order to improve access for those with visual disabilities. More information on this initiative can be found at the W3C's Web site at `www.w3.org`.

Video File Formats

There are also a variety of different video file formats available on the Internet. FrontPage supports only *AVI* files for inline video content. AVI is the Windows standard video format.

Other popular video formats are:

- QuickTime

- RealVideo

- MPEG

You can create inline videos in these formats using a plug-in.

MIME Types

 MIME stands for *Multimedia Internet Mail Extensions*. In order for a server or a browser to interpret what type of file is being served, MIME types associate particular file extensions with the necessary application that will properly display the file.

MIME was first developed to allow for the transfer of non-text files via e-mail. It has come to be an essential protocol on the Web as well, particularly with respect to multimedia. Each MIME type consists of a general type name and a sub-type name. Examples of general type names are:

- application

- image

- text

- audio

- video

Table 15-1 shows the MIME types for the multimedia applications supported by FrontPage for background audio and inline video. MIME types for other applications are discussed in greater depth in *Part 3*.

MIME Type	Associated File Extensions
audio/x-wav	WAV
audio/x-aiff	AIF, AIFF, AIFC
audio/basic	AU
audio/x-pn-realaudio	RA, RAM
audio/midi	MID, MIDI
video/avi	AVI

Table 15-1: MIME types for FrontPage-supported inline video and audio files

Adding Background Audio to Your Site

Adding background audio to your site with FrontPage is as simple as incorporating any FrontPage component. The background sound is played the first time the page on which the sound resides is opened. You have the option of playing the sound a set number of times, or looping it so that it plays the whole time the page is displayed.

As always, be considerate of your users! Very large background sound files will cause delays in the download of the page. Very loud and long sound files may frighten away visitors. What better way to alert your co-workers (and superiors) that you have been surfing the 'Net instead of working on that important proposal than to come across a page with loud, intrusive background sound.

Exercise 15-1: Incorporating Background Audio

1. Launch your browser and go to `msdn.microsoft.com/downloads/sounds/default.asp`.

2. After this page loads in your browser, click the show toc hyperlink. Click the sound of your choice in the **TOC** list. Select a sound file from the list.

3. Right click the sound icon choose Save target as. Save this file as `C:\MY DOCUMENTS\MY WEBS\SOUND.WAV`.

If you saving the file with Netscape Navigator, hold <SHIFT> while you click the sound file name. A Save window will appear. Save the file as C:\MY DOCUMENTS\MY WEBS\SOUND.WAV.

4. Open your web on your server. Open INDEX.HTM for editing.

5. Select **File ▶ Properties**.

6. In the section labeled **Background Sound**, type `C:\MY DOCUMENTS\MY WEBS\SOUND.WAV` for **Location**, as shown in Figure 15-1 on the following page.

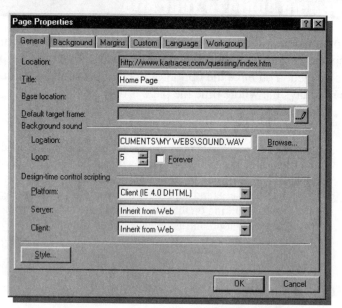

Figure 15-1: Page Properties dialog box

7. Under **Looping**, de-select **Forever**. Loop the file five times.

8. Click **OK**.

9. Save the file.

10. Click **OK** on the **Save Embedded Files** dialog box.

11. Switch to **Preview** tab.

 If your computer is equipped with a sound card and speakers, you should hear your background audio.

Adding Inline Video to Your Site

Adding inline video to your site is just like adding any inline image. Like the background sound, you can specify whether to loop the video or play it a set number of times. There are several more configurable options for inline video, as shown in Figure 15-2.

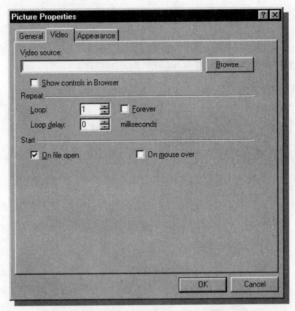

Figure 15-2: Video tab of Picture Properties dialog box

- <u>Show controls in Browser</u>: displays stop and play buttons underneath the video, allowing the user to stop and start as they choose.

- <u>Loop delay</u>: length of time between playing the video if it is set to loop more than once.

- <u>Start on file open</u>: video begins to play as soon as the page is loaded.

- <u>Start on mouse over</u>: video begins to play only when the user's mouse passes over the video.

Start on file open and **Start on mouse over** are not mutually exclusive. You can set it so that the video begins playing a set number of times when the site is first loaded. You can set it to repeat by selecting **on mouse over**.

Exercise 15-2: Incorporating an Inline Video

1. Open your web on your server. Open MYHOBBIES.HTM for editing.

2. Insert the text **and dancing** after "stamp collecting."

3. On the same line, choose **Insert ▶ Picture ▶ Video**.

4. Choose the file BABY.AVI from the images directory. Click **OK**.

5. Right-click the picture and select **Picture Properties**.

6. Set the video to loop 5 times and to begin playing on mouse over. Do not show controls in Browser.

7. Click **OK** to close the **Picture Properties** dialog box.

8. Save the file and preview in your browser.

 You should see the famous dancing baby of the Internet.

Exercise 15-3: Inline Video for Browsers Other Than IE

As with background sound, the code generated by FrontPage to display the inline video is specific to Internet Explorer. If you want users of Netscape Navigator to access the video as an inline video, perform the following steps.

1. In **Page View**, **Normal** tab, select the video by clicking it.

2. Select **Insert ▶ Advanced ▶ Plug-In**.

3. For data source, click **Browse** and select BABY.AVI from the IMAGES folder.

4. Specify the following as the message for users without plug-in support: **Plug-in required to view this video.**

5. Select **300 x 300** for dimensions in the **Plug-In Properties** dialog box, as shown in Figure 15-3 on the following page.

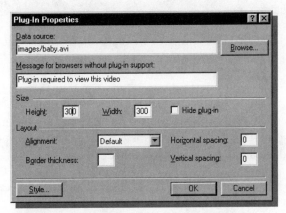

Figure 15-3: Plug-In Properties dialog box

6. Click **OK** to close the **Plug-In Properties** dialog box.

7. Save the file and switch to **Preview** tab.

If you use the plug-in method for including inline videos, you can use any video file format the browser can display—rather than just AVI—including QuickTime, MPEG, and RealPlayer.

Plug-ins are discussed in greater detail in *Part 3*.

Lesson Summary

► Multimedia is the term used to describe the incorporation of dynamic audio and video content in a Web site.

► Audio file formats supported by FrontPage include WAV, AIFF, AU, RealAudio, and MIDI.

► AVI is the only video file format supported by FrontPage 2000 for inline video, unless a plug-in is used. If a plug-in is employed by the user, other formats, such as QuickTime, MPEG, and RealVideo can be made into inline videos.

► MIME (*Multimedia Internet Mail Extensions*) types associate a file extension with a particular application.

► FrontPage enables you to incorporate a background sound in any page. The regular method of doing so works only for users of Internet Explorer. Special HTML code must be added to the page for users of Netscape Navigator and other browsers.

► Background sounds may loop infinitely or for a set number of times.

► When incorporating an inline AVI video without a plug-in, you can set the video to loop, configure whether controls appear in the browser, and whether the video will begin playing when the page is loaded, on mouse over, or both.

DDC Publishing • www.ddcpub.com

Lesson Review

Matching

___	1. Windows standard audio format	a. QuickTime
___	2. Macintosh standard video format	b. AU
___	3. Sun Microsystems standard audio format	c. MIDI
___	4. Windows standard video format	d. WAV
___	5. Macintosh standard audio format	e. AIFF
___	6. Sound file generated by synthesizers	f. AVI

Fill in the Blank

7. _____ _____ are the *Multimedia Internet Mail Extensions*.

8. _____ is the format supported by FrontPage for inline video without a plug-in.

9. _____ and _____ are the most cross-platform friendly of audio formats.

10. _____ _____ files have an extension of RA or RAM.

11. _____, _____, _____, and _____ are examples of waveform audio files.

True or False?

T / F   12. The inline video created by FrontPage can be viewed in any browser.

T / F   13. MIDI would be the best format in which to store Beethoven's Ninth Symphony.

T / F   14. A special HTML tag is required in order for visitors with Netscape Navigator to hear background sounds created with FrontPage.

T / F   15. A background sound can only be triggered once per page.

DDC Publishing • www.ddcpub.com

Lesson 16
Course Review

Applying What You Have Learned

Now that you have the skills necessary to create a dynamic, complex Web site, it is time to apply them. Be as creative as you would like when completing this final exercise. Feel free to add any additional pieces.

Exercise 16-1: Applying What You Have Learned

1. Ensure that all of your pages are linked in **Navigation View** in the appropriate place in the site hierarchy.

2. Add an additional page as a **Child Page** of *Stamp Collecting* for stamps from South America. Add a link to this page from the image map.

3. Recalculate hyperlinks to update the Table of Contents and Navigation Bars.

4. Create a linear navigation bar (vertical orientation) for the child pages of *Stamp Collecting* in a Shared Border on the left.

5. Modify the Shared Border at the bottom of the pages of your web to include the sentence `Created with Microsoft's FrontPage 2000`.

6. Apply an External Style Sheet of your choice to the entire site.

7. Modify the fields in your custom form to allow for visitors from outside the USA.

8. Create a Discussion Web on the topic of Stamp Collecting and link it to the appropriate page.

9. Add a Hover Button to STAMPS.HTM that links to the *South American Stamps* page.

10. Add background audio to the image map page.

11. Add any additional effects or pages that you would like.

"Consult my Website."

Mastering FrontPage 2000: Part 3
Advanced Web Site Publishing and Management

"In times of change, learners shall inherit the earth, while the learned are beautifully equipped for a world that no longer exists."

— Eric Hoffer

DDC Publishing • www.ddcpub.com

Part 3 Description

Welcome to *Mastering FrontPage 2000: Part 3*, the third section in *Mastering FrontPage 2000* series. This advanced-level section of the course is designed to provide an overview of some of the more sophisticated features of FrontPage 2000, for those who desire to create and manage complex Web sites.

Students learn to use advanced FrontPage features and apply them to a static web site through a series of hands-on exercises.

Please Note: Microsoft FrontPage 2000 can be used to develop and administer Web sites that are published to Windows, Macintosh, and UNIX Web servers. However, the full range of FrontPage 2000 features are best supported within the Microsoft development environment.

This course has been optimized for use in creating Web sites that will run on Web servers that support the FrontPage 2000 Server Extensions (such as Microsoft's Internet Information Server or Personal Web Server). Also, some of the FrontPage components may be viewed only in Microsoft's Internet Explorer. Such requirements are noted as they arise throughout this *Mastering FrontPage 2000* series.

Course Objectives

- Applying advanced FrontPage components

- Designing a database application

- Using FrontPage to develop client-side and server-side scripting

- Integrating Office 2000 applications into a FrontPage web

- Generating reports for analysis of a FrontPage web

- Managing a complex Web site

Part 3 Setup

Mastering FrontPage 2000: Part 3 requires minimal PC configuration and setup. To complete all of the lessons in this course, you will need:

- Microsoft FrontPage 2000 and Microsoft Office 2000

- A Web browser

- **Access to a Web server with FrontPage Server Extensions installed. The server MUST support Open Database Connectivity (ODBC) and Active Server Pages (ASP).** In a classroom setting, each student should be provided with a URL for publishing the web produced in class.

- Student files

- Lesson 18: *Web Databases* requires access to a database. It is suggested that you use the sample database that comes with FrontPage 2000 and Access (entitled "Northwind" or "Nwind").

During this entire course, you (or your students) will toggle back and forth between your Web browser and FrontPage 2000 as you edit the Web pages according to the exercises in this course.

Installing the Student Files

The student files necessary for *Mastering FrontPage 2000: Part 3* are archived on the Student Files CD-ROM. Follow these steps to install the student files:

1. Insert the Student Files CD-ROM into the appropriate drive on your computer.

2. Using Windows Explorer (file manager) or another file management utility, locate the file named FP-3.EXE and copy it to your Windows Desktop.

   - On the CD-ROM, single-click FP-3.EXE and right-click.

   - On the shortcut menu that appears, select **Copy**.

   - On your Desktop, be sure your mouse pointer is not on an icon or application and right-click.

   - Select **Paste**. This will copy the FP-3.EXE file from the Student Files CD-ROM to your Windows Desktop.

3. On your Desktop, double-click FP-3.EXE.

4. The **WinZip Self-Extractor** dialog box will appear. Click the **Unzip** button.

5. The files will be decompressed and stored in a folder called FP-3 on your desktop. If the files were decompressed and installed correctly, an alert box will appear that indicates this.

6. Open Windows Explorer.

7. If it does not currently exist, create a new MY WEBS folder inside the C:\MY DOCUMENTS folder.

8. Locate and open the FPSOURCEFILES folder inside the FP-3 folder on your Desktop. Locate the SOURCEWEB folder.

9. Copy the SOURCEWEB folder and paste it inside your C:\MY DOCUMENTS\MY WEBS folder.

10. Rename the pasted SOURCEWEB folder to FP2KADV.

11. Locate and open the FPSOURCEFILES folder from the FP-3 folder on your Desktop. Copy the final source file MARSALIS.DOC and paste it inside the C:\MY DOCUMENTS folder.

12. Launch FrontPage 2000.

13. Select **File ▶ Open Web**. For the folder name, type C:\MY DOCUMENTS\MY WEBS\FP2KADV.

14. Click **Open**.

DDC Publishing • www.ddcpub.com

Lesson 17
Advanced
FrontPage
Components

Lesson Topics

- ► What Are FrontPage Components?

- ► Include Page

- ► Scheduled Include Page

- ► Scheduled Picture

- ► Substitution

- ► Lesson Summary

What Are FrontPage Components?

FrontPage components are mini-applications included with FrontPage that are designed to make the creation of complex, dynamic Web sites as simple as possible. Without FrontPage, incorporating applications such as these into your Web site would require a great deal of time, and programming and/or scripting experience.

 As you remember from *Mastering FrontPage 2000: Part 2*, FrontPage components require the FrontPage Server Extensions to be installed on your Web server.

A number of these components have already been discussed in *Part 2*, such as:

- Table of Contents

- Navigation Bars

- Shared Borders

- Search Form

- Banner Ad Rotator

- Hit Counter

- Scrolling Marquee

- Hover Buttons

- Page Transitions

In this lesson, you will learn about four other FrontPage components:

- Include Page

- Scheduled Include Page

- Scheduled Picture

- Substitution

You are not limited to the components included with FrontPage 2000. You can also use FrontPage components created by third-party vendors. Some examples are: JustAddCommerce (www.richmediatech.com) and J-BOTS (www.websunlimited.com).

The FrontPage web included in the student files for this course is for a small business named "Saxophonics," a music store specializing in saxophones. You are the Webmaster for this site. Your task throughout this course will be to improve the site, incorporating what you have learned. The business is expanding, and its Web presence will mean the difference between a struggling small town brick-and-mortar music store and a successful international Web-based business!

Take a moment before beginning the first exercise to explore the "Saxophonics" FrontPage web, getting a sense of its layout, structure, and contents. View the web in a browser and in FrontPage's **Navigation** View. This web uses a FrontPage theme. You may modify the theme if you choose. The web also includes a Shared Border on the top of every page, and many pages include Navigation Bars.

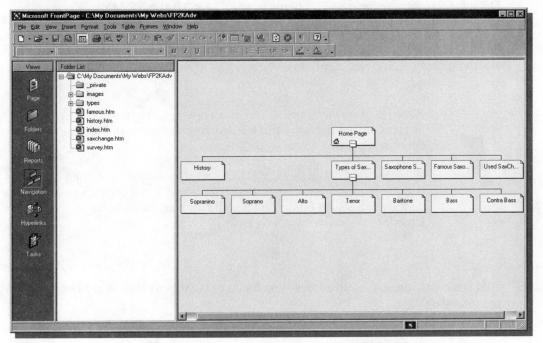

Figure 17-1: "Saxophonics" FrontPage web in Navigation View

Include Page

The *Include Page* component allows you to read one page of code into one or many other pages. The effect is similar to a Shared Border (discussed in *Part 2*). Choosing one method over the other is merely a matter of preference. With the Include Page component, you can insert shared data anywhere in the page; you are not limited to a border.

To use the Include Page component, you first need to create the page that will be shared. This is the "difficult part." After you create this page, you can include it as many times as you would like anywhere in your FrontPage web.

You can save your shared page to any part of your FrontPage web. One option is to save it in the _PRIVATE directory, because Web browsers cannot access files in that folder.

Exercise 17-1: Creating a Page to be Included in Other Pages

In this exercise, you will create a page that will be shared across your FrontPage Web using the Include Page component.

1. Open the *Saxophonics* web in FrontPage (C:\MY DOCUMENTS\MY WEBS\FP2KADV).

2. Create a new page, removing the top Shared Border (right-click page, select **Shared Borders**, deselect **Top**, and apply to current page.)

When removing the Shared Border on a single page, be sure to check that the **Current Page** option is selected. By default, the **All Pages** option is selected.

When you click OK in the dialog box, you will not receive a warning if you have forgotten to change the default setting. If this occurs, you must create a Shared Border for the entire site *again* because the Undo feature will *not correct the error*.

3. Add and center the name and address line for *Saxophonics*, as shown in Figure 17-2 on the following page.

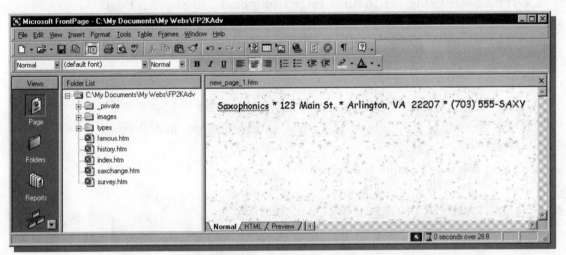

Figure 17-2: Creating the Include Page

4. Save the page as INCLUDEPAGE1.HTM within the _PRIVATE directory.

5. Close the page.

The file you just created will be shared throughout the FrontPage web.

Exercise 17-2: Using the Include Page Component to Share a Page

In this exercise, you will add the file created in Exercise 17-1 to selected pages within your FrontPage web.

1. Open INDEX.HTM for editing.

2. Insert the cursor at the end of the navigation bar at the bottom of the page. Press <RETURN>.

3. Select **Insert ▶ Component ▶ Include Page**.

4. Type (or browse to) the path and filename of the page to be included (_PRIVATE/INCLUDEPAGE1.HTM). Click **OK**.

5. Save the file.

6. Preview INDEX.HTM in a browser, then close the page.

When you preview INDEX.HTM in a browser, it should appear similar to Figure 17-3.

The HTML code for the Include Page component reads:

```
<!--webbot bot="Include" U-
Include="_private/IncludePage1.htm" TAG="BODY" -->
```

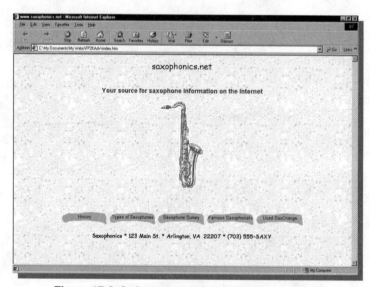

Figure 17-3: Index page with Include Page added

Exercise 17-3: Adding the Include Page to Another Page

In this exercise, you will again use the Include Page component to add the page created in Exercise 17-1 to another page in your web.

1. Open SAXCHANGE.HTM for editing.

2. Insert the cursor just beneath the top Shared Border (and just above the "Used SaxChange" header.)

3. Select **Insert ▶ Component ▶ Include Page**.

4. Again type (or browse to) _PRIVATE/INCLUDEPAGE1.HTM, and click **OK**.

5. Save the file and preview SAXCHANGE.HTM in your browser. Close the page.

When you preview SAXCHANGE.HTM in a browser, it should appear similar to Figure 17-4. Note that the Include Page is near the top of the page. The ability to place the Include Page anywhere in the page distinguishes the Include Page from the Shared Border.

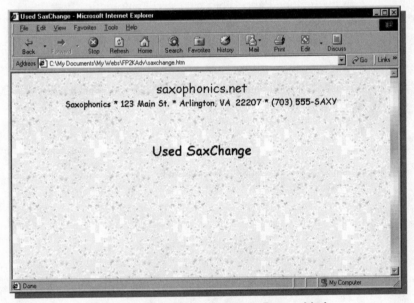

Figure 17-4: Page with Include Page added

Exercise 17-4: Modifying the Include Page

In this exercise, you will update the phone number within the Include Page. This will then update the pages that share the Include Page.

 Saxophonics traded in its local number for a toll-free number. Now you will need to modify the Include Page.

1. Open _PRIVATE/INCLUDEPAGE1.HTM for editing.

2. Change the phone number to read: **1–800–555–SAXY**.

3. Save and close the file.

4. Preview both INDEX.HTM and SAXCHANGE.HTM in a browser.

 The pages will display the new phone number, as shown in Figure 17-5. With the Include Page component, you need only edit the Include Page; other pages will automatically reflect the changes.

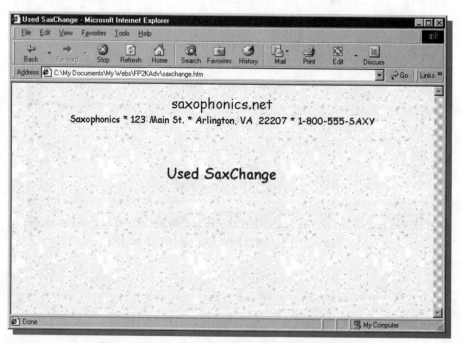

Figure 17-5: Page with modified Include Page

DDC Publishing • www.ddcpub.com

Scheduled Include Page

Some Web sites contain time-sensitive content. FrontPage makes it simple for you to maintain such content with the *Scheduled Include Page* Component. You will not have to worry about your site being "out-of-date" if you are unable to manually remove your content.

The **Scheduled Include Page Properties** dialog box (accessible via **Insert ▶ Component ▶ Scheduled Include Page**) is shown in Figure 17-6.

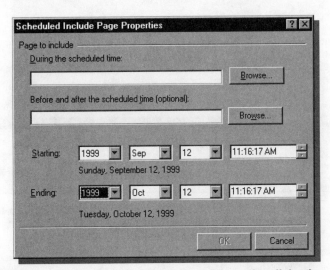

Figure 17-6: Scheduled Include Page Properties dialog box

You can specify the Include Page duration to be a period of time anywhere from a few seconds to several years. You can optionally specify a page to occupy the Include Page spot before and after the scheduled Include Page (this could be useful for messages such as "Coming Soon!").

Exercise 17-5: Creating the Scheduled Include Page

In this exercise, you will create the page that will be scheduled to appear for a certain period of time on another page within the web.

1. Create a new page, removing the top Shared Border.

2. Add the text **This is National Jazz Appreciation Month!**, as shown in Figure 17-7 below. Make this text stand out; use a bright color and a large, bold typeface.

3. Center the text.

4. Save the page as INCLUDEPAGE2.HTM in the _PRIVATE directory.

5. Close the page.

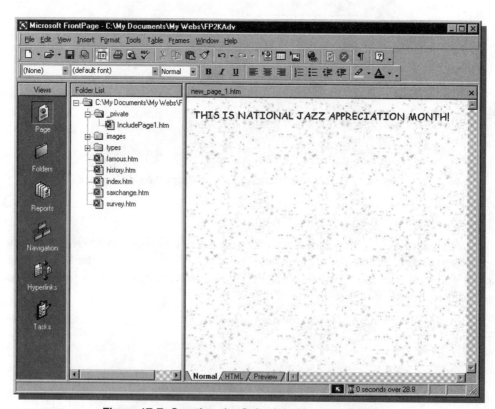

Figure 17-7: Creating the Scheduled Include Page

Exercise 17-6: Scheduling the Include Page

In this exercise, you will schedule the page created in Exercise 17-5 to appear for one month within your home page.

1. Open INDEX.HTM for editing.

2. Insert the cursor directly underneath the saxophone graphic, above the navigation bar.

3. Select **Insert ▶ Component ▶ Scheduled Include Page**.

4. In the box labeled **Page to include during the scheduled time**, type (or browse to) _PRIVATE/INCLUDEPAGE2.HTM.

5. For the timeframe, set the Include Page to expire at the end of the current month.

6. Click **OK**. Save and close the file. Preview INDEX.HTM in your browser.

 When you preview INDEX.HTM in a browser, it should appear similar to Figure 17-8.

Figure 17-8: Home page with Scheduled Include Page added

Scheduled Picture

The *Scheduled Picture* component is similar to the Scheduled Include Page, except that it is used specifically for image files. The same properties are used to determine the duration of the file.

The **Scheduled Picture Properties** dialog box, accessed by selecting **Insert ▶ Component ▶ Scheduled Picture,** is shown in Figure 17-9.

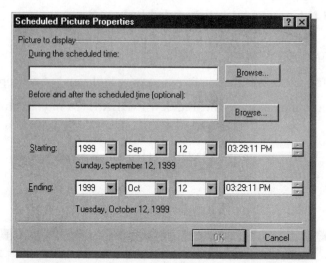

Figure 17-9: Scheduled Picture Properties dialog box

Saxophonics is having a sale on a particular brand of saxophones. The sale is for a limited time only. You need to schedule an image created to advertise this sale.

Exercise 17-7: Scheduling a Picture

In this exercise, you will schedule an image file to appear for only two weeks.

1. Open SAXCHANGE.HTM for editing.

2. Insert the cursor beneath the heading "Used SaxChange."

3. Select **Insert ▶ Component ▶ Scheduled Picture**.

4. In the box labeled **Picture to display during the scheduled time**, type (or browse to) IMAGES/SALE.GIF.

5. Set the ending date for two weeks from today. Click **OK**.

6. Save and close the file. Preview SAXCHANGE.HTM in your browser.

 When previewed in a browser, SAXCHANGE.HTM should resemble Figure 17-10.

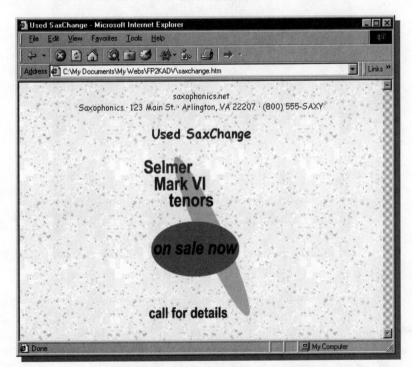

Figure 17-10: Page with Scheduled Image

Substitution

The *Substitution* component allows you to create a parameter and include it wherever you want within your FrontPage web. When you want to modify it, you need only modify the parameter, and the text wherever inserted throughout the site will be automatically updated.

 You could create a parameter called "Motto." If the company motto changes, you simply update the "Motto" parameter and, wherever it appears in the web, it will also be updated.

To use the Substitution component, you first have to create the parameter. This is done in the **Tools** menu, under **Web Settings**. Select the **Parameters** tab (shown in Figure 17-11) and click **Add**. You must then enter the name and current value of the parameter.

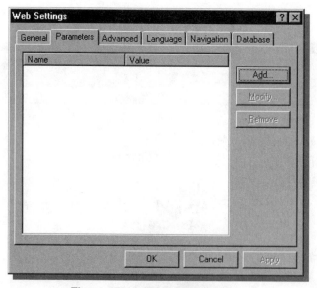

Figure 17-11: Parameters tab

To add the parameter to your Web pages, insert the cursor where you want the parameter to appear, then select **Insert ▶ Component ▶ Substitution**. You are presented with a drop-down menu of parameters (shown in Figure 17-12 on the following page). Select the one you want, and its value will be inserted (or "substituted") into your Web page text.

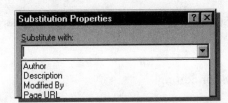

Figure 17-12: Substitution Properties dialog box

To change the value of the parameter, you go back into **Tools ▶ Web Settings**, select the **Parameters** tab, highlight the one you want to change, and click **Modify**. You can also remove parameters under this tab.

Saxophonics is going to have a featured artist every few months. You will need to create a parameter for this, and update its value when necessary.

Exercise 17-8: Creating a Parameter

In this exercise, you will create the parameter "Featured Artist." The initial value for this parameter will be "Stan Getz."

1. Select **Tools ▶ Web Settings**.
2. Click the **Parameters** tab.
3. Click **Add**.
4. In the **Name:** box, type `Featured Artist`.
5. In the **Value:** box, type `Stan Getz`.
6. Click **OK**.
7. Click **Apply**, then click **OK**.

Exercise 17-9: Using the Substitution Component

In this exercise, you will substitute the parameter created in Exercise 17-8 for text within your FrontPage web.

1. Open FAMOUS.HTM for editing.

2. Center the cursor under the heading "Some Famous Saxophonists."

3. Type **Our featured artist**: and press <SPACE> once.

4. Select **Insert ▶ Component ▶ Substitution**.

5. Select **Featured Artist** from the drop-down menu. Click **OK**.

6. Save and close the page.

7. Open INDEX.HTM for editing.

8. Center the cursor under the "Scheduled Include Page" text.

9. Type **Our featured artist**: and press <SPACE> once.

10. Select **Insert ▶ Component ▶ Substitution**.

11. Select **Featured Artist** from the drop-down menu.

12. Click **OK**. Save and close the page.

13. View the page in your browser.

 When viewed in a browser, INDEX.HTM will resemble Figure 17-13.

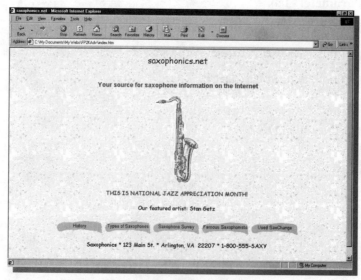

Figure 17-13: Home page with Substitution

Exercise 17-10: Changing Parameter Value

In this exercise, you will change the parameter value, which will automatically update your Substitutions.

1. Select **Tools ▶ Web Settings**.

2. Select the **Parameters** tab.

3. Click **Featured Artist** to highlight it, then click **Modify**.

4. In the **Value:** box, type `Candy Dulfer`.

5. Click **OK**.

6. Click **Apply**, then click **OK**.

7. Preview INDEX.HTM or FAMOUS.HTM in your browser.

 When previewed in a browser, INDEX.HTM and FAMOUS.HTM both show the new value for the **Featured Artist** parameter, as shown in Figure 17-14.

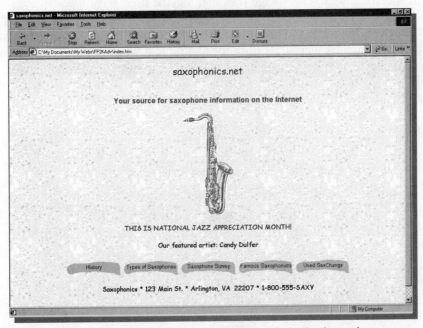

Figure 17-14: Home Page with updated Substitution value

Lesson Summary

▶ FrontPage components are mini-applications included within FrontPage.

▶ FrontPage components take care of the "difficult work" involved in creating dynamic Web sites.

▶ This lesson covers four of the more advanced components: Include Page, Scheduled Include Page, Scheduled Picture, and Substitution.

▶ The Include Page component allows you to insert the contents of one page into another or many other pages in your FrontPage web. The Include Page is "shared" by these pages.

▶ When using Include Pages within many pages of a site, the contents of the source page can be modified and all other pages will be automatically updated by FrontPage.

▶ It is a good idea to save your shared page in the _PRIVATE directory, where Web users cannot access it.

▶ The Scheduled Include Page component enables you to include a page within another page for a specified length of time. This is helpful when creating time-sensitive content. You can schedule a page to be included for as little as seconds, or as long as years.

▶ The Scheduled Picture component is similar to the Scheduled Include Page component, except it is specifically used for image files that may be time-sensitive.

▶ The Substitution Component requires the creation of a parameter, for which the value can be altered. The parameter then substitutes for regular text within your FrontPage web. When the parameter's value is changed, all of the substitutions are also updated.

Lesson Review

Matching

1. Schedules an image to appear for a specified length of time

2. FrontPage application that saves time and effort by scripting behind the scenes

3. Enables a page to be shared by other pages

4. Allows a page to be shared by other pages for a specified length of time

5. Setting whose value can substitute for regular text

a. Component

b. Include Page component

c. Scheduled Include Page component

d. Scheduled Picture component

e. Parameter

Fill in the Blank

6. Time-sensitive elements can be scheduled using the _____ _____ components.

7. A _____ is an object for which you define a value, to then be substituted for regular text.

8. Time-sensitive text can be scheduled using _____ _____ _____ component.

True or False?

T / F 9. You cannot schedule an image for longer than one month.

T / F 10. You must define a parameter before you can substitute text with it.

T / F 11. A Scheduled Include Page must be inserted into a Shared Border.

DDC Publishing • www.ddcpub.com

Lesson 18
Web Databases

Lesson Topics

▶ Databases & the Web

▶ Requirements for FrontPage Databases

▶ Creating Database Connections

▶ Database Results Wizard

▶ Creating a Database Using Form Results

▶ Creating a Database Query Form

▶ Lesson Summary

Databases & the Web

Adding a database to your Web site can be exciting. Databases give the World Wide Web an added depth. Your users can add data in real-time, and search for data that is up-to-date. Using a relational database system such as Access or Microsoft SQL Server gives you more capacity and flexibility than a mere flat-file spreadsheet. Many powerful Web applications rely on database connectivity.

FrontPage Makes Databases Easier

Creating a database and integrating it into your Web site does not have to be difficult. FrontPage 2000 includes some very useful database tools that enable you to create simple database applications without advanced programming.

Before you plan to add a database, check with your ISP or web hosting provider. Because databases can be resource-intensive, some providers do not allow database connectivity, or will charge you an additional fee for database use.

This lesson includes:

- requirements for FrontPage databases

- creating database connections

- creating a Microsoft Access database file using form results

- designing a database query form using Database Results Wizard

Leading database creation and management programs such as Access, Oracle, and Microsoft SQL Server are beyond the scope of this course and are not taught in this lesson. Instead the focus is on FrontPage tools you can use to add these applications to your Web site.

Requirements for FrontPage Databases

FrontPage easily integrates database applications into your Web site, but there are several requirements for using databases with FrontPage. These concern the type of database you are using, and the type of Web server your site is hosted on.

Type of Database

Most common database programs support *Open Database Connectivity (ODBC)*, a standard method of making a connection to a database. FrontPage requires that you use an ODBC-compliant database. In addition, your Web server must have the correct ODBC drivers for your database. Most ODBC drivers are included with Windows-based machines.

Windows includes drivers for the following ODBC-compliant databases and database management systems:

- Access

- dBASE

- Excel

- FoxPro

- Oracle

- Paradox

- SQL Server

- Sybase

Web Server Type

To use a database with FrontPage, your Web server must support *Active Server Pages (ASP)*, a Microsoft technology which is used by FrontPage to connect to databases. Both Microsoft Internet Information Server (IIS) and Microsoft Personal Web Server (PWS) support ASP.

Your Web server must also have the FrontPage 2000 Server Extensions installed. The Extensions have been discussed in various contexts throughout this course. It is possible to use FrontPage to develop a Web site without having the Server Extensions installed on your Web server. However, you will not be able to use a database with FrontPage.

Creating Database Connections

To access a database from FrontPage, you need to tell FrontPage how to connect to that database. As discussed in the previous section, FrontPage can only make connections to ODBC-compliant databases.

To configure a database connection, select **Tools** ▶ **Web Settings** and click the **Database** tab, as shown in Figure 18-1.

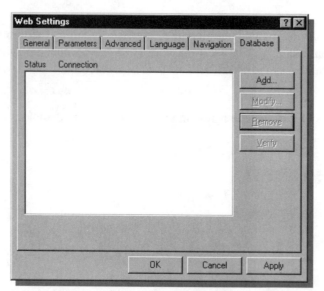

Figure 18-1: Web Settings dialog box, Database tab

You can *add* a new database connection or *modify* or *remove* an existing connection. You can also *verify* a database connection; verification ensures that the database is still available to FrontPage.

To add a database, click **Add**. The **New Database Connection** dialog box will appear, as shown in Figure 18-2.

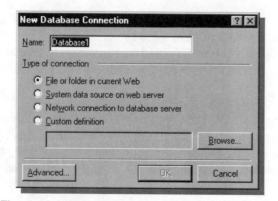

Figure 18-2: New Database Connection dialog box

Names & Types

You must name any database connection you establish. The name does not have to be the same as the database filename, but you may find it helpful to be consistent, especially if you have multiple databases.

You must also select the type of connection. Four connection type options are available:

- File or folder in current Web: the file must be imported into FrontPage; useful for Access or Excel files

- System data source on web server: the most common choice for Web databases. Requires the configuration of an ODBC data source using the Windows ODBC Data Source Administrator

- Network connection to database server: for Intranet use, or for large Web sites with dedicated database servers

- Custom definition: for databases whose drivers require more parameters than can be configured in a standard FrontPage database connection

Locating the Database File

You will then select **Browse** to locate the file or connection.

After clicking **OK** in the **New Database Connection** dialog box, you will be returned to the **Database** tab of the **Web Settings** dialog box. You can then highlight the connection you created, and click **Verify**. If the file exists, and all necessary parameters are passed to the database, you will be rewarded with a green checkmark next to the connection name. If not, there will be a broken chain link. If you do not verify the connection, there will be a question mark. These icons are shown in Figure 18-3.

Figure 18-3: Verifying database connections

Database Results Wizard

There is another way to create a new database connection: the *Database Results Wizard*. This wizard is designed to easily create a database query and format the results. This section will examine each step of the Database Results Wizard.

To begin, select **Insert ▶ Database ▶ Results**. This launches the Database Results Wizard, which has five steps.

Step one is to specify the database connection. To create a new connection, click **Create**. (This opens the **Web Settings** dialog box discussed in the previous section.) Otherwise, you can use the sample database that comes with FrontPage and Access (entitled "Northwind"), or you can select an existing database connection. These options are shown in Figure 18-4.

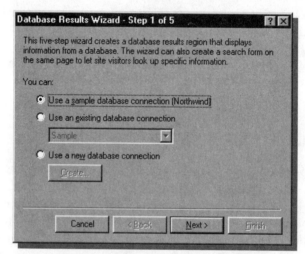

Figure 18-4: Database Results Wizard (Step #1)

Next, you will learn how to select the record source to query, or create a custom query, as shown in Figure 18-5.

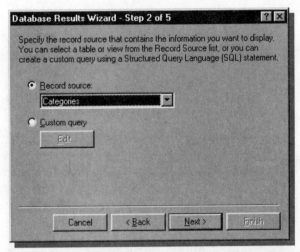

Figure 18-5: Database Results Wizard (Step #2)

Figure 18-6 shows the third step of the Database Results Wizard. This step allows you to choose which fields are returned from the query, and if they will be filtered or sorted in a particular manner.

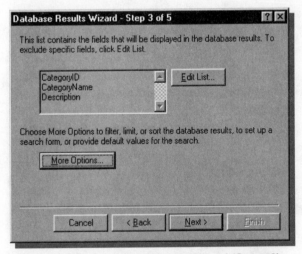

Figure 18-6: Database Results Wizard (Step #3)

The next step is to select a formatting option. You can choose to use a table, a list, or a drop-down list. Each of these options has its own set of features to configure. The options for a "table" are shown in Figure 18-7.

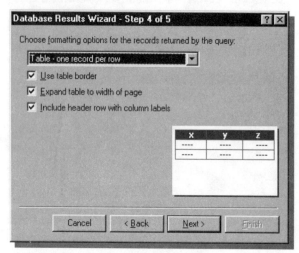

Figure 18-7: Database Results Wizard (Step #4)

Finally, you can determine if the records will be grouped for display. This step is shown in Figure 18-8.

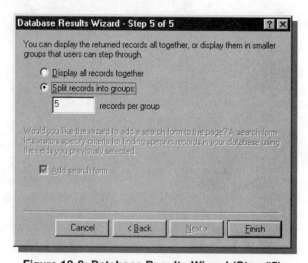

Figure 18-8: Database Results Wizard (Step #5)

Exercise 18-1: Using the Database Results Wizard

In this exercise, you will use the Database Results Wizard to query the sample Northwind database.

 To complete the exercises in this lesson, you must have access to a Web server with FrontPage 2000 Server Extensions installed and Active Server Pages support.

1. Publish your web. Open your published web from the server and create a new page. Position your cursor below the Shared Border area

2. Select **Insert ▶ Database ▶ Results**.

3. In step one of the Database Results Wizard, choose to use the sample database connection.

4. In step two, select **Employees** as the record source.

5. In step three, do not edit any of the fields.

6. For step four, select **Table - one record per row** and accept the default options.

7. In step five, select **Split records into groups.** Enter 5 for the number of records per group.

8. Click Finish.

9. Save the page as DATABASETEST.ASP. Note that the file type is automatically changed to Active Server Pages.

 A page with database results must be named with the .ASP extension, since FrontPage uses Active Server Pages to handle its database connections.

 The resulting page should resemble Figure 18-9 on the following page.

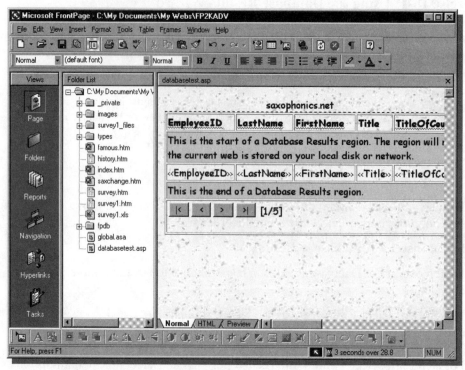

Figure 18-9: Results page created by Database Results Wizard

You will now need to publish your web to the server in order to test the database and results pages.

This page previewed in a browser should resemble Figure 18-10 on the following page.

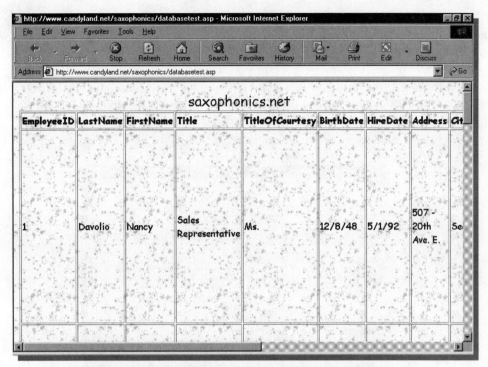

Figure 18-10: Results page as previewed in a browser

You can see that accepting all of the defaults offered by the Database Results Wizard may not format your data the way you want. You may need to experiment with the options offered. To edit your results page after it has been created, you can right-click within the database results region and select **Database Results Properties**. This will launch the Database Results Wizard for editing.

After the preceding exercise, you will also notice the presence of another new file in your FrontPage web. This file, called GLOBAL.ASA, sets application variables for your Web site. You will not need to open or edit this file.

Creating a Database Using Form Results

If you already have a database, it is easy to integrate it into your FrontPage web using the Database Results Wizard. However, you can also have FrontPage create a database for you.

You can make a form (forms are discussed in detail in *Part 2*) and have the form results sent to an Access database file. This is specified in the **Form Properties** box, as shown in Figure 18-11.

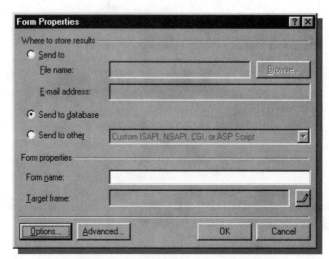

Figure 18-11: Form Properties dialog box

Select **Send to database**, then click **Options**. The options box is shown in Figure 18-12 on the following page.

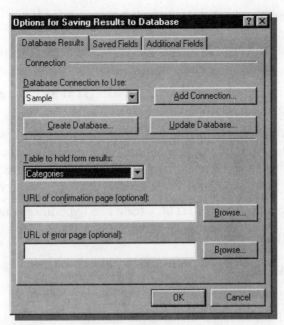

Figure 18-12: Options for Saving Results to Database dialog box

Click **Create Database**. FrontPage will create the database based on your form fields. When the operation is complete, you will receive a confirmation message indicating that the database has been created, and the name of the database connection you should use. You can see a sample of this in Figure 18-13.

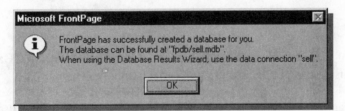

Figure 18-13: Database creation confirmation

FrontPage likes to create and store databases in a folder called FPDB, which it also creates within your FrontPage web.

It is time to set up the Saxophonics Used SaxChange. You will first create the form for saxophone sellers to enter their information into your database (which FrontPage will create for you). Then you will create a search form for saxophone buyers to search your database.

Exercise 18-2: Creating a Database Using Form Results

In this exercise, you will create a form to collect data and use it to create a database.

1. From your published web, open SAXCHANGE.HTM for editing. Delete the shared border at the top of the page.

2. Create these two new pages in your web: SELL.ASP and BUY.ASP. When you save each of these files, an alert box may appear warning you that changing a filename extension may make the file unusable and asking if you are sure you want to change the filename. Click **Yes.**

3. Switch back to SAXCHANGE.HTM. Create two hyperlinks at the bottom of the page:

   - **Sell a saxophone** – SELL.ASP

   - **Buy a saxophone** – BUY.ASP

4. Open SELL.ASP for editing and delete the shared border at the top of the page. Set the title of this page to `Sax for sale`.

5. At the top of the page, type the heading `Yes, I Want to Sell a Saxophone!`

6. Create a form that collects the following data:

   - Name

   - E-mail

   - City

   - State

   - Type of saxophone: Sopranino, Soprano, Alto, Tenor, Baritone, Bass, Contra Bass (use radio buttons for the types of saxophones).

   - Price range: $1-250, $251-500, $501-750, $751-1000, $1000+ (use radio buttons).

   - Comments

7. Be sure to define the Name properties of each field and to create the group names for both the Type and Price radio buttons.

8. Save the file. Preview SELL.ASP in your browser.

When previewed in a browser, your form page should appear similar to Figure 18-14.

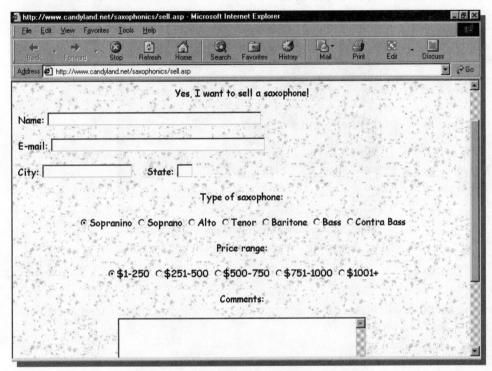

Figure 18-14: Form to sell a saxophone

9. Right-click the form, and choose **Form Properties**. Select **Send to database**, then click **Options**.

10. Click **Create database**. FrontPage will create a database called SELL.MDB, which it will place within a folder called FPDB. You will receive a confirmation message indicating that the data connection name is **sell**. Click **OK**.

11. For **URL of confirmation page**, type **SAXCHANGE.HTM**. Click **OK**.

12. Click **OK** again to exit the **Form Properties** dialog box. Save and close SELL.ASP.

The SELL.MDB database has been created within your web by FrontPage. You do not need to know how to use Access, and you do not have to have Access installed on your Web server to do this.

Creating a Database Query Form

You have already taken a brief tour of the Database Results Wizard. You can also use the Database Results Wizard to create a search form.

In step three of the Database Results Wizard, where you choose which fields to display, there is a **More Options** button. If you click that, you will see a screen resembling Figure 18-15.

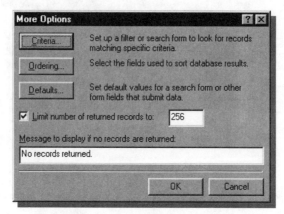

Figure 18-15: More Options dialog box

Clicking **Criteria** will bring you to another screen in which you can specify search form fields, as shown in Figure 18-16.

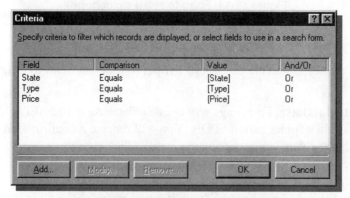

Figure 18-16: Criteria for search fields

You can then add or modify existing search form fields. When the Database Results Wizard is complete, your results page will have a search form instead of the entire contents of the database. Your users can then search the database using the fields you selected using the Database Results Wizard.

Exercise 18-3: Creating a Database Query Form

In this exercise, you will create a database query form for users who wish to buy a saxophone. Your search form will query the SELL.MDB database you created in Exercise 18-2.

1. Open BUY.ASP for editing and delete the shared border at the top of the page. Set the title of this page to **Buy a sax**.

2. Launch the Database Results Wizard (select **Insert ▶ Database ▶ Results**).

3. Select **Use an existing database connection**, and choose **sell** from the drop-down list. Click **Next**.

4. The only option for **Record Source** is **Results**, so click **Next**.

5. Click **Edit List**, and remove **ID**, **Remote_computer**, **User_name**, and **Browser_type**. Click **OK** to return to Database Results Wizard.

6. Click **More Options**, then click **Criteria**. Click **Add**.

7. From **Field Name**, select **State**. For **And/Or**, select **Or**. Click **OK**.

8. Repeat the last step, adding **Type** and **Price**. When finished, click **OK** twice.

9. Click **Next** to proceed to next Database Results Wizard screen. Choose to format your results as a list, specifically a bullet list (**List options**). Click **Next**.

10. Select **Display all records together**, and check the box next to **Add search form**. Click **Finish**.

11. To verify the database connections choose **Tools ▶ Web Settings ▶ Database** tab. Click the first connection and click **verify**. After verifying each database connection, click **OK**.

12. Save and close the page. Preview BUY.ASP in your browser.

 BUY.ASP previewed in your browser should resemble Figure 18-17 on the following page.

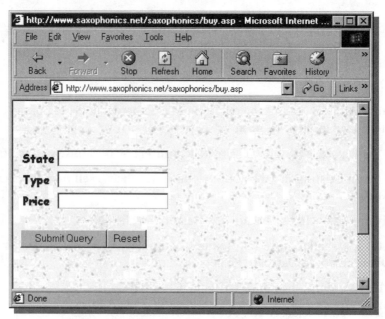

Figure 18-17: Search form to query database

Do not forget to publish your site and test all pages you have created in this lesson.

Lesson Summary

▶ Databases can make your Web site more powerful.

▶ Before you plan a database application, check with your ISP or hosting provider to ensure that database connectivity is supported.

▶ To use a database with FrontPage, your Web server must support ODBC (Open Database Connectivity) and ASP (Active Server Pages). The FrontPage 2000 Server Extensions must also be installed.

▶ You must identify a database for FrontPage to be able to use it. This is done via database connections, or data source names.

▶ The Database Results Wizard allows you to design queries and format query results.

▶ You can create a database using the results from a form. You can then use a feature of the Database Results Wizard to create a search form to query this database.

▶ FrontPage stores information about your database connection within a GLOBAL.ASA file.

Lesson Review

Matching

___ 1. Server requirements to enable an active database

___ 2. Filters which records are displayed in a search form

___ 3. Five-step process for creating queries and formatting query results

___ 4. Type of database file generated by FrontPage form results

___ 5. Another name for a database connection

a. Database Results Wizard

b. Microsoft Access

c. Criteria

d. FrontPage 2000 Extensions

e. Open Database Connectivity (ODBC)

Fill in the Blank

6. The _____ _____ _____ is a five-step process for creating database queries and formatting query results.

7. _____ _____ Pages can be used to query a database.

8. FrontPage's sample database is called _____ .

True or False?

T / F   9. A database connection must be configured to use a database within FrontPage.

T / F   10. FrontPage can automatically generate a search form to query your database

T / F   11. FrontPage can generate an Oracle database from form results.

T / F   12. Some ISPs may not allow you to have a database on your Web site.

Lesson 19
Scripting &
Active Content

Lesson Topics

► Scripting Basics

► Client-Side Scripting: JavaScript

► Client-Side Scripting: DHTML

► Lesson Summary

Scripting Basics

In the broadest sense, a *script* is a set of instructions on how to perform an action. Thus far, much of the scripting used to build your Web site has been invisible to you. FrontPage is appealing because you do not need to do your own scripting to produce special effects and components; the program does the scripting for you.

However, if you want to add your own scripts to your site, FrontPage has some tools to help you out.

This lesson does not endeavor to teach you scripting languages, which is beyond the scope of this course. Instead, you will receive a broad overview of how scripting can be integrated into your FrontPage web.

Scripting Languages & the Web

There are a number of types of scripts used on the Web. CGI scripts, commonly written in Perl or C, are used to submit information to the server, where it is processed. CGIs are an example of *server-side scripting*. Depending on the application, CGIs can be difficult to design and implement.

Client-side Scripting

The focus of this lesson will be on *client-side scripting*. Client-side scripts are written directly into your Web page. When a visitor to your site requests the page, the visitor's browser processes and executes the script instructions. This type of script is less resource-intensive, since it does not depend on the Web server to process information.

Some of the tasks that scripting languages can help you accomplish are:

- Animation

- Browser detection

- Calculations

- Form field control

- Pop-up messages

Choosing a Scripting Language

As you probably know by now, the two major Web browsers handle various Web technologies in different ways. When planning to incorporate scripts into your site, you need to examine the possibilities for scripting languages, and how they are supported by different browsers (and older versions of those browsers).

Two commonly-used scripting languages are JavaScript and VBScript. Both exist as client-side and server-side languages; this lesson will focus on their client-side applications.

JavaScript

JavaScript was the first scripting language used in Web development. It was developed by Netscape Communications and is supported (but not uniformly) by both Netscape Navigator, Netscape Communicator, and Internet Explorer. Microsoft has developed its own version of JavaScript, called *JScript*.

JavaScript is not the same as *Java*. Java is an object-oriented programming language (developed by Sun Microsystems), whereas JavaScript is a scripting language. JavaScript was originally named LiveScript; the name was changed to take advantage of Java's popularity. (For an in-depth examination of JavaScript, see DDC's *Mastering JavaScript Series*.)

VBScript

VBScript is Microsoft's script version of its *Visual Basic* programming language. It only runs in Internet Explorer, which is why JavaScript is more widely used for client-side Web applications. For more information regarding VBScript, see DDC's *Mastering VBScript*.

Browser Compatibility

However you decide to address your scripting needs, you want to be certain that your target users will be able to take advantage of your coding.

When developing scripts, be sure to test them in different browsers, and different versions of those browsers.

Older browsers that do not support scripting will attempt to interpret the code as HTML. This could cause the browser to display your script code as normal text. This is unprofessional and will mark your Web site as being designed by an amateur. How can you resolve this problem?

Many developers enclose their scripts in HTML comment tags. This prevents the browser from displaying the code if it is not going to process the script itself. An example of this is shown below.

```
<SCRIPT>
<!-- Start hiding from old browsers.
[your script goes here]
// Stop hiding script from old browsers. -->
</SCRIPT>
```

Client-Side Scripting: JavaScript

As mentioned earlier, JavaScript is the most popular client-side scripting language on the Web. In this section, you will add two short scripts to your FrontPage web. One allows the user to find out the current time; the other generates the date and time the page was last updated.

Exercise 19-1: Writing a Clock Script

1. Create a new file called TIME.HTM and open it for editing.

2. Select the **HTML** tab.

3. Insert a line just after the <BODY> tag and enter the code shown below.

```
<P ALIGN="CENTER">
<FONT SIZE="1" COLOR="#000000" FACE="Verdana, Arial,Helvetica">
<STRONG><CENTER><H2>Days until the annual SAX Jazz show and sale:</H2>
<SCRIPT LANGUAGE="JavaScript">
<!--
var now = new Date();
var then = new Date("July 4, 2001");
var gap = then.getTime() - now.getTime();
gap = Math.floor(gap / (1000 * 60 * 60 * 24)+1);
document.write(" Only  " + gap + " days left to get ready!");
// -->
</SCRIPT></CENTER></STRONG></FONT>
```

4. Save the file. Preview TIME.HTM in your browser.

5. Close the file.

 Your page should resemble Figure 19-1.

Figure 19-1: Clock script as previewed in a browser

Client-Side Scripting: DHTML

DHTML (Dynamic HTML) is a combination of client-side scripting with standard HTML elements. The scripting language accesses page elements through the *DOM* (Document Object Model (DOM)).

The DOM is a set of rules governing how a script can refer to HTML elements.

Because a DHTML script modifies the HTML elements directly, its effects are rendered in the browser, thus requiring no server-side processing.

The problem, as with other scripting technologies, is that Netscape and Microsoft have both developed different implementations of the DOM. Technically, there are great differences; what is important for you to remember is that you need to test your scripting in different browsers and work with them to ensure cross-browser compatibility.

DHTML is only viewable in Internet Explorer 4.0 or later, and Netscape Navigator 4.0 or later.

DHTML & FrontPage

You can hand-code DHTML in FrontPage by working within the HTML tab of **Page** View. However, FrontPage also allows you to create DHTML using the DHTML Effects toolbar. FrontPage writes the coding for you. The DHTML Effects toolbar is shown in Figure 19-2.

Figure 19-2: DHTML Effects toolbar

To create a DHTML effect, highlight the text or picture you want to modify, then select **Format ▶ Dynamic HTML Effects**. This launches the DHTML Effects toolbar.

You can select from the following events:

- Click

- Double-click

- Mouse over

- Page load

Then, depending on the type of selection (text or image), you can choose to apply formatting (such as font size, color, border, etc.) or to apply a new picture. Close the toolbar, and your DHTML effect is ready to preview.

Exercise 19-2: Creating DHTML Effects

In this exercise, you will use the DHTML Effects toolbar to create a visual effect.

1. Open INDEX.HTM for editing.
2. Highlight the text: "Your source for saxophone information on the Internet."
3. Select **Format ▶ Dynamic HTML Effects**.
4. On the DHTML Effects toolbar, select **Mouse over**.
5. Choose to apply **Formatting**, then **Choose font**.
6. Change the appearance of the text; change the color, make it all caps (upper case), and other text formatting changes.
7. Click **OK**. The effect is in place, even though there is no visual confirmation on the toolbar.
8. Click the **X** to close the DHTML Effects toolbar. Save the file.
9. Preview the file in either the Preview tab or in your browser. Move your mouse over the affected text.

You should see the text change as you select it using the DHTML Effects toolbar. If you select the HTML tab, you can see the DHTML scripting that FrontPage wrote for you, as shown below. (Your DHTML script may be slightly different, depending on the effects you chose.)

```
<HEAD>
<SCRIPT LANGUAGE="JavaScript" fptype="dynamicanimation">
<!-
function dynAnimation() {}
function clickSwapImg() {}
//-->
</SCRIPT>
<SCRIPT LANGUAGE="JavaScript1.2" fptype="dynamicanimation"
src="animate.js">
</SCRIPT>
</HEAD>
<BODY onload="dynAnimation()" LANGUAGE="Javascript1.2">
<H3 ALIGN="center" dynamicanimation="fpAnimformatRolloverFP1"
fprolloverstyle="color: #FF0000; text-transform: uppercase"
onmouseover="rollIn(this)" onmouseout="rollout(this)"
LANGUAGE="Javascript1.2"><FONT FACE="Arial">Your source for saxophone
information on the Internet</FONT></H3>
```

Lesson Summary

▶ FrontPage generally does your scripting for you, but you can also add your own scripts to your FrontPage web.

▶ Scripts are used on the Web to fulfill a variety of tasks.

▶ There are two types of scripts: server-side and client-side.

▶ Server-side scripts require information to be passed from the browser to the server, where it is then processed. The results are passed back to the browser. CGI scripts are an example of server-side scripts.

▶ Client-side scripts are processed by the browser. They do not tax the server, and results are generated fairly rapidly.

▶ JavaScript and VBScript are two commonly used scripting languages. They both exist in server-side and client-side form.

▶ JavaScript is the most popular client-side scripting language on the Web. It was developed by Netscape, and is supported by the most recent versions of both Netscape browsers and Internet Explorer. Microsoft has its own version of JavaScript, called JScript.

▶ VBScript was created by Microsoft, and is a scripting version of Visual Basic. It is only supported in Internet Explorer.

▶ DHTML (Dynamic HTML) combines client-side scripting with the DOM (Document Object Model) to directly modify HTML elements.

▶ It is important to keep browser compatibility in mind when designing and testing scripts.

Lesson Review

Matching

___ 1. Passing data to the server to be processed   a. VBScript

___ 2. Microsoft version of JavaScript   b. JScript

___ 3. Microsoft alternative to JavaScript   c. JavaScript

___ 4. Most popular client-side Web scripting language   d. Server-side scripting

Fill in the Blank

5. _____ is the company which created JavaScript.

6. Client-side scripting involves processing data in the _____ .

7. _____ is a scripting version of Visual Basic.

8. ASPs may be written in Perl, VBScript, or _____ .

True or False?

T / F   9. JavaScript is exactly like Java, but easier to learn.

T / F   10. JScript and VBScript were both developed by Microsoft.

T / F   11. CGI scripts are server-side scripts.

T / F   12. Netscape browsers will only run VBScript, and not JavaScript.

T / F   13. DHTML is only supported in Internet Explorer.

Lesson 20
Integrating
Office 2000

Lesson Topics:

▶ Sharing Data Among Office 2000
  Applications

▶ Integrating FrontPage and Word

▶ Integrating FrontPage & Excel

▶ Integrating FrontPage & PowerPoint

▶ Inserting Office Components

▶ Lesson Summary

Sharing Data Among Office 2000 Applications

In Lesson 18: *Web Databases*, you saw how FrontPage 2000 interacts with Access 2000 to allow you to use a database with your site. You can also integrate other companion applications in the Office 2000 suite with FrontPage 2000, including:

- Word 2000

- Excel 2000

- PowerPoint 2000

This compatibility allows users to easily share documents and data among the various applications in the Office suite.

The advantages of sharing data from one application to the others are many:

- Ensure consistency of data

- Eliminate duplication of effort

- Quick conversion of existing documents to Web documents

The methods of sharing objects and data with FrontPage will vary depending on the companion application.

Integrating FrontPage and Word

Word is Office 2000's comprehensive word processing application. Word files generally have a .DOC file extension. Word is used to create documents that are primarily text-based, though it is possible to incorporate images into Word documents.

Copying from Word to FrontPage

The simplest way to share data between Word and FrontPage is to Copy and Paste using the Clipboard. You can copy text (or other objects) in Word to the clipboard, and then from the clipboard into FrontPage

FrontPage offers two options for copying objects from Word into FrontPage:

- standard Copy & Paste

- Copy & Paste special

With the standard copy and paste, you simply copy an object in Word and paste it into FrontPage, either by selecting **Edit ▶ Paste** or by right-clicking and selecting **Paste**. One drawback to this method is that all of the styles defined in the Word document will be carried over to the web page.

An alternative to the standard copy and paste is **Paste Special**, which allows you to control how copied text is brought into FrontPage. Instead of selecting **Paste**, you would instead select **Paste Special**, which opens the **Convert Text** dialog box, as shown in Figure 20-1.

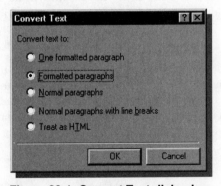

Figure 20-1: Convert Text dialog box

The Convert Text dialog box allows you to control the way FrontPage formats the copied text:

- <u>One formatted paragraph</u>: converts the text into a single paragraph, replacing paragraph breaks with line breaks

- <u>Formatted paragraphs</u>: copies the text as is, preserving formatting and paragraphs

- <u>Normal paragraphs</u>: copies the text, converting text to the Normal style as defined for your Web site (as defined by a Theme or Style Sheet)

- <u>Normal paragraphs with line breaks</u>: same as above, but substitutes line breaks for paragraph breaks

- <u>Treat as HTML</u>: interprets any HTML within the copied text. You would use this option if you had created an HTML file in Word and wanted to convert the HTML file into a FrontPage document.

The method of pasting you choose depends on what type of text is being copied into FrontPage.

Saving a Word Document as HTML

Another simple way of making your Word documents Web-ready is to choose the **Save As Web Page** option in Word 2000. This automatically converts an existing Word document into an HTML file or files. If your document is complex or includes images, Word will save the document as multiple files, and the entire document will be saved as a Web folder. This folder or the individual folders can be imported into or opened in FrontPage for editing.

If your document includes tables or images, using the **Save As Web Page** option in Word is not the most reliable way to make your Word documents Web-ready. Documents converted from Word to HTML in this way frequently lose much of their formatting and may require a significant amount of clean-up after being brought into FrontPage.

If you convert your Word documents to HTML in this way, you will then need to import the file or files created into FrontPage in order to edit them in FrontPage.

Exercise 20-1: Importing Word Content into FrontPage

In this exercise, you will share information from a Word document with FrontPage.

1. In **Folders** View, create a new folder named FAMOUS.

2. Go back into the Web Settings and change the Variable for Famous Artists to
   Branford Marsalis.

3. Move the file FAMOUS.HTM from the root directory into the FAMOUS folder and
   rename as INDEX.HTM. Open this file and add a link from the name "Branford
   Marsalis" in this page to MARSALIS.HTM. Save and close INDEX.HTM.

4. Create a new FrontPage document in the FAMOUS folder. Save this file as
   MARSALIS.HTM. Open this file for editing.

5. Open the file MARSALIS.DOC in Word.

6. Highlight the entire document and copy it to the clipboard.

7. Use the **Paste Special** option to paste the object on the clipboard into MARSALIS.HTM
   as **Normal paragraphs with line breaks**.

8. Save and close the file. Preview MARSALIS.HTM in your browser.

 The resulting FrontPage document as previewed in the
browser is shown in Figure 20-2.

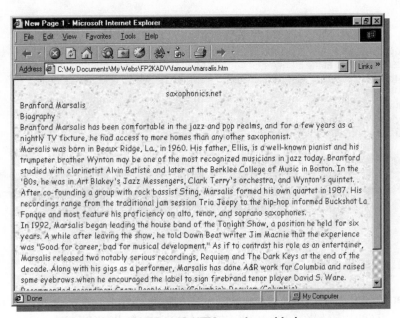

Figure 20-2: MARSALIS.HTM previewed in browser

9. Return to MARSALIS.DOC in Word.

10. Select **File ▶ Save As Web Page**. Save as MARSALIS2.HTM.

11. Select **File ▶ Web Page Preview**.

 Figure 20-3 displays MARSALIS2.HTM as previewed in a browser. Note that the **Save As Web Page** option retained more of the Word document's formatting than the **Paste Special** option. This will not always be the case. When sharing information between Word and FrontPage, you may need to try several different options to determine which is best for the particular document with which you are working.

12. Close Word.

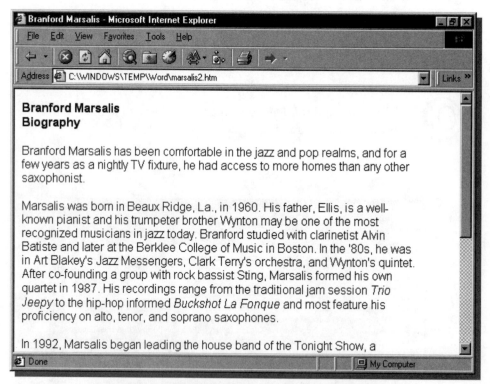

Figure 20-3: MARSALIS2.HTM previewed in browser

Sending Data from FrontPage to Word

As you learned in Lesson 18, it is possible to use FrontPage forms to send data to an Access database. You can also save form results as a Word file, to be used in creating a mail merge document. To do so, you need only specify that FrontPage store the results of the form to a file with a .DOC extension.

Integrating FrontPage & Excel

Excel is Office 2000's spreadsheet application. Excel can be used to organize data into tables, charts, and graphs, and to perform calculations and operations on the data. Excel files are generally referred to as workbooks and have a .XLS file extension.

Copying from Excel to FrontPage

Just as with Word, the simplest way to share data between Excel and FrontPage is by copying and pasting from the clipboard. You can copy selected cells or charts to the clipboard and from the clipboard into FrontPage.

When copying and pasting table cells or charts through the clipboard, formatting is not preserved.

Saving Excel Documents as Web Documents

Just as Word 2000 allowed you to save a Word document as an HTML file, Excel 2000 allows you to save selected cells, sheets, or charts as Web pages, or to save an entire worksheet as a set of Web files. When selecting the latter option, Excel creates a frame-based Web page whose interface is similar to that of Excel. When you select **File ▶ Save As Web Page** in Excel, the **Save As** dialog box allows you several option as shown in Figure 20-4.

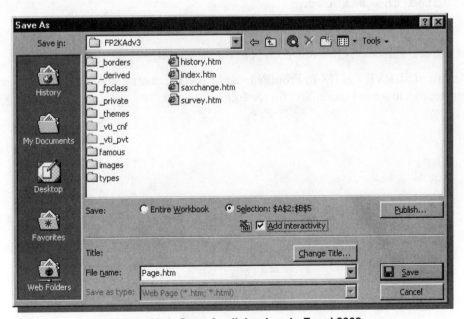

Figure 20-4: Save As dialog box in Excel 2000

- Entire workbook: saves the entire workbook, including all tables, charts, graphs, and worksheets as a set of files. Excel then creates a frames based page whose interface is similar to that of Excel.

- Selection: if you select a particular range of cells or a given chart before choosing the Save As Web Page option, you can elect to save only your selection as a Web document

- Add interactivity: enables you to create an interactive spreadsheet, in which visitors to your site can input their own data. This will be discussed in greater detail later in this lesson.

Once you save an Excel document as a Web document, you will need to import that document into FrontPage in order to edit the document using FrontPage.

Exercise 20-2: Integrating Excel and FrontPage

In this exercise, you will share information from an Excel document with FrontPage.

1. Open SURVEY.HTM in **Page** View, **Normal** tab and delete the shared border from the top of the page.

2. Insert the heading **Survey**. Beneath this heading, insert the text **In a previous survey we asked site visitors how many years they had studied the saxophone.**

3. Locate the file SURVEY1.XLS and open it in Excel.

4. In Sheet 2, select the chart and copy it to the clipboard.

5. Return to SURVEY.HTM in FrontPage and paste the chart below the text. Center the image, as shown in Figure 20-5 on the following page.

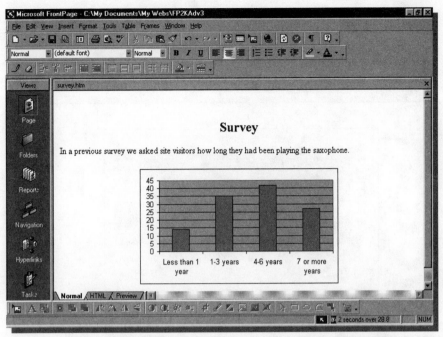

Figure 20-5: Excel chart pasted into FrontPage document

6. Save changes to SURVEY.HTM. Agree to save the embedded image file as SURVEY1.GIF in the IMAGES folder. Close the file.

7. Return to Excel, and select **File ▶ Save As Web Page**. Save the entire workbook as SURVEY1.HTM.

8. Select **File ▶ Web Page Preview**.

A frames-based web page with tabs for navigating among the worksheets is created, as shown in Figure 20-6 on the following page.

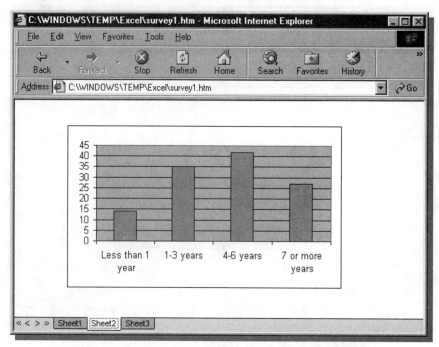

Figure 20-6: Excel worksheet saved as a Web Page

 If you select **View ▶ Source** on the resulting file, what you will see is called XML, the Extensible Markup Language. XML is a relatively new subset of SGML (Standard Generalized Markup Language), of which HTML is also a subset. XML is more flexible than HTML and allows for the creation of more dynamic and complex pages. The frames page created by Excel is created using XML. XML is well beyond the scope of this course. If you want to learn more about XML, see the World Wide Web Consortium's XML specifications at: www.w3.org/XML.

 If you wish to incorporate the imported workbook in your FrontPage web, you will need to Import all of the files that comprise the workbook.

9. Close Excel.

10. In FrontPage **Folders** View, select **File ▶ Import**. Select SURVEY1.HTM and the folder SURVEY1_FILES, as shown in Figure 20-7 on the following page. (Hint: Click **Add file** and then locate SURVEY1.HTM in C:\MY DOCUMENTS\MY WEBS\FPK2ADV; click **Add folder** and locate folder C:\MY DOCUMENTS\MY WEBS\FPK2ADV\SURVEY1_FILES.)

DDC Publishing • www.ddcpub.com

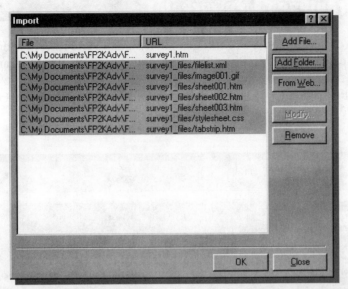

Figure 20-7: Importing the Excel-created Web page into FrontPage

 You should now be able to open SURVEY1.HTM in FrontPage. To do so, right-click on the file and choose **Open With** and select FrontPage. The resulting Frames page is shown in Figure 20-8.

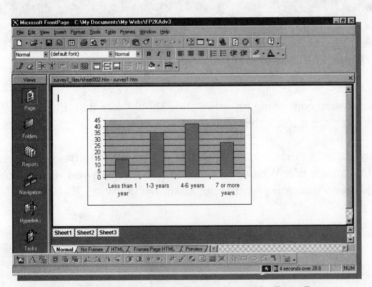

Figure 20-8: SURVEY1.HTM as viewed in FrontPage

Sending Data from FrontPage to Excel

Just as you can save form results to an Access database or to a Word document, so too can you save the results to an Excel workbook. To do so, you need only specify that FrontPage store the results of the form to a file with a .XLS extension.

Integrating FrontPage & PowerPoint

Just as you can use the **Save As Web Page** option in Word and Excel to convert documents to HTML, you can also do so in PowerPoint to convert slide shows into frames-based webs. As with Excel, this process creates a number of files and folders, including text and image files. The resulting files and folders do not work well when imported into FrontPage. Figure 20-9 shows a PowerPoint presentation converted to a Web page.

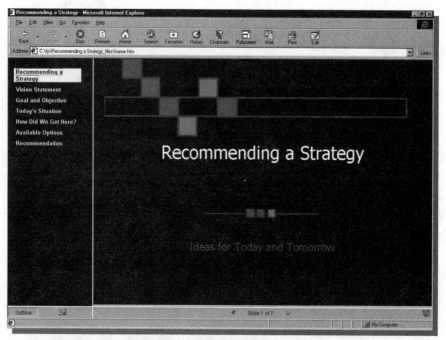

Figure 20-9: PowerPoint presentation converted to a Web page

This is sufficient when converting an entire slide show. Note that, like the converted Excel worksheet, the interface mimics that of PowerPoint.

If instead you want to import only a single slide, PowerPoint allows you to save a single slide as a JPEG or GIF image file. When you choose **Save As** in PowerPoint and choose one of these formats, PowerPoint will prompt you, as shown in Figure 20-10.

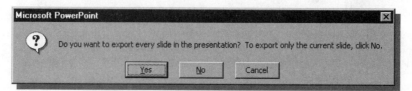

Figure 20-10: Exporting a single PowerPoint slide to JPEG or GIF format

Choosing **No** creates an image file containing only the slide in question. This image can then be incorporated into a FrontPage document.

Inserting Office Components

FrontPage also allows you to insert Office objects as components, not unlike the other FrontPage components you have already seen in Lesson 17 of this course. The Office components that can be used in FrontPage are:

- Office Spreadsheet

- Office PivotTable

- Office Chart

Only visitors with Office 2000 installed can use Office components. They will not work with Netscape browsers or with versions of Internet Explorer prior to IE 5. You can divert your visitors without IE 5 or better (and Office) to another page.

Office Spreadsheet Component

The Office Spreadsheet component allows users to enter data in a spreadsheet that can be set to perform calculations in real-time.

To insert an Office Spreadsheet component, select **Insert ▶ Component ▶ Office Spreadsheet**.

Spreadsheet properties can be adjusted in a number of ways. You can click and drag with the mouse to resize the spreadsheet object. You can also use the ActiveX Control properties dialog box to adjust several of the object's attributes, as shown in Figure 20-11.

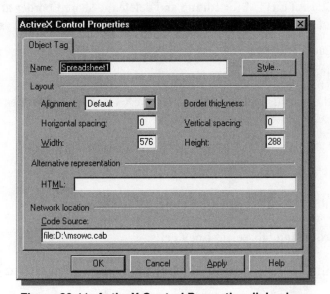

Figure 20-11: ActiveX Control Properties dialog box

- Name: name given to the object (necessary if the spreadsheet will be linked to an Office Chart)

- Width and Height: define the size of the spreadsheet (alternative to clicking and dragging)

- Alignment: as with other in-line images, defines text flow around the object

- Horizontal and Vertical spacing: used to define buffer between object and surrounding text

- Border thickness: defines the thickness of the border around the object

- HTML: URL for an alternative page that displays if a user's browser does not support the Office components

When creating the Spreadsheet object, you can use the Spreadsheet Property Toolbox just as you would in Excel to define the properties of individual cells.

Exercise 20-3: Inserting an Office Spreadsheet Component

In this exercise you will insert an Office Spreadsheet component and define its properties.

1. Open SAXCHANGE.HTM in **Page** View, **Normal** tab.

2. At the bottom of the page insert the text **Calculate your Sax's worth**. Create a hyperlink from this text to a new page, called CALCULATE.HTM.

3. Open CALCULATE.HTM for editing and delete the shared border at the top of the page. Set the title of this page as **Calculate the value of your sax**.

4. Insert the Header **Sax Value Calculator** at the top of the new page.

5. Insert an Office Spreadsheet Component.

6. Right-click the spreadsheet and choose **ActiveX Control Properties.** Set the name of the object to **SaxCalc**. Accept defaults for all other values.

7. In cell A1:

   - Insert the text **Years Owned**.

   - Right-click the cell and choose **Property Toolbox**.

   - In the **Protection** tab, select **Lock cells**.

   - In the **Title Bar** tab, change the title to **Saxophone Value Calculator**.

   - Close the **Property Toolbox**.

8. In cell A2:

   - Insert the text **Price at Purchase**.

   - Right-click the cell and choose **Property Toolbox**.

   - In the **Protection** tab, select **Lock cells**.

   - Close the **Property Toolbox**.

9. In cell A3:

   - Insert the text **Current value**.

   - Right-click the cell and choose **Property Toolbox**.

   - In the **Protection** tab, select **Lock cells**.

   - Close the **Property Toolbox**.

10. In cell B1:

    - Right-click the cell and choose **Property Toolbox**.

    - In the **Protection** tab, de-select **Lock cells**.

    - In the **Format** tab, set the **Number** format to **General Number**.

    - Close the **Property Toolbox.**

11. In cell B2:

    - Right-click the cell and choose **Property Toolbox**.

    - In the **Protection** tab, de-select **Lock cells**.

    - In the **Format** tab, set the **Number** format to **Currency**.

    - Close the **Property Toolbox.**

12. In cell B3:

    - Insert the formula **=B2-(B1*0.1*B2)**.

    - Right-click the cell and choose **Property Toolbox**.

    - In the **Protection** tab, de-select **Lock cells**.

    - In the **Format** tab, set the **Number** format to **Currency**.

- In the **Calculations** tab, set to **Automatic calculation**.

- Resize the columns so that all text is visible.

- In the **Show/Hide** tab, hide the toolbar, column headers, and row headers.

- Close the **Property Toolbox.**

13. Resize the spreadsheet so it displays only cells A1…C4.

14. Save the file and preview CALCULATE.HTM in your browser.

15. In your browser, type:

- **Years Owned**: 7

- **Price at Purchase**: $5000

 The resulting calculation appears, as shown in Figure 20-12.

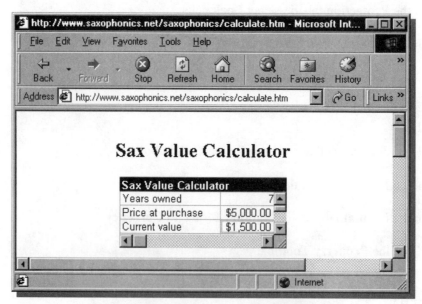

Figure 20-12: Office Spreadsheet component

Office Chart Component

The Office Chart component can be used in conjunction with the Office Spreadsheet component to create graphs and charts on the fly, based on data entered through the Spreadsheet component.

To insert an Office Chart component, select **Insert ▶ Component ▶ Office Chart**. This opens the first screen of the Office Chart Wizard, as shown in Figure 20-13.

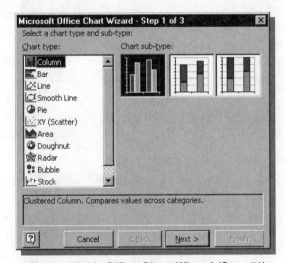

Figure 20-13: Office Chart Wizard (Step #1)

In this screen, you would select the type of chart, each of which has several sub-types.

The second screen of the Office Chart Wizard is displayed in Figure 20-14.

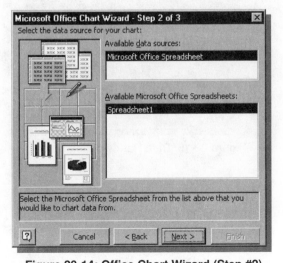

Figure 20-14: Office Chart Wizard (Step #2)

In this screen, you select the source of the data for the chart. This is defined by the **Name** attribute of the available Spreadsheets.

The third and final screen of the Office Chart Wizard is displayed in Figure 20-15.

Open Data
Range
dialog box →

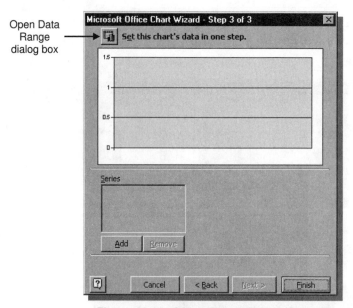

Figure 20-15: Office Chart Wizard (Step #3)

In this screen, you define the data from the spreadsheet that is to be graphed and can also define labels for the graph. Clicking the **Set this chart's data in one step** button opens the Data Range dialog box, as shown in Figure 20-16.

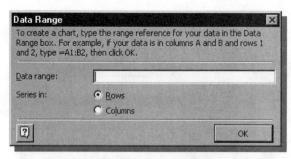

Figure 20-16: Data Range dialog box

Here you define specifically what data from your spreadsheet is to be charted. You would define a range of data cells and rows.

Exercise 20-4: Inserting an Office Chart Component

In this exercise, you will insert a chart that illustrates the depreciation of your instrument's value.

1. Open CALCULATE.HTM in **Page** View, **Normal** tab.

2. Insert your cursor below the Spreadsheet component and choose **Insert ▶ Component ▶ Office Chart**.

3. In the first screen of the Office Chart Wizard, select the **Column** chart type and the **Clustered Column** sub-type. Click **Next** to continue.

4. In the second screen of the Office Chart Wizard, select the **SaxCalc** object from the available spreadsheets (this should be the only choice). Click **Next** to continue.

5. In the third screen of the Office Chart Wizard, click the **Set this chart's data in one step** button.

6. Enter the formula **=A2:B3** for the Data range. Select to display the Series in **Columns**. Click **OK** to continue.

7. Click **Finish**.

8. Save the changes to calculate the following data and preview CALCULATOR.HTM in your browser.

    -   Enter **7** for **Years Owned**

    -   Enter **$5000** for **Price at Purchase**

 The chart will automatically display the values for the price at purchase and the current value, as shown in Figure 20-17 on the following page.

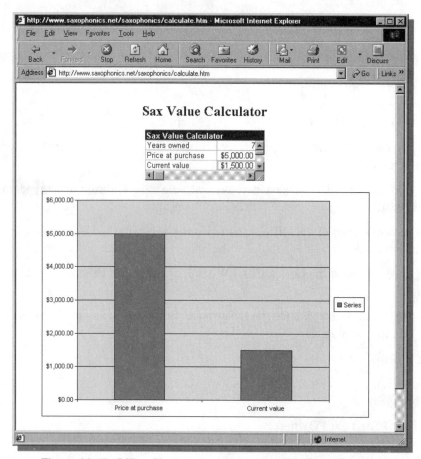

Figure 20-17: Office Chart component as previewed in browser

Office PivotTable Component

The third and final Office component that can be inserted into a FrontPage document is the PivotTable. This is the most complex of the three components. PivotTables summarize data from a table based on different criteria.

 If you had a table that showed you had 500 saxophones in stock, by type and by brand, a PivotTable could be used to summarize the total number of alto saxes, regardless of brand, or the total number of Selmer saxes, regardless of type.

Lesson Summary

▶ As you have already seen in Lesson 18: *Web Databases*, FrontPage is designed to work well with the other Microsoft Office programs. Files may be easily shared between Access, Word, Excel, PowerPoint, and FrontPage.

▶ Word documents are text documents. They have the .DOC filename extension.

▶ Excel documents are spreadsheets. They have the .XLS filename extension.

▶ PowerPoint documents are slide presentations. They have the .PPT filename extension.

▶ You can use the Clipboard to copy and paste from Word and Excel documents into FrontPage (and vice versa). This is generally the easiest method of moving data between these applications.

▶ You can also use the **Save As Web Page** function in Word, Excel, and PowerPoint. The resulting file(s) can then be imported into your FrontPage web. However, the HTML formatting used in this method is not always perfect, and you may need to "clean up" the code in FrontPage. This is especially true for PowerPoint files.

▶ When creating FrontPage forms, in addition to the standard choices, you can also choose to save form results as either a Word or Excel file. To do this, when selecting the name of the file to store the results, use the corresponding filename extension (.DOC or .XLS).

▶ Office components are similar to FrontPage components. They are mini-programs that perform certain functions within your Web pages.

▶ There are three Office components: Office Spreadsheet, Office Chart, and Office PivotTable.

▶ The Office Spreadsheet component allows your site visitors to perform real-time calculations.

▶ The Office Chart component creates charts and graphs based on the Office Spreadsheet Component.

▶ The Office PivotTable component is a complex tool that summarizes spreadsheet data into a table, based on custom queries.

▶ To use the Office components, your Web site visitors must have both Internet Explorer 5.0 and Office 2000 installed on their personal computers.

Lesson Review

Matching

___ 1. Filename extension for an Excel spreadsheet

a. Office Spreadsheet component

___ 2. Interactive spreadsheet program in a Web page

b. .PPT

___ 3. Filename extension for a PowerPoint presentation

c. Office 2000

___ 4. Microsoft's suite of integrated applications

d. .XLS

___ 5. Summarizes spreadsheet data into a table

e. Office PivotTable component

Fill in the Blank

6. Four Microsoft Office programs may be integrated with FrontPage: _____, _____, _____, and _____.

7. _____ _____ _____ is used to create charts and graphs from the Office Spreadsheet component.

8. Word, Excel, and PowerPoint all have the _____ _____ _____ _____ option, which allows you to save a file in HTML format.

True or False?

T / F 9. Users must have IE 5.0 and Office 2000 to use the Office components on your Web site.

T / F 10. Cutting and pasting to and from the Clipboard is generally the easiest method of sharing data between Office applications.

Lesson 21
FrontPage
Reports

Lesson Topics:

- ► FrontPage Reports

- ► Site Summary Report

- ► Detailed Reports

- ► Using Reports

- ► Lesson Summary

FrontPage Reports

One of FrontPage 2000's strengths is its reports capability. The built-in reporting functions enable you to effectively manage your site's content. FrontPage Reports are especially useful if you have a complex site.

Reports View

You can access FrontPage Reports through **Reports** View, one of the six FrontPage views. (You have already worked extensively with **Page** View and **Navigation** View throughout this *Mastering FrontPage 2000* series.)

When you select **Reports** View within an open FrontPage web, you will be presented with the **Site Summary** Report, as shown in Figure 21-1.

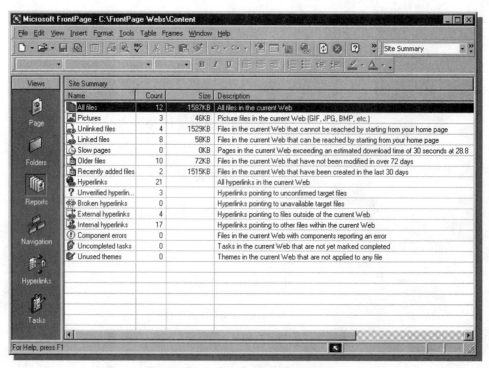

Figure 21-1: Site Summary Report

From the Site Summary Report, you can then generate detailed reports. To switch between reports, select **View ▶ Reports** from the main menu. Each of these report types and their features will be discussed in this lesson.

Report Options

You have some control over certain report settings. To change your Reports, select **Tools** ▶ **Options** ▶ **Reports View** tab. The **Reports** View tab is shown in Figure 21-2.

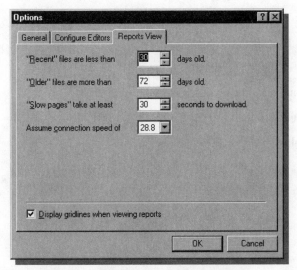

Figure 21-2: Reports View Options

You can modify the following:

- The maximum age, in days, of a "recent file"

- The minimum age, in days, of an "older file"

- The minimum download time, in seconds, of a "slow page"

- The connection speed to use for calculating download time

- The appearance of gridlines in your Reports

Exercise 21-1: Setting Reports View Options

In this exercise, you will configure the options available for **Reports** View.

1. Open your published *Saxophonics* (FP2K) web in FrontPage.
2. Select **Tools ▶ Options ▶ Reports View** tab.
3. Define **Recent files** as less than 7 days old.
4. Define **Older files** as more than 15 days old.
5. Define **Slow pages** as taking at least 15 seconds to download.
6. Assume **Connection speed** of 28.8.
7. Choose to display gridlines.
8. Click **OK**.

Site Summary Report

The Site Summary Report, as the name suggests, provides a broad overview of your FrontPage web's status, including file counts, file sizes, hyperlinks, etc.

Most of the Site Summary line items link to detailed reports, which will be discussed in the next section of this lesson.

As mentioned in the previous section, the Site Summary Report becomes available when you select **Reports** View. The Site Summary Report is shown in Figure 21-3.

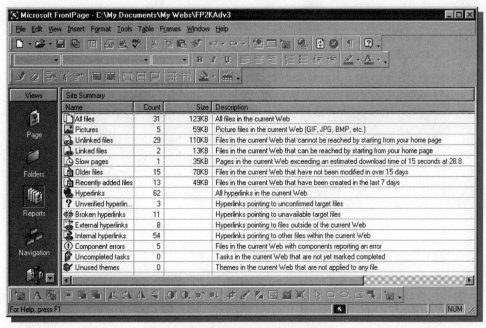

Figure 21-3: Site Summary Report

Detailed Reports

Most of the Site Summary line items can be expanded into detailed reports. To create these detailed reports, simply double-click the corresponding line item within the Site Summary. You can also use the Reports drop-down list that appears on the Standard toolbar when **Reports** View is selected, as shown in Figure 21-4.

All Files

The **All Files** Report provides the following details for all files in your FrontPage web:

Name	Title	In Folder
Orphan	Size	Type
Modified Date	Modified By	Comments

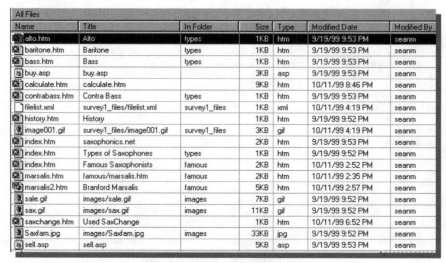

Name	Title	In Folder	Size	Type	Modified Date	Modified By
alto.htm	Alto	types	1KB	htm	9/19/99 9:53 PM	seanm
baritone.htm	Baritone	types	1KB	htm	9/19/99 9:53 PM	seanm
bass.htm	Bass	types	1KB	htm	9/19/99 9:53 PM	seanm
buy.asp	buy.asp		3KB	asp	9/19/99 9:53 PM	seanm
calculate.htm	calculate.htm		9KB	htm	10/11/99 8:46 PM	seanm
contrabass.htm	Contra Bass	types	1KB	htm	9/19/99 9:53 PM	seanm
filelist.xml	survey1_files/filelist.xml	survey1_files	1KB	xml	10/11/99 4:19 PM	seanm
history.htm	History		1KB	htm	9/19/99 9:52 PM	seanm
image001.gif	survey1_files/image001.gif	survey1_files	3KB	gif	10/11/99 4:19 PM	seanm
index.htm	saxophonics.net		2KB	htm	9/19/99 9:53 PM	seanm
index.htm	Types of Saxophones	types	1KB	htm	9/19/99 9:52 PM	seanm
index.htm	Famous Saxophonists	famous	2KB	htm	10/11/99 2:52 PM	seanm
marsalis.htm	famous/marsalis.htm	famous	2KB	htm	10/11/99 2:35 PM	seanm
marsalis2.htm	Branford Marsalis	famous	5KB	htm	10/11/99 2:57 PM	seanm
sale.gif	images/sale.gif	images	7KB	gif	9/19/99 9:52 PM	seanm
sax.gif	images/sax.gif	images	11KB	gif	9/19/99 9:52 PM	seanm
saxchange.htm	Used SaxChange		1KB	htm	10/11/99 6:52 PM	seanm
Saxfam.jpg	images/Saxfam.jpg	images	33KB	jpg	9/19/99 9:52 PM	seanm
sell.asp	sell.asp		5KB	asp	9/19/99 9:53 PM	seanm

Figure 21-4: All Files Report

Recently Added Files

The **Recently Added Files** Report, shown in Figure 21-5, includes files added since the date you set in your Reports Options. The Report includes the following information:

- Name

- Title

- Created Date

- Modified By

- Size

- Type

- In Folder

Name	Title	Created Date	Modified By	Size	Type	In Folder
marsalis.htm	famous/marsalis.htm	10/11/99 2:26 PM	seanm	2KB	htm	famous
marsalis2.htm	Branford Marsalis	10/11/99 2:57 PM	seanm	5KB	htm	famous
survey1.gif	images/survey1.gif	10/11/99 3:54 PM	seanm	4KB	gif	images
image001.gif	survey1_files/image001.gif	10/11/99 4:19 PM	seanm	3KB	gif	survey1_files
filelist.xml	survey1_files/filelist.xml	10/11/99 4:19 PM	seanm	1KB	xml	survey1_files
tabstrip.htm	survey1_files/tabstrip.htm	10/11/99 4:19 PM	seanm	1KB	htm	survey1_files
sheet001.htm	survey1_files/sheet001.htm	10/11/99 4:19 PM	seanm	3KB	htm	survey1_files
sheet002.htm	survey1_files/sheet002.htm	10/11/99 4:19 PM	seanm	8KB	htm	survey1_files
sheet003.htm	survey1_files/sheet003.htm	10/11/99 4:19 PM	seanm	2KB	htm	survey1_files
stylesheet.css	survey1_files/stylesheet.css	10/11/99 4:19 PM	seanm	1KB	css	survey1_files
survey1.htm	survey1.htm	10/11/99 4:19 PM	seanm	11KB	htm	
calculate.htm	calculate.htm	10/11/99 5:56 PM	seanm	9KB	htm	
stock.htm	New Page 1	10/11/99 9:10 PM	seanm	1KB	htm	

Figure 21-5: Recently Added Files detailed report

Recently Changed Files

The **Recently Changed Files** Report, shown in Figure 21-6, includes files modified since the date you specified in your Reports Options. It uses the same data categories as the **Recently Added Files** Report, except the **Created Date** data is replaced with **Modified Date**.

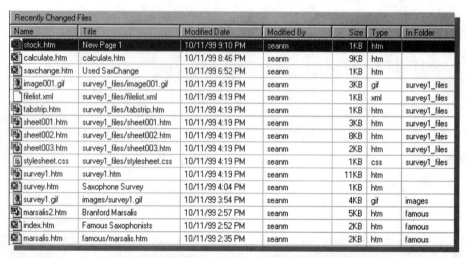

Name	Title	Modified Date	Modified By	Size	Type	In Folder
stock.htm	New Page 1	10/11/99 9:10 PM	seanm	1KB	htm	
calculate.htm	calculate.htm	10/11/99 8:46 PM	seanm	9KB	htm	
saxchange.htm	Used SaxChange	10/11/99 6:52 PM	seanm	1KB	htm	
image001.gif	survey1_files/image001.gif	10/11/99 4:19 PM	seanm	3KB	gif	survey1_files
filelist.xml	survey1_files/filelist.xml	10/11/99 4:19 PM	seanm	1KB	xml	survey1_files
tabstrip.htm	survey1_files/tabstrip.htm	10/11/99 4:19 PM	seanm	1KB	htm	survey1_files
sheet001.htm	survey1_files/sheet001.htm	10/11/99 4:19 PM	seanm	3KB	htm	survey1_files
sheet002.htm	survey1_files/sheet002.htm	10/11/99 4:19 PM	seanm	8KB	htm	survey1_files
sheet003.htm	survey1_files/sheet003.htm	10/11/99 4:19 PM	seanm	2KB	htm	survey1_files
stylesheet.css	survey1_files/stylesheet.css	10/11/99 4:19 PM	seanm	1KB	css	survey1_files
survey1.htm	survey1.htm	10/11/99 4:19 PM	seanm	11KB	htm	
survey.htm	Saxophone Survey	10/11/99 4:04 PM	seanm	1KB	htm	
survey1.gif	images/survey1.gif	10/11/99 3:54 PM	seanm	4KB	gif	images
marsalis2.htm	Branford Marsalis	10/11/99 2:57 PM	seanm	5KB	htm	famous
index.htm	Famous Saxophonists	10/11/99 2:52 PM	seanm	2KB	htm	famous
marsalis.htm	famous/marsalis.htm	10/11/99 2:35 PM	seanm	2KB	htm	famous

Figure 21-6: Recently Changed Files Report

Older Files

The **Older Files** Report, shown in Figure 21-7, uses the same data categories as the **Recently Changed Files** Report, but it includes files not modified since the date you set in your Reports Options.

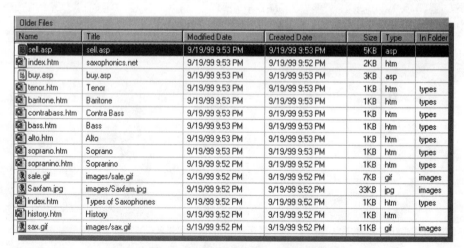

Name	Title	Modified Date	Created Date	Size	Type	In Folder
sell.asp	sell.asp	9/19/99 9:53 PM	9/19/99 9:53 PM	5KB	asp	
index.htm	saxophonics.net	9/19/99 9:53 PM	9/19/99 9:52 PM	2KB	htm	
buy.asp	buy.asp	9/19/99 9:53 PM	9/19/99 9:53 PM	3KB	asp	
tenor.htm	Tenor	9/19/99 9:53 PM	9/19/99 9:53 PM	1KB	htm	types
baritone.htm	Baritone	9/19/99 9:53 PM	9/19/99 9:53 PM	1KB	htm	types
contrabass.htm	Contra Bass	9/19/99 9:53 PM	9/19/99 9:53 PM	1KB	htm	types
bass.htm	Bass	9/19/99 9:53 PM	9/19/99 9:53 PM	1KB	htm	types
alto.htm	Alto	9/19/99 9:53 PM	9/19/99 9:53 PM	1KB	htm	types
soprano.htm	Soprano	9/19/99 9:53 PM	9/19/99 9:53 PM	1KB	htm	types
sopranino.htm	Sopranino	9/19/99 9:52 PM	9/19/99 9:52 PM	1KB	htm	types
sale.gif	images/sale.gif	9/19/99 9:52 PM	9/19/99 9:52 PM	7KB	gif	images
Saxfam.jpg	images/Saxfam.jpg	9/19/99 9:52 PM	9/19/99 9:52 PM	33KB	jpg	images
index.htm	Types of Saxophones	9/19/99 9:52 PM	9/19/99 9:52 PM	1KB	htm	types
history.htm	History	9/19/99 9:52 PM	9/19/99 9:52 PM	1KB	htm	
sax.gif	images/sax.gif	9/19/99 9:52 PM	9/19/99 9:52 PM	11KB	gif	images

Figure 21-7: Older Files Report

Unlinked Files

The **Unlinked Files** Report, shown in Figure 21-8, also uses the same data categories as the **Recently Changed Files** and **Older Files** Reports. However, it presents information on files that are not linked to by any other files in your FrontPage web.

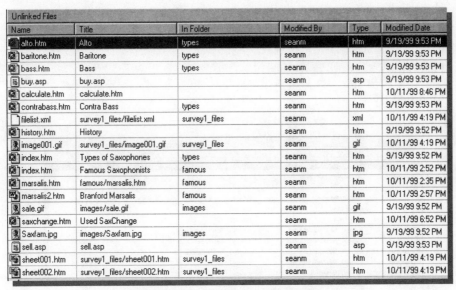

Figure 21-8: Unlinked Files Report

Slow Pages

The **Slow Pages** Report, shown in Figure 21-9, provides the following data for files that download more slowly than the speed you specified in your Reports Options:

- Name
- Title
- Download Time
- Size
- Type
- In Folder
- Modified Date

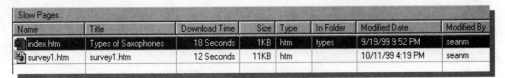

Figure 21-9: Slow Pages Report

Broken Hyperlinks

The **Broken Hyperlinks** Report, shown in Figure 21-10, provides the following information regarding hyperlinks to pages that are no longer available:

- Status

- Hyperlink

- In Page

- Page Title

- Modified By

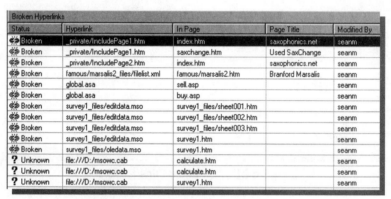

Figure 21-10: Broken Hyperlinks Report

Component Errors

The **Component Errors** Report, shown in Figure 21-11, provides the following information regarding FrontPage components that do not work correctly:

- Name

- Title

- Errors

- Type

- In Folder

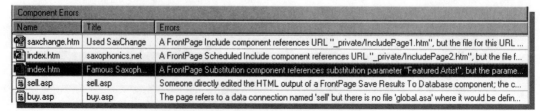

Figure 21-11: Component Errors Report

Review Status

The **Review Status** Report, shown in Figure 21-12, provides the following details regarding pages in your FrontPage web:

- Name

- Title

- Review Status

- Assigned To

- Review Date

- Reviewed By

- Type

- In Folder

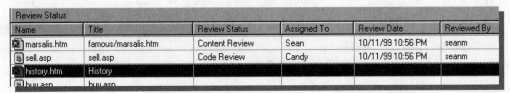

Figure 21-12: Review Status Report

Assigned To

The **Assigned To** Report, shown in Figure 21-13, provides the following details regarding file assignments:

- Name

- Title

- Assigned To

- Assigned Date

- Assigned By

- Comments

- Type

- In Folder

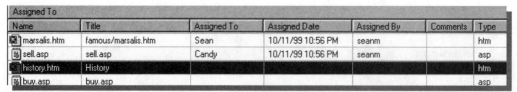

Name	Title	Assigned To	Assigned Date	Assigned By	Comments	Type
marsalis.htm	famous/marsalis.htm	Sean	10/11/99 10:56 PM	seanm		htm
sell.asp	sell.asp	Candy	10/11/99 10:56 PM	seanm		asp
history.htm	History					htm
buy.asp	buy.asp					asp

Figure 21-13: Assigned To Report

Categories

The **Categories** Report, shown in Figure 21-14, includes the following data about files in the web that have been assigned to categories:

- Name

- Title

- Category

- Type

- In Folder

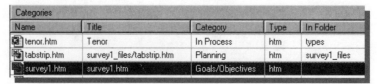

Name	Title	Category	Type	In Folder
tenor.htm	Tenor	In Process	htm	types
tabstrip.htm	survey1_files/tabstrip.htm	Planning	htm	survey1_files
survey1.htm	survey1.htm	Goals/Objectives	htm	

Figure 21-14: Categories Report

Publish Status

The **Publish Status** Report, shown in Figure 21-15, provides the following details about all the pages in your FrontPage web:

- Name

- Title

- Publish

- Modified Date

- Review Status

- Size

- Type

- In Folder

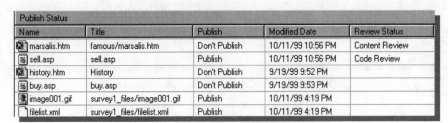

Figure 21-15: Publish Status Report

Checkout Status

If you are have enabled source control, you can use the **Checkout Status** Report, shown in Figure 21-16, to keep track of your documents. This Report contains the following data:

- Name

- Title

- Checked Out By

- Version

- Locked Date

- Type

- In Folder

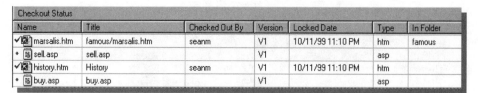

Name	Title	Checked Out By	Version	Locked Date	Type	In Folder
✓ marsalis.htm	famous/marsalis.htm	seanm	V1	10/11/99 11:10 PM	htm	famous
sell.asp	sell.asp		V1		asp	
✓ history.htm	History	seanm	V1	10/11/99 11:10 PM	htm	
buy.asp	buy.asp		V1		asp	

Figure 21-16: Checkout Status Report

Using Reports

FrontPage Reports are available so you can improve your site. As your site grows and changes, you will want to ensure that the quality of the site remains constant. Running Reports from time to time can assist you in managing your site.

Exercise 21-2: Generating Reports

In this exercise, you will take a look at some of the detailed reports for your FrontPage web, and use them to make changes, if necessary.

1. Open your published *Saxophonics* (FP2K) web in FrontPage.
2. Select **Reports** View.
3. Open the **Broken Hyperlinks** Report. If there are any broken hyperlinks, repair them.
4. Switch to the **Component Errors** Report by selecting **View ▶ Reports ▶ Component Errors**. If there are any component errors, investigate them and make changes if necessary.

Lesson Summary

▶ FrontPage Reports are accessed via **Reports** View.

▶ When **Reports** View is selected, the default is the Site Summary Report.

▶ The Site Summary Report contains data on the number and size of files, number and validity of hyperlinks, and other line items.

▶ Most of the line items in the Site Summary Report can be selected to generate a detailed report.

▶ Detailed reports are also accessible via the Reports menu within the main toolbar.

▶ There are thirteen detailed reports in FrontPage: All Files, Recently Added Files, Recently Changed Files, Older Files, Unlinked Files, Slow Pages, Broken hyperlinks, Component Errors, Review Status, Assigned To, Categories, Publish Status, and Checkout Status.

▶ Report Options may be modified through the **Tools** ▶ **Options** ▶ **Reports View** tab.

▶ You should use Reports to maintain the integrity of your Web site.

▶ You may switch between Reports by selecting **View** ▶ **Reports** from the main menu.

Lesson Review

Matching

_____ 1. FrontPage view that provides information about the status of your web

a. Broken hyperlinks

_____ 2. Detailed report only available if source control is enabled

b. Site Summary

_____ 3. Detailed report used to correct hyperlinks

c. Reports View

_____ 4. FrontPage's basic Report

d. Component Errors

_____ 5. Detailed report that tests FrontPage components

e. Checkout Status

Fill in the Blank

6. _____ _____ is the starting point for generating FrontPage Reports.

7. The _____ _____ Report lists files that are not linked to by any other pages in your FrontPage web.

8. You can keep track of which files have been published using the _____ _____ Report.

True or False?

_T / F_   9. The Slow Pages detailed report always assumes a connection speed of 14.4 bps.

_T / F_   10. A FrontPage web must be open in order to generate Reports for it.

_T / F_   11. All Site Summary Report line items link to detailed reports.

DDC Publishing • www.ddcpub.com

Lesson 22
Site Management
& Administration

Lesson Topics

► Managing Your Site with Tasks

► Review Status & Categories

► Enabling Source Control

► Setting Browser Compatibility

► Subwebs

► Security in FrontPage 2000

► Lesson Summary

Managing Your Site with Tasks

As you learned in Lesson 21: *FrontPage Reports*, FrontPage 2000 provides an assortment of tools that help you keep track of all of the details involved in managing a Web site. Such Reports let you see the status of what you've done. In this lesson, you will learn how *Tasks* help you maintain control over what has yet to be done.

 You can create a Task in **Page**, **Folders**, **Reports**, **Navigation**, or **Tasks** View.

Tasks View Basics

You can think of a Task as a type of interactive To-Do-List. As you will learn in this lesson, when it comes to the Task options available, FrontPage offers a lot of flexibility, control, and interactivity among project members and leaders. Tasks help you to track what work needs to be done on your site, who is responsible for it, and when it is completed.

When you use a wizard to create a web, FrontPage automatically adds a list of immediate Tasks for that web, as shown in Figure 22-1. Note that the default **Assigned To** information varies, as shown in Table 22-1 on the following page.

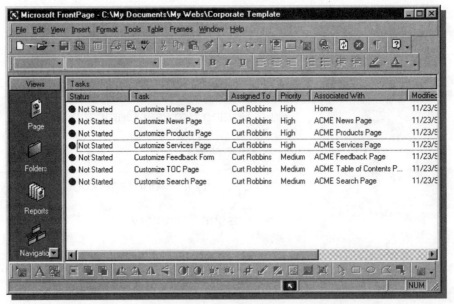

Figure 22-1: A wizard-created Task list shown in Tasks View

Task columns	Description
Status	Shows whether a Task is In Progress, Completed, or Not Started
Task	The description of the Task to be performed
Assigned To	Display of who is responsible for completing the Task. By default, FrontPage will show what it believes to be the name of the Web Administrator. In some cases this may default to the name of the company that built your computer and installed your version of Windows.
Priority	Shows user-assigned priority levels of High, Medium, or Low
Associated With	Displays the page or file associations for the Task
Modified Date	Shows the date and time of the last edit
Description	An explanation of the Task

Table 22-1: Tasks View column descriptions

No Tasks

If you do not use a wizard to create your web, no Tasks are assigned. It is up to you, as the site administrator, to create Tasks and assign them to the members of the team that will be building and maintaining your site. In this case, the **Tasks** View appears initially as a blank slate.

Creating a Task

Now that you know that you should create a series of Tasks to help you track the progress of your work and remind you of work you need to do, you need to know the steps involved in doing this. You can create Tasks using the methods listed below:

- Choose **Edit ▶ Tasks ▶ Add Task**. This option works in any view. If you use this option while in **Page** View, FrontPage automatically associates the Task with the file you have open.

- From **Tasks** View, right-click the **Information Viewer** and choose **New Task**.

- From **Folder** View, right-click on the filename to which you wish to assign a Task. Choose **Add Task** from the resulting menu.

- Click the down arrow to the right of the **New Page** icon and choose **Task**.

Any of these options will bring up the **New Task** dialog box, as shown in Figure 22-2.

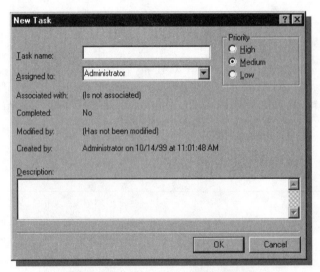

Figure 22-2: New Task dialog box

Using the **New Task** dialog box, you can set the following parameters:

- <u>Task name</u>: a short name used to identify the Task

- <u>Assigned to</u>: name of the team member responsible for a particular Task

- <u>Priority</u>: relative importance of a given Task; may be High, Medium, or Low

- <u>Description</u>: a longer explanation of the selected Task

Choosing Your Tasks

Determining which Tasks to add does not have to be a daunting chore. For example, you can preview your FrontPage Reports to see what has yet to be completed on your web. You can see from the Site Summary Report, shown in Figure 22-3, that the user has not yet verified the 4,458 hyperlinks on the Web site. That is one obvious need for a Task.

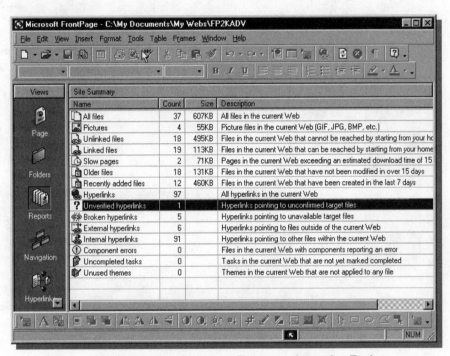

Figure 22-3: Using Site Summary Report to determine Tasks

From Folders View

Another way to determine what Tasks remain is to view the web in **Folders** View, as shown in Figure 22-4. There you can select the filename of a page or pages that you know needs updating or refinement.

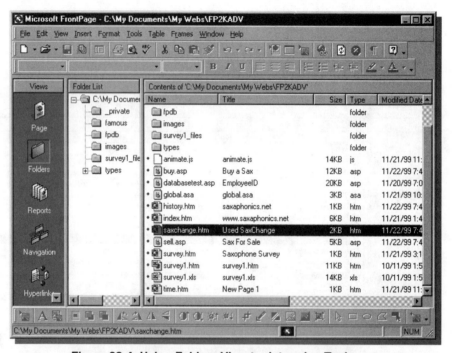

Figure 22-4: Using Folders View to determine Tasks

Other Methods

Other ways to trigger ideas for the Tasks you need to add to your web are:

- Check your IMAGES folder for any graphics that may need to be edited.

- Search the appropriate folders within your MY DOCUMENTS folder for any files in Word or other Microsoft Office applications that need to be edited or imported into your web.

- View your Calendar in Outlook for any upcoming status meetings or reports that are due.

Completing a Task

Once you have determined your Tasks and assigned personnel and priorities, you will want to get to work on completing the Tasks.

In **Tasks** View, double-click on a task to open it. When the task is associated with a file, FrontPage automatically adds a **Start Task** button to the resulting **Task Details** dialog box shown in Figure 22-5. Click **Start Task** to begin your work.

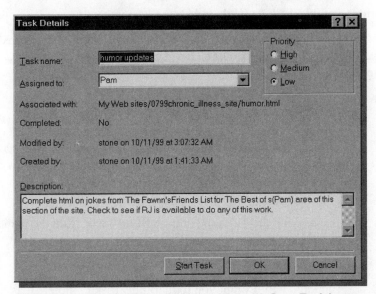

Figure 22-5: The Task Details dialog box with Start Task button

When you begin work on a Task in this manner, FrontPage gives you the option of marking the Task completed when you save the page or file.

Once you have a Task associated with a file or Web page, it is a good idea to start your work on that Task in **Task** View. That way you can have FrontPage update the status on it for you.

Editing a Task

The only constant in your workday is change. There will be times when such changes will affect your Tasks list: new team member assignments, departing team members, updated deadlines, etc. FrontPage allows you to edit any of the Task properties assigned in the **New Task** dialog box. To edit a Task, you can click the Task to select it, then select **File ▶ Properties**.

Exercise 22-1: Creating and Completing a Task

In this exercise, you will create and assign a task for your web.

1. Open the *Saxophonics* web in **Folders** View.

2. Open the FAMOUS folder and right-click INDEX.HTM.

3. Select **Add Task**. Create a Task and name it `Add CPD to list`.

4. Set the priority of this Task as **High** and assign it to yourself.

5. In the **Description** field, type `Add Sean Flannery and Ian Early from the Cherry Poppin' Daddies to the list of famous saxophonists.`

6. Click **OK** to add the Task.

 If you switch to **Tasks** View, you will note that this Task has been added to the list with a status of **Not Started**.

7. In **Tasks** View, right-click the Task and choose **Start Task**. Add the names to the list and save.

 FrontPage will prompt you to mark the Task completed, as shown in Figure 22-6.

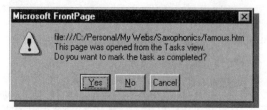

Figure 22-6: Prompt to mark Task completed

8. Choose **Yes** to mark the Task completed.

 When you return to **Tasks** View, you will see that the Task now displays a status of **Completed**.

Review Status & Categories

The **Tasks** View is only one way FrontPage assists in the administration of your site. There are several other tools that can assist in tracking the management of your FrontPage web. Among these tools are:

- Review Status

- Categories

Review Status

Review Status allows you to determine whether a given file is ready to be published. You may have several authors working on different parts of the Web site. Before publishing a file, you may require that it go through some review, to ensure that files published to your Web site meet a certain standard.

By default, FrontPage allows four types of **Review Status**:

- Code Review

- Content Review

- Legal Review

- Manager Review

You can add additional Review Status types if you so desire. Each Review Status type does not hold any intrinsic meaning to FrontPage, so you can assign any meaning to them you desire.

Setting File Review Status

You can set the Review Status of a file in three ways:

1. With the file open, right-click anywhere in the page and select **Page Properties**. Click the **Workgroup** tab and choose a Review Status from the drop-down menu, as shown in Figure 22-7.

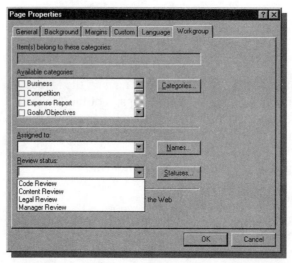

Figure 22-7: Selecting a Review Status for a file

2. If the file is closed, right-click the filename in **Folders** View and select **Properties**. Click the **Workgroup** tab and proceed as above.

3. Set the Review Status for any file using the Review Status Report. Select the Review Status Report from the Reports toolbar and click Review Status field for the appropriate file. You can then choose a Review Status code from the Review Status Master List or add your own custom status code, as shown in Figure 22-8.

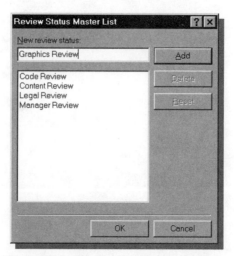

Figure 22-8: Review Status Master List

Categories

Categories can be used to classify the various files of your Web site into particular groups. You can then use these Categories to manage your files or to insert a list of files of a given Category onto a page. This is useful in developing a Site Map.

By default, FrontPage includes the following Categories:

Business	Competition	Expense Report
Goals / Objectives	Ideas	In Process
Miscellaneous	Planning	Schedule
Travel	VIP	Waiting

Add Your Own

Similar to Review Status codes, you can add custom Category types. The Categories themselves do not hold any intrinsic meaning to FrontPage, so you can assign any meaning to them that you require.

Setting the Category of a File

Setting a file's Category is very similar to setting its Review Status. A Web page may fall into more than one Category.

To set a Category on an open file, right-click anywhere in the page and select **Page Properties**. Click the **Workgroup** tab and choose a Category from the menu, as shown in Figure 22-9 on the following page.

If the file is closed, right-click the filename in **Folders** View and select **Properties**. Click the Workgroup tab and proceed as above. You can configure the Category for multiple files simultaneously by selecting all of the files in question in **Folders** View (hold <SHIFT> for a contiguous list, <CTRL> for discontiguous files), right-clicking any filename, and proceeding as described above.

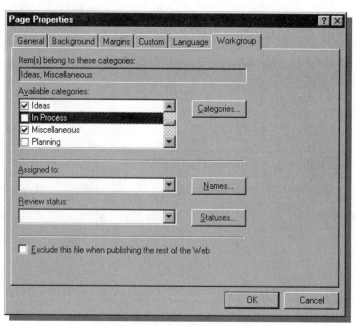

Figure 22-9: Categorizing a file

Adding Additional Categories to the Master List

As with Review Status codes, you can add additional Categories to the Master List. To do so, select the **Categories** button from the **Workgroup** tab of the **Page Properties** dialog box, as shown in Figure 22-9. This opens the **Master Category List**, as shown in Figure 22-10.

Figure 22-10: Master Category List

Exercise 22-2: Categorizing Your Files

In this exercise, you will create and set Categories for the pages in your FrontPage Web.

1. In **Folders** View, select BUY.ASP, CALCULATE.HTM, and SELL.ASP.

2. Right-click and select **Properties**. Choose the **Workgroup** tab.

3. Click **Categories**. Create a new Category titled **Sax Exchange Files**. Click **ADD** and then click **OK** to close the dialog box.

4. Select **Sax Exchange Files** from the Categories menu, as shown in Figure 22-11.

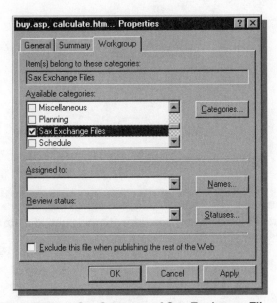

Figure 22-11: Set Category of Sax Exchange Files

5. Click **OK** to close the **Page Properties** dialog box.

6. Open SAXCHANGE.HTM for editing.

7. Delete the following text: "Buy a Saxophone," "Sell a Saxophone," "Calculate your Sax's worth."

8. In place of that text, select **Insert ▶ Component ▶ Categories**.

9. Select **Sax Exchange Files** and click **OK**.

10. Save these changes and preview SAXCHANGE.HTM in your browser.

The Categories component automatically inserts the names of the files in the Category, as shown in Figure 22-12.

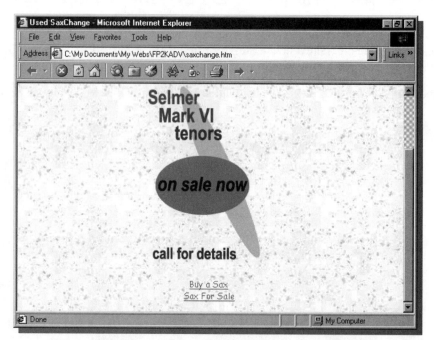

Figure 22-12: Category component previewed in a browser

You can modify the titles of these pages in the **Page Properties** dialog box of each page to make the titles more descriptive.

Enabling Source Control

Work done on a networked system – such as an Intranet or a web or Web site project – can pose problems which you must anticipate in advance. For example, suppose two different people each have an assigned Task involving the same page. You can avoid this potential conflict by enabling the Check-in/Check-out feature in FrontPage.

The *Document Check-In/Check-Out* feature prevents more than one user from opening and editing a document at the same time. When the feature is enabled, it requires users to "check out" a document before they can edit it. Once a document is "checked-out" by a particular user, no other user can "check-out" the same document.

Enabling Document Check-in/Check-out

To enable the Document Check-in/Check-out feature, select **Tools ▶ Web Settings**. This opens the **Web Settings** dialog box, as shown in Figure 22-13.

Enable document check-in and check-out

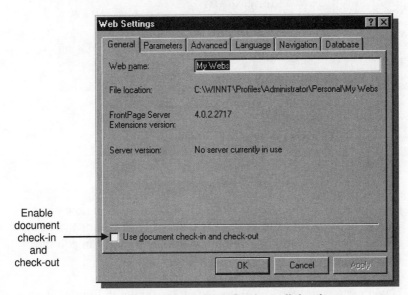

Figure 22-13: Web Settings dialog box

At the bottom left corner of the **General** tab of the **Web Settings** dialog box, you will note a check box for enabling document check-in and check-out.

Exercise 22-3: Enabling the Check-in/Check-out Feature

In this exercise, you will enable the FrontPage Check-in/Check-out feature using the **Web Settings** dialog box.

1. If it is not already, open the *Saxophonics* web.

2. Choose **Tools** ▶ **Web Settings**. (This option works in any view.)

3. At the bottom of the **Web Settings** dialog box, **General** tab, click the **Use document check-in and check-out** check box.

4. Choose **Apply**.

5. In the resulting warning box, click **Yes** to apply the setting, as shown in Figure 22-14.

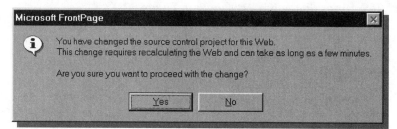

Figure 22-14: Warning dialog box

6. Click **OK**.

Once you enable the Check-in/Check-out feature, you now have what FrontPage refers to as **Source control**. This means that in an environment with multiple authors, only one person can edit the file at a time.

If you view your web in **Folders** View, as shown in Figure 22-15 on the following page, you will note that there is now an indicator next to each file name:

- a dot (•) indicates that the file is not checked out

- a check (✓) indicates that you have checked out the file

- a padlock (🔒) indicates that another user has checked out the file

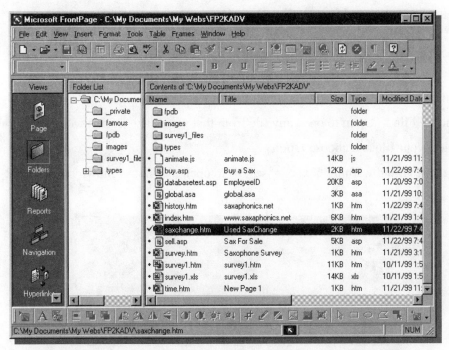

Figure 22-15: Check-in/Check-out Status indicated in Folders View

Remember: for the Check-in/Check-out feature to work with published pages or a published web, your Web server must support (and have installed) FrontPage Server Extensions.

Checking Out a Document

Once the Document Check-In/Check-Out feature is enabled, FrontPage will require that documents be "checked-out" before they can be edited. It is possible to open documents in READ-ONLY mode without checking them out. When a document is opened in READ-ONLY mode, it cannot be edited or overwritten.

Exercise 22-4: "Checking-out" a Web Document

In this exercise, you will learn how to check out a **Source Control** file.

1. If it is not already, open the *Saxophonics* web.

2. Choose **File ▶ Open** to open any file from that web. (This option works in any view.)

3. Select your file and choose **Open**.

4. In the resulting warning box, choose **Yes** to open the file, as shown in Figure 22-16.

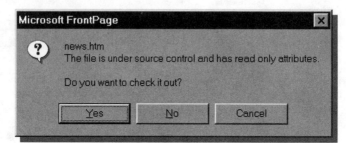

Figure 22-16: Document Check-out dialog box

 The file is now "checked-out" to you. No other users may open the file until you check it back in.

Checking In a Document

To check in a file, save the changes and close the open file. You can also close the file without making any modifications. FrontPage publishes the last saved version of that file.

For those webs running with FrontPage Security in place, the page author still has control over a document once it is checked in. For example, an author can check in a file without accepting any of the changes made to that file while it was checked out. You will learn more about FrontPage Security later in this lesson.

Setting Browser Compatibility

As emphasized throughout this course, Web technologies are by no means standardized. Netscape and Internet Explorer vary widely in the features they support. Other, less-used browsers also exist – and may not support the latest Web applications. The version of a browser is also an issue; many people do not upgrade their browsers every time a new version is released.

You have seen that many of FrontPage's special features are not supported in all browsers. If you desire to reach as many Internet users as possible, you may not want to use some FrontPage components. But you do not have to sort through them yourself to figure out which ones to eliminate. FrontPage can do it for you.

Compatibility Options

FrontPage has compatibility settings. To access them, select **Tools ▶ Page Options** and click the **Compatibility** tab, as shown in Figure 22-17.

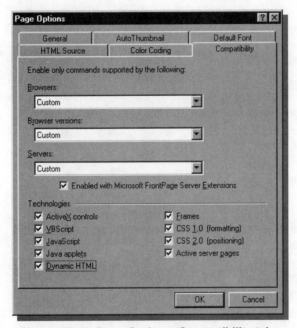

Figure 22-17: Page Options, Compatibility tab

You can choose to target the following elements:

- Browsers

  - Microsoft Internet Explorer only

  - Netscape Navigator only

  - Both Internet Explorer and Navigator

  - Microsoft Web TV

  - Custom (select from the Technologies options)

- Browser versions

  - 4.0 browsers and later

  - 3.0 browsers and later

  - Custom

- Servers

  - Microsoft Internet Information Server 3.0 and later

  - Apache server

  - Custom

By default, **Custom** is selected for these three options, and all of the Technologies options are selected. They include:

- ActiveX controls
- VBScript
- JavaScript
- Java applets
- Dynamic HTML
- Frames
- CSS 1.0 (formatting)
- CSS 2.0 (positioning)
- Active server pages

Figure 22-18 and Figure 22-19 show examples of how selecting choices for the three categories affect the Technologies options available.

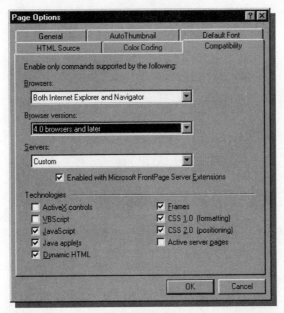

Figure 22-18: Compatibility Options — example #1

In Figure 22-18, the following options are enabled:

- <u>Browsers</u>: both Internet Explorer and Navigator

- <u>Browser versions</u>: 4.0 browsers and later

These options enabled the following technologies:

- JavaScript

- Java applets

- Dynamic HTML

- Frames

- CSS 1.0 (formatting)

- CSS 2.0 (positioning)

In Figure 22-19, the same browsers are enabled, but **3.0 browsers and later** is selected for the **Browser versions** option. This leaves only JavaScript, Java applets, and Frames available as Technology Options

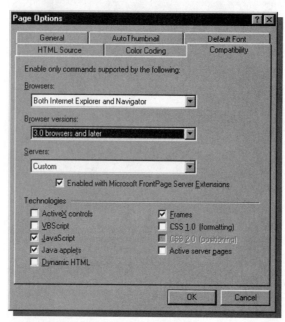

Figure 22-19: Compatibility options — example #2

When you apply these selections, the Technologies not supported by your choices will no longer be available to you in FrontPage. For example, with the choices shown in Figure 22-19, you will not be able to add a database because **Active server pages** is not selected. If you manually select **Active server pages**, you are creating a **Custom** definition.

Subwebs

Subwebs in FrontPage 2000 are mini-webs embedded in a larger FrontPage web. In earlier versions of FrontPage, it was only possible to have subwebs within a root web. In FrontPage 2000, you can embed subwebs within subwebs.

A subweb has all of the properties and characteristics of any FrontPage web. You can create a new subweb at any time, or you can convert an existing folder within a web to a subweb. Likewise, a subweb may be converted into a folder.

Advantages of Using Subwebs

The principle advantage of using subwebs is that they enable you to more effectively manage areas within your site. Just as with a standard web, each subweb can be assigned its own properties, such as:

- Theme

- Style Sheets

- Permissions

- Reports

- Tasks

If you have a Web site with many authors, you can make each author's area of responsibility into a subweb. Each author is then free to make stylistic choices without affecting other areas of the site. This is also advantageous if you do not want authors to have the ability to modify content outside of their area.

Creating a New Subweb

The process for creating a new subweb is similar to the process for creating any kind of new web. From the main menu, select **File ▶ New ▶ Web**. You would then check the box next to **Add to Current Web**, as shown in Figure 22-20 on the following page.

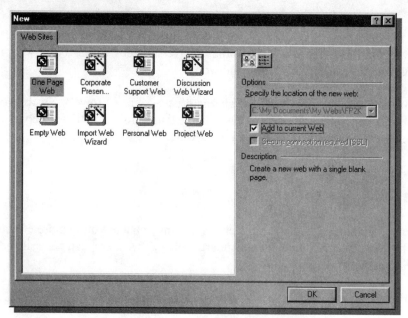

Figure 22-20: Creating a new subweb

Converting Folders Into Subwebs

To convert a folder into a subweb, right-click the name of the folder and select **Convert to Web** (this works in any view where you have selected to display the Folder List). You will be prompted by FrontPage, as shown in Figure 22-21.

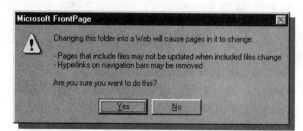

Figure 22-21: Converting a folder to a subweb

FrontPage is warning you that converting a folder into a subweb results in several changes:

- Pages that include files may not be updated when these included files changed.

- Hyperlinks on navigation bars may be removed.

When any web is created, certain configuration changes are made to the folder. An IMAGES folder and a _PRIVATE are automatically added, as are a number of hidden files and folders upon which FrontPage depends.

Exercise 22-5: Converting a Folder into a Subweb

In this exercise, you will convert the TYPES folder into a subweb.

1. Open the *Saxophonics* web in **Folders** View.

2. Right-click the TYPES folder and select **Convert to Web**.

3. Click **Yes** when asked if you are sure that you want to do this.

 The TYPES folder is now displayed as a subweb, as shown in Figure 22-22.

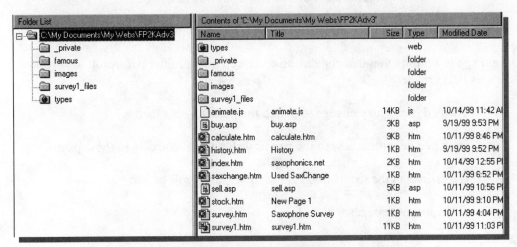

Figure 22-22: Folder List with TYPES folder as a subweb

Converting a Subweb Into a Folder

To convert a subweb into a folder, right-click the name of the subweb in the Folder List and select **Convert to Folder**. You will be prompted by FrontPage, as shown in Figure 22-23.

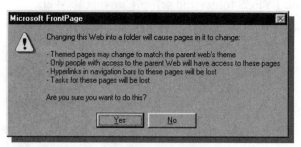

Figure 22-23: Converting a subweb to a folder

FrontPage is warning you that converting a subweb into a folder will result in several changes being made:

- Themed pages may change to match the parent web's theme.

- Only people with access to the parent web will have access to these pages.

- Hyperlinks in the navigation bars to these pages will be lost.

- Tasks for these pages will be lost.

Exercise 22-6: Converting a Subweb into a Folder

In this exercise, you will convert a subweb into a folder.

1. In the open *Saxophonics* web, right-click the **Types** subweb.

2. Select **Convert to Folder**.

3. Click **Yes** when asked if you are sure that you want to do this.

 The TYPES subweb is now displayed as a regular folder again.

 Remember that when you converted TYPES into a subweb, FrontPage automatically added IMAGES and _PRIVATE folders. These folders remain when the web is converted back into a folder.

Security in FrontPage 2000

As with all new technologies, the World Wide Web has solved many of its problems, and has in many cases created new, unanticipated challenges. One of the primary concerns facing everyone who works on the Web, as a user, developer, or administrator, is security.

Security Concerns on the Web

Concerns about security on the Internet include:

- Protection of sensitive data in transit

- Limiting ability to browse a Web site or portions thereof

- Limiting access to deleting, changing, or creating site content

A number of protocols have developed on the Internet to address these security concerns. FrontPage has incorporated a number of security features that enable you to take advantage of these protocols.

Secure Data Transfer

As you have learned, FrontPage allows you to use the HyperText Transfer Protocol (HTTP) to upload your files to the server. With FrontPage you also have the option of using a *Secure Socket Layer (SSL)* to encrypt the data as it is transferred. This prevents malicious individuals operating *packet sniffers* from stealing your data as it is transferred.

Secure Socket Layer (SSL) is a program layer created by Netscape for managing the security of message transmissions in a network. Netscape's idea is that the programming for keeping your messages confidential ought to be contained in a program layer between an application (such as your Web browser or HTTP) and the Internet's TCP/IP layers.

"Sockets" refers to the sockets method of passing data back and forth between a client and a server program in a network or between program layers on the same computer. Netscape's SSL uses the public key encryption scheme from RSA, which also includes the use of a digital certificate.[7]

---

[7] From www.whatis.com.

A packet sniffer is a program that monitors and analyzes network traffic. They have legitimate uses in keeping traffic flowing efficiently, but can also be used illegitimately to capture data being transmitted on a network. A network router reads every packet of data passed to it, determining whether it is intended for a destination within the router's own network or whether it should be passed further along the Internet.

A router with a sniffer, however, may be able to read the data in the packet as well as the source and destination addresses. Traffic sent in clear text, including passwords or other sensitive materials, can be read by a malicious individual.[8]

To use SSL to transfer data to your site, your server must be configured to allow secure connections via port 443. A thorough discussion of the encryption technology used in SSL is beyond the scope of this course.

If your server is configured to accept SSL connections, select **File ▶ Publish Web**, as you would normally to publish your web. Select **Secure connection required (SSL)** as shown in Figure 22-24 if your server requires or allows SSL connections. Click **Publish** to upload the web to your server. Your data will be protected in transit.

Figure 22-24: Publishing via Secure Socket Layer

---

[8] From www.whatis.com.

Using FrontPage to Manage Site Security

FrontPage recognizes three levels of access:

- <u>Browse</u>: allows users to view pages

- <u>Author</u>: allows users to create, edit, delete, and view pages

- <u>Administrator</u>: allows users to change settings, add new Webs, and other administrative tasks

Each layer of security includes the layers below it. In other words, users with Administrator access always have Author and Browse access as well. Users with Author access always have Browse access as well.

Limiting Browse Access

You can "password-protect" areas of your site by placing different restrictions on different areas of your site. You can restrict access to your entire web or to a particular subweb to particular users or groups. FrontPage also allows you to restrict users from a certain domain name or IP address range from accessing all or part of your site.

You must open your site on the server in order to administer security. When you publish your site from one machine to another, security settings are not transferred.

FrontPage security can be set by choosing **Tools ▶ Security ▶ Permissions** from the menu bar. This opens the **Permissions** dialog box. A slightly different dialog box appears if you are editing Permissions for a root web or for a subweb. The **Permissions** dialog box for a subweb is shown in Figure 22-25 on the following page.

DDC Publishing • www.ddcpub.com

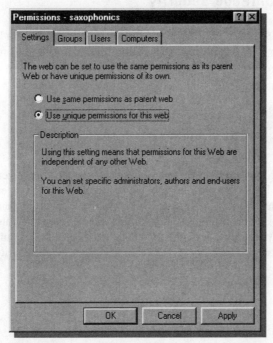

Figure 22-25: Setting Permissions for a subweb

Here you can opt to use the same Permissions on the subweb as for the root web, or to set unique Permissions for the subweb. If you want to password-protect a particular area of your site contained in the subweb, use unique Permissions.

There are three additional tabs on the **Permissions** dialog box. For a root web, however, these are the only three tabs:

- Groups: defines the list of groups that exists on the server and the access level of each.

- Users: lists the specific users with Administrator and Author level permissions. Selecting **Only selected users have browse access** will password-protect your web. You will then need to also specify what users, if any, have Browse level Permissions.

- Computers: allows you to restrict access by domain name, IP address, or computer name. This is useful if your web is intended as an Intranet. You can specify that only computers located within your network can access your site.

Limitations of FrontPage Security

The ability to use the security features in FrontPage is dependent on the server and the operating system your site is running. You cannot use FrontPage to manage your security if you are using Microsoft Personal Web Server. If you are running on Windows NT, all server administrators will automatically have Administrator level access.

The ability to use FrontPage to administer site security is very powerful, and can be very dangerous. In a Windows NT system, it is easy to inadvertently grant Administrator access to the group. If you do that, literally anyone can not only modify or delete your site content, but can change your server settings (which includes Permissions) and can effectively lock you out of your own site. As with all security issues, use caution when modifying FrontPage Permissions.

Lesson Summary

▶ **Tasks** View is another tool to assist you in the management of your site. **Tasks** View helps you to create an interactive To-Do-List for your site and assign Tasks to particular individuals.

▶ Tasks can be added in any view and may or may not be associated with a particular page of your site. You can use a variety of methods to determine what tasks need to be set for your web. When you save a page that is associated with a Task, FrontPage will prompt you to mark that Task as completed.

▶ You can set Review Status and Categories for any pages within your web. FrontPage assigns no intrinsic meaning to these, and you are free to use the ones provided or to create your own. Both the Review Status and Categories of a given page are set in the **Page Properties** dialog box. A given file can belong to more than one Category simultaneously. The list of files included in a given Category can be inserted as a FrontPage component on any page within your web. This is useful in creating a Site Map.

▶ FrontPage allows you to activate Source Control on your web. This requires users to "check-out" and "check-in" files in order to modify them. This prevents multiple users from modifying the same page concurrently. It is possible to open a document "checked-out" by another user, but no modifications may be made. This is known as READ ONLY mode.

▶ Setting browser compatibility allows you to specify what scripting languages and protocols can be used within your web. This ensures your site reaches the target audience, with respect to browser type and version.

▶ Subwebs are miniwebs embedded within a larger FrontPage web. FrontPage 2000 does not limit the number of subweb layers that can be created.

▶ Subwebs enable an administrator to more effectively manage the areas of a site. Different subwebs beneath the same root web can have unique Themes, Permissions, Tasks, Reports, and Styles.

▶ A new subweb can be added to an existing web, or a folder within a given web can be converted into a subweb. It is also possible to convert subwebs back into folders. When a folder is converted to a subweb or vice versa, certain configuration changes are made. These changes should be taken into account before a subweb is created or removed.

▶ Security is a major issue on the Internet. FrontPage has incorporated security support that addresses some of the most common security concerns.

▶ A Secure Socket Layer (SSL) enables you to connect to your Web server securely. FrontPage allows you to use the Secure Socket Layer to publish to your site.

▶ FrontPage recognizes three levels of Permissions: Administrator, Author, and Browse. FrontPage permissions can only be set on the server, they cannot be published to a server. Not all server software supports FrontPage security.

Lesson Review

Matching

___ 1. Encrypting data for transfer to the server

a. Categories

___ 2. Interactive To Do List for your site

b. Source Control

___ 3. Document Check-In/Check-Out

c. Secure Socket Layer (SSL)

___ 4. FrontPage component that can be used in creating site maps

d. Tasks View

Fill in the Blank

5. The four types of review status built into FrontPage are _____ , _____ , _____ , and _____ .

6. A _____ is a web that is within another web.

7. In **Folders** View, a _____ beside a filename indicates you have this file open (checked-out).

8. The three levels of FrontPage Permissions are _____ , _____ , and _____ .

True or False?

T / F   9. FrontPage automatically creates default Tasks for every web or Web site.

T / F   10. Users with Author Permissions can create new subwebs.

T / F   11. FrontPage always provides the means to handle your Web site or web security.

T / F   12. Security settings on a subweb must always be the same as for the root web.

T / F   13. A subweb cannot have subwebs of its own.

Appendices

- ► Appendix A: Common HTML Tags
- ► Appendix B: FrontPage Server Extensions
- ► Appendix C : Servers Supporting Extensions
- ► Appendix D: Glossary

Appendix A: Common HTML Tags

There are two different types of HTML code: elements and attributes. Elements are the actual HTML tags, while attributes are used to define and enhance those tags.

Tag	Description
A	Anchor
Body	Document body
BR	Forced line break
BUTTON	Push button
CENTER	Align center
CITE	Citation
CODE	Computer code fragment
DD	Definition description
DIV	Generic language/style container
DL	Definition list
DT	Definition term
EM	Emphasis
FONT	Local change to font
FORM	Interactive form
FRAME	Subwindow
FRAMESET	Window subdivision
H1	Heading size 1
H2	Heading size 2
H3	Heading size 3
H4	Heading size 4
H5	Heading size 5
H6	Heading size 6
HEAD	Document head
HR	Horizontal Rule
HTML	Document root element
I	Italicize text
IFRAME	Inline subwindow
IMG	Embedded image

LI	List item
META	Generic document information
NOFRAMES	Alternate content container for non-frame-based rendering
NOSCRIPT	Alternate content container for non-script-based rendering
OL	Ordered list
OPTION	Selectable choice
P	Paragraph
PRE	Preformatted text
S	Strike through text style
SCRIPT	Script statements
SELECT	Option selector
SMALL	Small text style
SPAN	Style container
STRIKE	Strike though text style
STRONG	Strong emphasis
STYLE	Style information
TABLE	Table body
TD	Table data cell
TEXTAREA	Multi-line text field
TH	Table header cell
TITLE	Document title
TR	Table row
TT	Teletype or mono-spaced text style
U	Underline text style
UL	Unordered list

Reference Table A-1: Common HTML tags

Name	Related Elements	Description
Action	FORM	Server-side form handler
Align	CAPTION	Relative to table
Align	APPLET, IFRAME, IMG, INPUT, OBJECT	Vertical or horizontal alignment
Align	LEGEND	Relative to fieldset
Align	TABLE	Table position relative to window
Align	HR	Horizontal rule width
Align	DIV, H1, H2, H3, H4, H5, H6, P	Align, text alignment
Align	COL, COLGROUP, TBODY, TD, TFOOT, TH, THEAD, TR	Align table attributes
Alink	BODY	Color of selected links
Alt	APPLET	Short description
Alt	AREA, IMG	Short description
Alt	INPUT	Short description
Background	BODY	Texture tile for document background
Bgcolor	TABLE	Background color for table cells
Bgcolor	TR	Background color for table row
Bgcolor	TD, TH	Cell background color
Bgcolor	BODY	Document background color
Border	IMG, OBJECT	Link border width
Cellpadding	TABLE	Spacing within cells
Cellspacing	TABLE	Spacing between cells
Class	All Elements but: BASE, BASEFONT, HEAD, HTML, META, PARAM, SCRIPT, STYLE, TITLE	Space separated list of classes
Color	BASEFONT, FONT	Text color
Colspan	TD, TH	Number of columns spanned by cell
Dir	All Elements but: APPLET, BASE, BASEFONT, BDO, BR, FRAME, FRAMESET, HR, IFRAME, PARAM, SCRIPT	Direction for weak/neutral text

Headers	TD, TH	List of id's for header cells
Height	IFRAME	Frame height
Height	IMG, OBJECT	Override height
Height	APPLET	Initial height
Height	TD, TH	Height for cell
Href	A, AREA, LINK	URL for linked resource
http-equiv	META	HTTP response header name
Id	All Elements but: BASE, HEAD, HTML, META, SCRIPT, STYLE, TITLE	Document-wide unique id
Ismap	IMG	Use server-side image map
Link	BODY	Color of links
Marginheight	FRAME, IFRAME	Margin height in pixels
Marginwidth	FRAME, IFRAME	Margin width in pixels
Maxlength	INPUT	Maximum characters for text fields
Method	FORM	HTTP method used to submit the form
Multiple	SELECT	Default is single selection
Name	BUTTON, TEXTAREA	Name of button or text area
Name	APPLET	Allows applets to find each other
Name	SELECT	Field name
Name	FRAME, IFRAME	Name of frame for targeting
Name	A	Named link end
Name	INPUT, OBJECT	Submit as part of a form
Name	MAP	For reference by usemap
Name	PARAM	Property name
Name	META	Metainformation name
Noresize	FRAME	Disallows users to resize frames
Noshade	HR	Horizontal rule appears with no shade fill
Nowrap	TD, TH	Suppresses word wrap
Onblur	A, AREA, BUTTON, INPUT, LABEL, SELECT, TEXTAREA	The element lost the focus

Onchange	INPUT, SELECT, TEXTAREA	The element value was changed
Onclick	All Elements but: APPLET, BASE, BASEFONT, BDO, BR, FONT, FRAME, FRAMESET, HEAD, HTML, IFRAME, ISINDEX, META, PARAM, SCRIPT, STYLE, TITLE	A pointer button was clicked
Ondblclick	All Elements but: APPLET, BASE, BASEFONT, BDO, BR, FONT, FRAME, FRAMESET, HEAD, HTML, IFRAME, ISINDEX, META, PARAM, SCRIPT, STYLE, TITLE	A pointer button was double clicked
Onfocus	A, AREA, BUTTON, INPUT, LABEL, SELECT, TEXTAREA	The element got the focus
Onkeydown	All Elements but: APPLET, BASE, BASEFONT, BDO, BR, FONT, FRAME, FRAMESET, HEAD, HTML, IFRAME, ISINDEX, META, PARAM, SCRIPT, STYLE, TITLE	A key was pressed down
Onkeypress	All Elements but: APPLET, BASE, BASEFONT, BDO, BR, FONT, FRAME, FRAMESET, HEAD, HTML, IFRAME, ISINDEX, META, PARAM, SCRIPT, STYLE, TITLE	A key was pressed and released
Onkeyup	All Elements but: APPLET, BASE, BASEFONT, BDO, BR, FONT, FRAME, FRAMESET, HEAD, HTML, IFRAME, ISINDEX, META, PARAM, SCRIPT, STYLE, TITLE	A key was released
Onload	BODY	The document has been loaded
Onload	FRAMESET	All the frames have been loaded
Onmouseover	All Elements but: APPLET, BASE, BASEFONT, BDO, BR, FONT, FRAME, FRAMESET, HEAD, HTML, IFRAME, ISINDEX, META, PARAM, SCRIPT, STYLE, TITLE	A pointer was moved onto
Onreset	FORM	The form was reset
Onselect	INPUT, TEXTAREA	Some text was selected
Onsubmit	FORM	The form was submitted
Onunload	FRAMESET	All the frames have been removed

Onrunload	BODY	The document has been removed
Rows	FRAMESET	List of lengths
Rows	TEXTAREA	Number of rows in text block
Rowspan	TD, TH	Number of rows spanned by cell
Size	HR	Horizontal rule size
Size	FONT	Font size
Size	INPUT	Specific to each type of field
Size	BASEFONT	Base font size for font elements
Size	SELECT	Rows visible
Span	COL	Column attributes
Span	COLGROUP	Default number of columns in group
Src	SCRIPT	URL for an external script
Src	INPUT	For fields with images
Src	FRAME, IFRAME	Source of frame content
Src	IMG	URL of image to embed
Target	A, AREA, BASE, FORM, LINK	Render in this frame
Text	BODY	Document text color
Title	STYLE	Advisory title
Title	All Elements but: BASE, BASEFONT, HEAD, HTML, META, PARAM, SCRIPT, STYLE, TITLE	Advisory title amplification
Type	A, LINK	Advisory content type
Type	OBJECT	Content type for data
Type	PARAM	Content type for value when valuetype=ref
Type	SCRIPT	Content type of script language
Type	STYLE	Content type of style language
Type	INPUT	What kind of widget is needed
Type	LI	List item style
Type	OL	Numbering style
Type	UL	Bullet style

Type	BUTTON	For use as form button
Valign	COL, COLGROUP, TBODY, TD, TFOOT, TH, THEAD, TR	Vertical alignment in cells
Value	OPTION	Defaults to element content
Value	PARAM	Property value
Value	INPUT	Required for radio and checkboxes
Value	BUTTON	Sent to server when submitted
Value	LI	Reset sequence number
Vlink	BODY	Color of visited links
Width	HR	Horizontal rule width
Width	IFRAME	Frame width
Width	IMG, OBJECT	Override width
Width	TABLE	Table width
Width	APPLET	Initial width
Width	COL	Column width specification
Width	COLGROUP	Default width for enclosed columns
Width	TD, TH	Width for cell
Width	PRE	Preformatted width

Reference Table A-2: HTML attributes

Appendix B: FrontPage Server Extensions Features

The following is a list of features that require FrontPage Server Extensions to function properly:

- Hit counter

- Banner ads

- Hover buttons

- Marquees

- Search form

- Confirmation field

- Discussion groups

- User registration

- Table of Contents

Appendix C: Servers Supporting Extensions

Operating System	Web Server
Windows NT Server	Microsoft Internet Information Server 3.0 and higher
Windows NT Workstation	Microsoft Peer Web Services
Windows 98	Microsoft Personal Web Server
Windows 95	▪ Microsoft FrontPage Personal Web Server ▪ Netscape FastTrack 2.0, 3.01 ▪ Netscape Enterprise Server 3.x, 3.51 ▪ O'Reilly WebSite Pro 2.0
Digital Unix 3.2c, 4.0	Apache 1.2.6, 1.3.3
Linux 2.0.34 (MIPS)	NCSA 1.5.2
Linux 3.0.3 (Red Hat)	Netscape Enterprise Server 3.x, 3.51
BSDi 3.1, 4.0	Netscape FastTrack 2.0, 3.01
SCO OpenServer 5	Stronghold 2.3

Reference Table C-1: Operating Systems and Web servers that support FP 2000 Server Extensions

Appendix D: Glossary

Anchor

An element in an HTML document from which a link is accessed by a user. Anchors may be either text or inline images, and provide access to various data, including other Web pages, binary files, Gopher and FTP servers, and launching E-mail client applications. Anchors also provide a method for advancing to another section of the same Web page or a specific location in a different Web page.

Animated GIF

An advanced capability of the GIF 89a image file format that allows several discrete GIF images to be archived in a single GIF image. Animated GIFs are then referenced in an HTML document for use as inline images. No special tagging or attributes are required to use an animated GIF, although advanced control functions that allow infinite or limited looping are available. Browsers capable of displaying animated GIF files automatically detect and display the animated GIF, the individual GIF images comprising the master GIF are displayed in rapid succession, creating the illusion of animation.

ANSI Character Set

A set of 256 characters, numbered from 0 to 255, established by ANSI, the American National Standards Institute. HTML scripters may use them to establish character entities. The standard HTML character entity syntax applies, but the character entity element (copy, reg, deg) is a pound sign (#) followed by the ANSI character number, such as 112 or 241. Thus, a character entity featuring an ANSI character would have a syntax of .

ASCII

The acronym for *America Standard Code for Information Interchange*. A universal, cross-platform plain text file format. The ASCII format does not support text formatting (such as bold, italic, or underline) and will not store layout information, such as margins, tabs, or embedded objects. Also known as *DOS text* or *plain text*, ASCII is the format in which an HTML document must be stored.

Attribute

An HTML element that modifies or enhances the behavior of a tag by providing additional instructions to a Web browser. Not all HTML tags have attributes. Multiple attributes may be used simultaneously with a single tag (providing they do not logically negate or interfere with each other). Netscape Communications Corporation, Microsoft Corporation, and CERN are rapidly introducing new attributes to existing HTML tags.

Body

The larger portion of the HTML document that is interpreted and displayed by a Web browser as a Web page. It can contain hypertext link anchors, inline images, content data, and multimedia objects. The Body, combined with the Head, comprises an entire HTML document.

Character Reference

An HTML element that begins with an ampersand (&), followed by a predefined term, and ends with a semicolon (;). For example, the copyright symbol (©), may be created with the sequence ©. The degree sign may be generated with the ° character reference. Character references may also be created using the ANSI character set. (see *ANSI Character Set*)

Empty Tag

One of two categories of HTML tag types. An empty tag is a single tag; it does not require opening and closing tags. Empty tags may have attributes. Examples of empty tags are the horizontal rules <HR>, paragraph breaks <P>, and line breaks, <BR>.

Form

An advanced capability of HTML that allows text fields, buttons, check boxes, and scrolling lists to be incorporated into Web documents. Typically, a CGI script is running on the same server that is hosting the form in order to process the user-entered data.

GIF (Graphics Interchange Format)

Introduced by CompuServe in 1987 (and updated in 1989), GIF is the most common image file format found on the Internet and is one of the preferred formats for inline images. Available in both 87a and 89a formats, GIF is an inherently compressed format, meaning that GIF files require less space than non-compressed image formats (BMP). The GIF format has a maximum color depth of 256 (8 bit) and is not a lossy format. GIF 89a offers the ability to create transparent images.

Head

The Head of an HTML document is the minority of the document and contains global instructional information and other Web browser cues that are not directly displayed by the browser to a user. The Head, combined with the Body, comprises an entire HTML document.

Heading Styles

HTML 4.0 provides six heading styles—or levels—denoted with the following tag syntax: <H1>...</H1>. Heading Level 1 is the largest header and Heading Level 6 is the smallest. There are no absolute point sizes for Heading Levels, only a relative scale from largest to smallest.

Horizontal Rule

A horizontal line that, by default, has a width that spans the Web page. The horizontal rule is inserted with the <HR> tag and has many associated attributes for adjusting width, thickness, and justification.

HTML (HyperText Markup Language)

The authoring language used to develop Web pages. The standard for HTML is currently under development. The International Standards Organization ratifies and publishes the HTML standard, but many independent browser developers have added significant and numerous extensions to the HTML language.

HTTP (HyperText Transfer Protocol)

The protocol for transporting HTML documents across the Internet. HTTP requires that TCP/IP be running on both the client and server computers. HTTP is the transfer protocol used by HTML authors when scripting anchor tags that refer to documents and multimedia data that reside on Web servers.

Hypermedia

The fusion of hypertext (see *Hypertext*) and multimedia. Hypermedia is available in the form of audio, video, animation, and special image and multimedia data types on the World Wide Web. Hypermedia information is located, downloaded, and consumed in the technical framework of the Web and hypertext navigation systems, including standard Web browsers and the HTTP transfer protocol. Many high-end multimedia data formats require special Netscape Navigator or Microsoft Internet Explorer plug-ins.

Hypertext

A term coined by computer visionary Ted Nelson in 1965. Hypertext is text that contains links to other pieces of text, or to various types of media, including sound, video, animation, and images. Hypertext allows a user to navigate through an information hyperspace in a user-defined, non-linear sequence.

Inline Image

Any image displayed in a Web page by an HTML browser. Inline images are GIF or JPEG format.

JPEG (Joint Photographic Experts Group)

JPEG is an increasingly popular image file format on the Internet. The JPEG image file format is recognized by leading Web browsers for use as inline images. JPEG can support a color depth of 16.7 million (24 bit) but is a lossy compression ratio. JPEG is rapidly gaining popularity among Web authors and publishers because it provides greater compression ratios for images and, thus, creates images that are fewer bytes in size than other image file formats, including GIF. JPEG was designed for compressing high-resolution, photographic quality images. (see *Inline image*)

List

There are two categories of HTML lists: ordered and unordered. Ordered lists are more commonly called numbered lists. Unordered lists are typically called bullet lists. Lists are created using the list tag family, involving either the <OL> (ordered list) or <UL> (unordered list) tag in conjunction with the <LI> (list item) tag.

Non-empty Tag

One of the categories of HTML tag categories. A non-empty tag set contains both an opening and closing tag. The vast majority of HTML tags are non-empty. The closing tag differs from the opening tag with the addition of a forward slash following the opening wicket (<B>dog</B>).

RGB Color Code

The six-letter codes that represent three (3) pairs of hexadecimal codes across a spectrum of values for the 1) red, 2) green, and 3) blue color attributes. In combination, these three hexadecimal code value pairs form a single color code. In HTML, RGB color codes are used to specify background colors and text colors (both unvisited and visited hypertext links).

Script

Term used to describe the contents of an HTML document; the combination of the content of a Web page and the HTML elements (tags, tag attributes, character entities) that instruct a Web browser how to interpret and display Web page content (non-HTML text).

Table

An HTML element created using a special tag family. Introduced by Netscape Communications Corporation, tables were not officially supported by HTML until version 3.2. Tables provide sophisticated layout and data management capabilities and allow for row spanning, column spanning, border and gridline attribute adjustment, cell data justification, and embedding of tables within tables.

Tag

An HTML tag is an element that is unseen by the user but is interpreted by the browser. A tag can be either empty or non-empty. Non-empty tags act upon text enclosed in a pair of opening and closing tags. An opening tag begins with a left wicket (<) followed immediately by the tag element and any attributes (and their associated values) and ends with a right wicket (>). Closing tags differ from opening tags with the addition of a forward slash (/) between the opening wicket and the tag element. An empty tag is a single tag that resembles an opening tag in a non-empty tag set.

Tiling

The process of repeating a background image in a Web page to create the illusion of a consistent, single backdrop pattern. Web browsers automatically tile image files (GIF or JPEG) that are referenced using the BACKGROUND attribute to the <BODY> tag.

Wicket

The commonly accepted term for the left angle bracket (<) and the right angle bracket (>) that are used to syntactically enclose HTML tag elements. Used as mathematical operators, these characters are called the "less than sign" and the "greater than sign."

Index

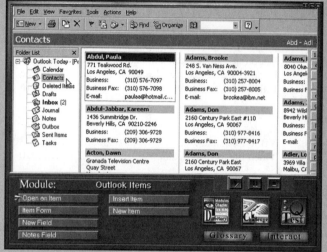

The Visual Reference Series

Each book shows you the 100 most important functions of popular software

We explain your computer screen's elements—icons, windows, dialog boxes—with pictures, callouts, and simple "Press this, type that" illustrated commands. You go right into software functions. No time wasted. The spiral binding keeps the pages open and your hands free to move your mouse and type.

$15ea.

Did we make one for you?

Cat. No.	Title
G29	Microsoft® Access 97
G43	Microsoft® Access 2000
G58	ACT!® 4.0
G21	Microsoft® Excel 97
G46	Microsoft® Excel 2000
G37	Microsoft® Internet Explorer 4.0
G59	Microsoft® FrontPage 2000
G33	The Internet
G19	Microsoft® Office 97
G40	Microsoft® Office 2000
G23	Microsoft® Outlook 97
G50	Microsoft® Outlook 98
G54	Microsoft® Outlook 2000
G22	Microsoft® PowerPoint® 97
G44	Microsoft® PowerPoint® 2000
G57	Microsoft® Publisher 2000
G36	Microsoft® Windows® 98
G53	Microsoft® Windows® 2000
G20	Microsoft® Word 97
G45	Microsoft® Word 2000
G70	Upgrading to Office 2000

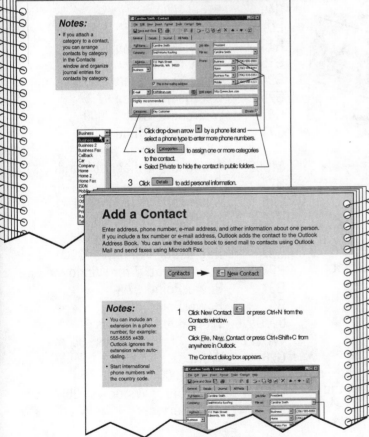

Preview our books online at: http://www.ddcpub.com

DDC *Publishing* to order call 800-528-3897 or fax 800-528-3862

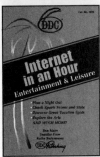

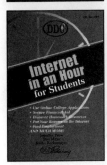

Microsoft® Office 2000 Advanced Skills:
An Integrated Approach

For use following Learning Office 2000, when students have mastered basic skills in each application. Each exercise incorporates more than one application. For example:

■ Embed charts and graphs in reports (Word & Excel)
■ Link tables to presentations (Word & PowerPoint)
■ Create a mail merge using a query (Access & Word)
■ Perform a merge with calculations (Excel & Access)

This book teaches students five different kinds of integration:

■ Survival Skill Integration ■ Productivity Integration ■ Power Integration
■ Web Page Integration ■ Internet Integration

These integration skills reflect the way power users work with Office in a real-world business setting using several different applications in combination to finish a complex task.

$29 *60 Exercises*
Cat. No. Z51
ISBN 1-56243-774-7
Includes CD-ROM

SUPPORT MATERIALS

Cat. No. Z51TE	Annotated Teacher Edition with Solution Files	$50
Cat. No. BTZ51	Tests in a three-ring binder	$100
Cat. No. SLZ5	Solutions on CD-ROM	$15
Cat. No. SLZ5SL	Solutions on CD-ROM Site License	$65
Cat. No. VA51	Visual Aids on Diskette (25 PowerPoint Slides)	$50
Cat. No. SLB51	Printouts of solutions in a three-ring binder	$50
Cat. No. DLZ51	Distance Learning Template CD-ROM	$150

Business Simulations with Microsoft® Office 2000
Know the pressures and rewards of being a regional sales manager in

In 25 realistic business simulation projects, students use critical thinking, communications, and cross-curriculum study skills. They hone computer skills as they:

■ Interact by e-mail with boss and coworkers
■ Prepare product presentations
■ Budget finances with spreadsheets and databases
■ Make key business decisions

$29 Spiral
Cat. No. LPZ35
ISBN 1-56243-861-1
Includes CD-ROM

$15 Solutions CD-ROM with Instructor Support Material.
Get hints, tips, and sample solutions. Cat. No. SLLP

Preview our books online at: http://www.ddcpub.com

 **275 Madison Avenue, New York, NY 10016**
phone 800-528-3897 • fax 800-528-3862

#8-2KZ51&LPZ35

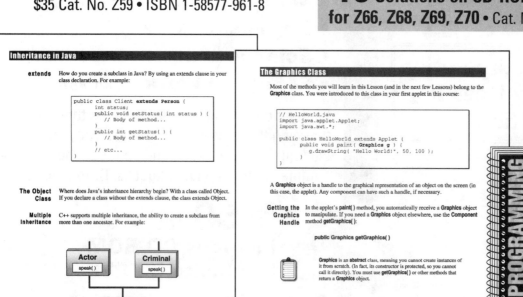

DDC Programming Series

Master Programming—Fast

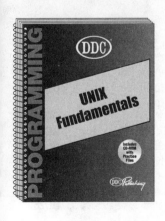

HTML 4.0 Fundamentals
7+ hours of training
$20 Cat. No. DC67 • ISBN 1-56243-834-4
Includes Data Disc with Student Files
Instructor's PowerPoint Slide Show $15 • Cat. No. IDCD

HTML 4.0 Intermediate
7+ hours of training
$20 Cat. No. DC68 • ISBN 1-56243-835-2
Includes Data Disc with Student Files
Instructor's PowerPoint Slide Show $15 • Cat. No. IDCD

Mastering JavaScript: Part 1
7+ hours of training
$20 Cat. No. DC69 • ISBN 1-56243-836-0
Includes Data Disc with Student Files
Instructor's PowerPoint Slide Show $15 • Cat. No. IDCD

Mastering JavaScript: Part 2
7+ hours of training
$20 Cat. No. DC70 • ISBN 1-56243-837-9
Includes Data Disc with Student Files
Instructor's PowerPoint Slide Show $15 • Cat. No. IDCD

Mastering Java Threads
14+ hours of training
$20 Cat. No. DC75 • ISBN 1-56243-842-5
Includes Data Disc with Student Files
Instructor's PowerPoint Slide Show $15 • Cat. No. IDCD

HTML 4.0 Advanced
7+ hours of training
$20 Cat. No. DC92 • ISBN 1-56243-970-7
Includes Data Disc with Student Files

Creating Web Graphics
7+ hours of training
$20 Cat. No. DC87 • ISBN 1-56243-960-X
Includes Data Disc with Student Files
Instructor's PowerPoint Slide Show $15 • Cat. No. IDCD

Converting Files for the Web
7+ hours of training
$20 Cat. No. DC54 • ISBN 1-56243-972-3
Includes Data Disc with Student Files

Transitioning C++ to Java
7+ hours of training
$20 Cat. No. DC86 • ISBN 1-56243-959-6
Includes Data Disc with Student Files

Perl Programming
Prerequisites: Fundamentals of UNIX. C Programming is recommended.
40+ hours of training
$40 Cat. No. DC97 • ISBN 1-56243-976-6
Includes Data Disc with Student Files

Advanced Perl Programming
Prerequisites: Perl Programming and Perl application development experience. Full comprehension of the extending and embedding material will require some C or C++ programming experience.
32+ hours of training
$40 Cat. No. DC98 • ISBN 1-56243-977-4
Includes Data Disc with Student Files

UNIX Fundamentals
Prerequisites: None
32+ hours of training
$40 Cat. No. DC99 • ISBN 1-56243-978-2
Includes Data Disc with Student Files

Advanced UNIX Tools
Prerequisites: Fundamentals of UNIX
32+ hours of training
$38 Cat. No. DC101 • ISBN 1-56243-980-4
Includes Data Disc with Student Files

Awk Programming
Prerequisites: The ability to write programs in a high level language (such as C or shell) is very helpful in completing the lab exercises and understanding the lectures. A good working knowledge of the UNIX environment is necessary.
16+ hours of training
$25 Cat. No. DC102 • ISBN 1-56243-981-2
Includes Data Disc with Student Files

Object-Oriented Analysis and Design Unified Modeling Language
Prerequisites: Familiarity with structured techniques such as functional decomposition is helpful.
40+ hours of training
$45 Cat. No. DC103 • ISBN 1-56243-982-0

SQL Programming
Prerequisites: None
16+ hours of training
$25 Cat. No. DC104 • ISBN 1-56243-983-9
Includes Data Disc with Student Files

Oracle for Application Developers
Prerequisites: Experience in a structured programming language.
40+ hours of training
$45 Cat. No. DC105 • ISBN 1-56243-984-7
Includes Data Disc with Student Files

**Preview our books
online at:
www.ddcpub.com**

to order call 800-528-3897 or fax 800-528-3862
275 Madison Avenue, New York, NY 10016

#2-2K PRO/OD

FREE CATALOG
AND
UPDATED LISTING

We don't just have books that find your answers faster; we also have books that teach you how to use your computer without the fairy tales and the gobbledygook.

We also have books to improve your typing, spelling and punctuation.

Return this card for a free catalog and mailing list update.

275 Madison Avenue,
New York, NY 10016

☐ Please send me your catalog
and put me on your mailing list.

Name

Firm (if any)

Address

City, State, Zip

Phone (800) 528-3897   Fax (800) 528-3862

SEE OUR COMPLETE CATALOG ON THE INTERNET @: http://www.ddcpub.com

---

FREE CATALOG
AND
UPDATED LISTING

We don't just have books that find your answers faster; we also have books that teach you how to use your computer without the fairy tales and the gobbledygook.

We also have books to improve your typing, spelling and punctuation.

Return this card for a free catalog and mailing list update.

275 Madison Avenue,
New York, NY 10016

☐ Please send me your catalog
and put me on your mailing list.

Name

Firm (if any)

Address

City, State, Zip

Phone (800) 528-3897   Fax (800) 528-3862

SEE OUR COMPLETE CATALOG ON THE INTERNET @: http://www.ddcpub.com

---

FREE CATALOG
AND
UPDATED LISTING

We don't just have books that find your answers faster; we also have books that teach you how to use your computer without the fairy tales and the gobbledygook.

We also have books to improve your typing, spelling and punctuation.

Return this card for a free catalog and mailing list update.

DDC *Publishing*

275 Madison Avenue,
New York, NY 10016

☐ Please send me your catalog
and put me on your mailing list.

Name

Firm (if any)

Address

City, State, Zip

Phone (800) 528-3897   Fax (800) 528-3862

SEE OUR COMPLETE CATALOG ON THE INTERNET @: http://www.ddcpub.com

**NO POSTAGE
NECESSARY
IF MAILED
IN THE
UNITED STATES**

BUSINESS REPLY MAIL
FIRST-CLASS MAIL PERMIT NO. 7321 NEW YORK, N.Y.

POSTAGE WILL BE PAID BY ADDRESSEE

275 Madison Avenue
New York, NY 10157-0410

**NO POSTAGE
NECESSARY
IF MAILED
IN THE
UNITED STATES**

BUSINESS REPLY MAIL
FIRST-CLASS MAIL PERMIT NO. 7321 NEW YORK, N.Y.

POSTAGE WILL BE PAID BY ADDRESSEE

275 Madison Avenue
New York, NY 10157-0410

**NO POSTAGE
NECESSARY
IF MAILED
IN THE
UNITED STATES**

BUSINESS REPLY MAIL
FIRST-CLASS MAIL PERMIT NO. 7321 NEW YORK, N.Y.

POSTAGE WILL BE PAID BY ADDRESSEE

275 Madison Avenue
New York, NY 10157-0410

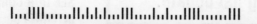